ADAPTER

IRELAND

a traveler's tools for living like a local

Steenie Harvey

AVALON
TRAVEL

ADAPTER KIT: IRELAND
First Edition
Steenie Harvey

Published by Avalon Travel Publishing,
5855 Beaudry Street, Emeryville CA 94608

Text and photographs © 2002 by Steenie Harvey
Illustrations and maps © 2002 by
Avalon Travel Publishing. All rights reserved.

Please send all
comments, corrections, additions,
amendments, and critiques to:

ADAPTER KIT: Ireland
AVALON TRAVEL PUBLISHING
5855 BEAUDRY ST.
EMERYVILLE, CA 94608, USA
email: info@travelmatters.com
website: www.travelmatters.com

Printed in the United States of America by R.R. Donnelley
First edition. First printing January 2002.

ISSN 1536-271X
ISBN 1-56691-444-2

Printing History
1st edition—January 2002
5 4 3 2 1

Editor: Kate Willis
Series Manager: Kate Willis
Copy Editor: Elizabeth Wolf
Graphics: Melissa Sherowski
Design & Production: Amber Pirker
Cartographers: Mike Morgenfeld, Kat Kalamaras
Map Editor: Naomi Dancis
Index: Leslie Miller

Front Cover Photo: Terry Donnelly
Back Cover Photos: Steenie Harvey

Photos on pages vii, 1, 3, 11, 23, 35, 37, 45, 57, 71, 73, 99, 111, 127, 141, 167, 175, 193, 209, 225, 241, 243, 255, 261: Steenie Harvey

Distributed by Publishers Group West, Berkeley, California

Contents

EARNING A LIVING

APPENDIX

Preface

A new life in Ireland. Sounds like a wonderful idea, but is it really possible? Well, I'd just like to tell you that dreams can come true. I should know, mine did ...

I haven't always been a writer, you know. And Ireland is my adopted home, rather than my place of birth. Back in the late 1980s, my life was in a rut. I lived in a dreary industrial English town and had an equally dreary job as an office clerk in a printing factory.

Although family life was great—wonderful husband, wonderful daughter—I felt crushed by the sheer grind of my day-to-day existence. I got up, went to work, caught a bus home, cooked dinner, and watched television. Day after day after day. But what's wrong with that? After all, thousands of people were in the same boat as me.

Then a bombshell dropped—my husband, Michael, lost his job. Maybe it was the shock of discovering our income had been cut in half, but we had this crazy idea. Why not move away, try a completely different lifestyle?

We knew Ireland, having spent several vacations there—and Michael has Irish blood passed down from his grandfathers. We had always enjoyed fantastic holidays in Ireland, and it seemed such a *gentle* place, so why not give it a try? I had always yearned to live in the countryside, and Ireland certainly had plenty of that.

To be frank, it was all very impulsive. And maybe if I had thought longer about it, I'd still be serving a life sentence in that wretched old printing works. At that time, 13 years ago, Ireland's unemployment figures were ghastly, and we had no jobs lined up. My parents thought we were completely crazy. But we went anyway.

We rented a furnished house in county Sligo for the first few months while we were hunting around for a cottage to buy. Our daughter, Maggie, was dispatched to the local convent school—and if you have teenage girls yourself, you can probably imagine her reaction to a mud-brown uniform with mud-brown socks to match.

It's hard to believe now, but we went to Ireland with the idea of buying a home for less than $15,000. It took some months of searching, but we did eventually hit gold. We found a cozy cottage overlooking Lough Key in county Roscommon. This was just how I'd pictured country living: a huge garden where we could grow all our own vegetables, room enough to have a dog and three cats, a shop and a couple of excellent pubs—all within a mile's walk. Plus we were surrounded by lovely neighbors—and, by the way, I can assure you that all those things you may have heard about Irish warmth and hospitality are true. (You'd best start developing a taste for strong tea and idle chit-chat now.)

Apart from the fact that we had to learn how to light fires and sweep chimneys (I was sure nobody had done this in England since Victorian times), the only fly in the ointment was our job situation. Michael had found work, but nobody seemed to want me. What could I do besides hiring myself out as a chimney sweep? My new enthusiasm for gardening seemed unlikely to pay dividends either. For some reason there didn't seem to be a market for tons of organically grown radishes, not in this corner of county Roscommon. Take it from one who knows: Do not sow four packets of radish seeds all at once.

Fortunately, I'd read one of those daft "You too can have a career as a writer" advertisements, and as luck would have it, the previous owner of our house had left behind an antique manual typewriter in the shed. Plus a collection of rubber Wellington boots with whiskey bottles buried inside them. I got really excited—until I discovered the bottles were all empty—but I did make use of the typewriter.

I decided to bash out a humorous article about our own search for the perfect Irish country cottage. I rambled on about real estate agents taking us to see hovels with tin roofs and no bathroom facilities—mere shacks with no front doors. In fact, we even saw one where cows were using the kitchen as a barnyard. This was the first thing I'd ever written, and believe it or not, the property editor of a daily newspaper published it. She was kind enough to ask me for a follow-up, a factual piece outlining the kind of homes that were on sale in this forgotten corner of western Ireland.

Thirteen years on, we're still living in the same little cottage. Our daughter has married an Irishman, and we've acquired a bunch of grandkids—six in total. ("What are you trying to do?" I ask her. "Repopulate the west of Ireland all by yourself?") And my writing career has soared ...

Not only have I had books published, I also spend a fair bit of time traveling around Europe on behalf of an American magazine, writing about real estate. Would this have happened if I hadn't moved to Ireland? Don't think so. Chances are I'd still be on the other end of a telephone, explaining to irate customers why their printing orders weren't ready.

But here's the thing: I've never been tempted to move on again. Flying back from Slovenia a week ago, the same tremendous thrill swept through me that I felt the first time I ever visited Ireland. My heart always lifts as the plane swoops over Dublin Bay, and once again I see my adopted homeland emerging from the mist.

I think what I'm trying to say is this: I love this country, and I can't imagine any reason why I'd want to say goodbye. After you've read this book, I very much hope that you too will come and experience the magic. It may be just for a visit, but then again, Ireland and its enchantments may keep you here forever. You have been warned!

—*Steenie Harvey*

Acknowledgments

For my ever-patient husband Michael, who endures my black moods and tantrums when the words look like gobbledygook. For my darlin' daughter Maggie for the endless tea and chitchat. For my editor at Avalon, Kate Willis, who keeps me afloat with all her good cheer and encouragement. A heartfelt thanks to you all.

And a dedication to my grandchildren whose happy little faces make me remember that there's more to life than work. Thomas, twins Harry and Paddy, Cassie, Tara and Jack—bless you.

PART I

Introduction

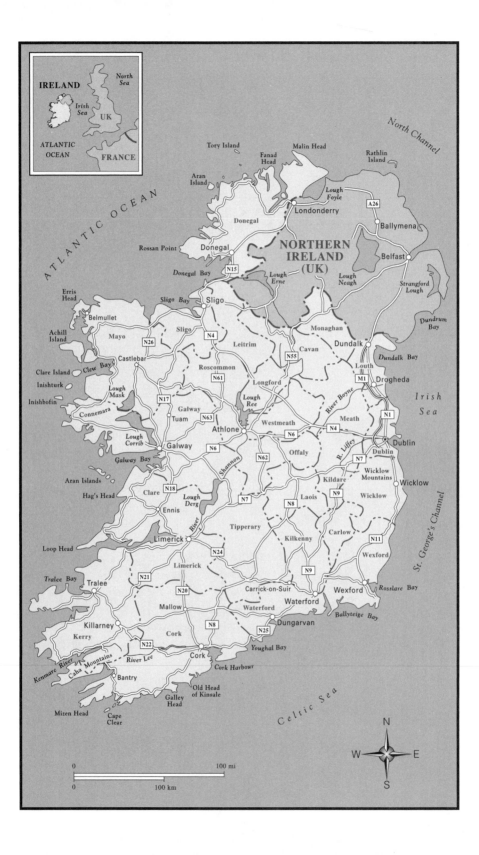

1 Welcome to Ireland

*W*rapped in a soft green cloak of ancient memories, Ireland is one of the most beautiful and fascinating small countries in the world. Cast adrift in the Atlantic Ocean to the west of Britain, this jewel of an island has become one of Europe's most desirable addresses for those wishing to swap the stresses of city life for old-fashioned rural bliss.

The renowned Irish welcome has never depended on the size of a person's bank balance, and whether you hope to rent or buy property, it's easy to acquire residency here. Maybe your idea of heaven is a little white-washed cottage, maybe a thatched farmhouse or even an ivy-clad Georgian mansion. A pretty bungalow with ocean views? A centuries-old castle? Somewhere there's a dream home waiting.

But why does Ireland exert such a pull on the imagination? After all, most people realize it's a divided island—the Republic of Ireland, the easygoing south, has a grim-faced neighbor called Northern Ireland. And here's another puzzle: All those lush green meadows on "the Emerald Isle" certainly didn't come from blue skies and unlimited sunshine. So what *does* make Ireland so special?

The Allure of Ireland

Most expatriates are enticed here for the same reasons vacationers are. Ireland lures expats and visitors alike with its unique amalgam of storybook scenery coupled with open spaces, safe streets, and a gentle way of life. Along with its absorbing tangle of history, the country also offers up colorful festivals and curious traditions. What's more, its vibrant culture of music, dance, and poetry remains wonderfully intact and accessible to everybody. The country is so proud of its literary and cultural heritage that resident writers, artists, and musicians are allowed generous tax breaks. Here you're never considered too young or too old to learn to play the fiddle, take up painting, or write a masterpiece.

In our polluted world, the notion of a clean, green environment is hard to resist. Europe's industrial revolution hardly touched provincial Ireland. Between the bright lights of Dublin and the Atlantic's fossil shores, much of the country remains pleasingly rural, a pastoral haven of small farmsteads, quiet lanes, and rolling pasturelands. Particularly in the wilder reaches of the west, old-fashioned ways stubbornly survive with many communities clinging like limpets to seasonal patterns that vanished from neighboring European countries generations ago.

Tradition is part and parcel of everyday life, not a tourist sideshow laid on by the heritage industry. Turf, those brown slabs of winter fuel, is still hand-cut from the bogs in many parts of Connemara. Some fishermen still put to sea in *currachs*, fragile, hide-bound rowing boats that have been used

Dublin's Trinity College dates back to 1592

© Steenie Harvey

since Celtic times. Visit a horse-fair such as Ballinasloe and you'll see deals conducted the old-fashioned way—with spits, handshakes, and the return of "luck money."

Yet the great paradox is that Ireland is also part of the new Europe, a modern country with good hospitals and world-class restaurants. The capital, Dublin, is no stuffy museum piece but a sophisticated city where you'll find cybercafés and a club scene alongside Ireland's renowned Georgian architecture, traditional theater, and legendary pub crawls. If you enjoy outdoor pursuits, there's plenty to keep you busy. The enviable array of activities includes sailing, hill walking, fishing, and "riding to hounds" (foxhunting), not to mention more than 350 superb golf

Here you're never considered too young or too old to learn to play the fiddle, take up painting, or write a masterpiece.

courses. And although some may take a dim view of blasting our furry and feathered friends to kingdom come, shooting is also a tremendously popular country pursuit. Sunday afternoon is a favorite time for gun clubs to go rough shooting, still today an almost exclusively male activity. Even under deluge conditions, the unfairer sex will happily slog through bog and ditch to bag whatever small game or wildfowl they and their gun dogs can flush out—partridge, snipe, teal, and rabbit, to name just a few.

Where Should You Live?

With the economy combining high growth with low inflation, most Irish people enjoy a good standard of living. Rather than laboring in smokestack industries, many of the country's young and highly educated workforce are employed in pharmaceuticals, telecommunications, and computers. Your new Irish neighbors are just as likely to be working at the cutting edge of technology as tending sheep and cattle.

In contrast to many Irish home buyers, most foreigners wish to escape the urban world of the workplace. Cities are fine for shopping trips, but most newcomers have a craving for nostalgia, preferring to seek out those quintessential Irish villages where everybody knows their neighbors. What they yearn for is a kind of Gaelic version of *Paradise Lost,* a picture-postcard country where traffic is a faint hum in the distance and timeless hamlets huddle below a backdrop of misty blue mountains. Thankfully that paradise is still pretty much intact.

It's impossible to pinpoint any one Irish county as *the* place to head for. The entire western seaboard is a rugged patchwork of lakes, mountains, and offshore islands as spine-tingling and heart-wrenchingly beautiful as imagination promised. Alternatively you may prefer the less well-known

Quiz: twenty teasers

1. The Republic of Ireland's flag is
   a) a gold harp on a green background.
   b) a gold shamrock on a green background.
   c) a tricolor of green, white, and orange bands.

2. What should you do with a crubeen?
   a) Eat it.
   b) Wear it.
   c) Show it to your doctor.

3. The name of Ireland's national airline is
   a) Aer Fungus.
   b) Aer Lingus.
   c) Irlandia.

4. A pishogue is
   a) a month-old piglet.
   b) a spade for digging turf.
   c) a fairy spell.

5. Area-wise, Ireland's largest county is
   a) Dublin.
   b) Cork.
   c) Galway.

6. What can be heard in Dáil Éireann?
   a) Political debate
   b) Opera music
   c) Silence

7. Roddy Doyle and Maeve Binchy are
   a) novelists.
   b) musicians.
   c) politicians.

8. A sheila-na-gig is
   a) a spinning wheel.
   b) a pagan fertility symbol.
   c) a pony and trap.

9. Which American director made *The Quiet Man?*
   a) Steven Spielberg
   b) Francis Ford Coppola
   c) John Huston

10. Ireland's president is
    a) Mary McAleese.
    b) Mary Robinson.
    c) Bertie Ahern.

11. What color are Irish mailboxes?
    a) red
    b) yellow
    c) green

12. A Ban Garda is
    a) a sticky tea-bread.
    b) a female police officer.
    c) a ban on immoral publications.

coastal villages of Ireland's sunnier southeast corner or the lush river valleys of an inland county such as Kilkenny.

Color is splashed everywhere. Donegal's village cottages sparkle white while those in West Cork are as bright and varied as a child's paintbox. Flowers refuse to be confined tidily to gardens, and Kerry's seasonal colorfest ranges from the pink springtime blaze of wild rhododendrons to summertime's hedgerows of crimson fuchsia flowers, charmingly known in the old Irish language as *Deora Dé* (the tears of God). You don't need a botany degree to appreciate a stroll along the crooked trackways of Clare's Burren region, a stony wilderness that blooms into a rock garden of orchids, gentians, and other rare wildflowers each spring. Just as beguiling for ramblers are the crescent moon coves of the far west, solitary golden sand beaches where you're far more likely to encounter fami-

13. Which Irish author penned *Ulysses*?
   a) W. B. Yeats
   b) James Joyce
   c) Samuel Beckett

14. Where are the Cliffs of Moher?
   a) Clare
   b) Kerry
   c) Donegal

15. In an Irish placename the word cnoc means
   a) fortress.
   b) church.
   c) hill.

16. How do you pronounce "lough," the usual word for a lake in Ireland?
   a) luff
   b) low
   c) lock

17. You go into a turf accountant's office to
   a) buy turf.
   b) place a bet.
   c) buy a horse.

18. The Battle of the Boyne took place in
   a) 1690.
   b) 1916.
   c) 1140.

19. The Romans called Ireland "Hibernia," meaning
   a) Land of Winter.
   b) Land of Water.
   c) Land of Dreams.

20. In Irish, a Meiriceánach is
   a) a mercenary.
   b) an American.
   c) a missionary.

Answers: 1-c; 2-a; 3-b; 4-c; 5-b; 6-a; 7-a; 8-b; 9-c; 10-a; 11-c; 12-b; 13-b; 14-a; 15-c; 16-c; 17-b; 18-a; 19-a; 20-b.

Score: 16-20 correct: Clever clogs! You've been here before, haven't you? 10-15 Well done! You obviously have a love for all things Irish. 5-9 Ah well, everyone admires a trier! Under 5. Hmm. I'd like to be in the doctor's office when you show him your crubeen. (It's a pig's trotter!)

lies of seals and otters than regiments of sunbathers armed with boom boxes and cell phones.

A Land of Myths and Legends

Complementing all the attractions for the eye is balm for the soul. The rich layer-cake of Irish myth and tradition is just one awaiting feast. The call of the past is another. Laced with pilgrim paths, replete with countless historical remains, Ireland once shimmered at the very edge of medieval Christendom. This remote island outpost of saints and scholars was where the maps ran out and the known world ended.

For anyone with even a smidgen of romance in their soul, the allure of long ago is irresistible. The early Irish bequeathed an incomparably rich legacy, not just of ornately carved crosses and high round towers but also of manuscript illumination, folklore, and gold and silver craftsmanship. Celtic metalsmiths produced sumptuous treasures, often decorated with stylized enamel animals and studded with amber and rock crystal. Masterpieces such as the Tara Brooch and Ardagh Chalice have never been equaled let alone surpassed.

> *A cliché it may be, but Ireland really is one of the friendliest, safest, and most relaxing countries in which to live.*

Have you ever yearned to slip through a crack in time and connect with the long-gone world of myth and magic? Countless localities resonate with even older messages than those left by the scholarly Celtic monks who doused Druidic bonfires with Christianity. Ireland is a land with a thoroughly pagan past, a twilight realm of mysterious stone circles, hollow hills, and prehistoric earthen burial mounds known as "fairy raths." Every mirror-bright lake and green-cloaked mountain seems spellbound by enchantments: Listen hard and you'll hear the westerly winds still carry the fading whisper of otherworldly voices.

It's always *a lovely day for a Guinness.*

© Steenie Harvey

The midsummer bonfires of St. John's Eve are but a continuation of the ancient fires lit in honor of the goddess Danu. Hallowe'en originates from the great feast of *Samhain*, when the door to the Celtic otherworld was said to creak fully open. The Garland Sunday pilgrimage to Croagh Patrick, now a holy mountain but once a pagan sun sanctuary, takes place around *Lughnasa*, a Celtic feast celebrating the harvest. So does Kerry's Puck Fair, an age-old festival in which a goat is hoisted aloft a platform to oversee the shenanigans. You never have to go far below the surface to find the pulse of Ireland's ever-present Celtic past.

Ireland's famous (or infamous) laid-back lifestyle is

another good reason to bid farewell to the rat race. A cliché it may be, but Ireland really is one of the friendliest, safest, and most relaxing countries in which to live. It's a caring society in which people are still more important than profits. Hospital treatment is free, and if you need medical attention, you'll find family doctors make house calls—even in the middle of the night.

Whether you're looking for a retirement destination, a vacation home, or a place to raise a young family, it's easy to fall in love with Ireland. Yes, the clouds do sometimes leak but, contrary to wicked rumors, the country does enjoy its share of dry days and sunshine. And although the country remains divided, immense progress has been made in solving the problems of Northern Ireland.

A Hundred Thousand Welcomes

The drawbacks? Well, Ireland isn't an inexpensive place to live—you'll certainly find the cost of running a car is higher than at home. And although it's still possible to buy a nice home for under $100,000, here as everywhere, price depends upon location. Be warned that a huge prosperity gap exists between Ireland's eastern seaboard and many western communities. For anything resembling a bargain-priced home, it's necessary to look to rural areas where the Celtic tiger has yet to roar. Dublin and its surrounding counties have benefited most from the booming economy, and this translates into property values. House prices in these pockets of affluence have surpassed those in many other major European cities. To

U2—Ireland's well-known rock band. Has fame gone to their heads?

© Steenie Harvey

experience the Dublin lifestyle, you may have to consider renting rather than buying.

But wherever you choose to live, you won't pay property taxes. And many of you will be able to travel around the country for absolutely nothing: All retirees ride free on the country's public transport systems. Seniors entitled to Irish citizenship or who are receiving social security pensions may also be able to benefit from free health and welfare plans for older people. Who says that age doesn't have its advantages?

Although relocating to another country is always a bold move, it's a blessing to know that in Ireland you'll be spared the constant frustration of trying to communicate in a foreign language (unless, of course, you live in one of the Gaeltacht areas where the ancient Irish language is still spoken). Sure, it may take a while to decipher the different Irish accents, but folks here do speak English.

Some Americans come here to enjoy new adventures. For others it feels more like coming home. Largely due to the tragic potato famine of the 1840s and the resulting Irish diaspora, an estimated 70 million people worldwide have what you might call emerald green blood coursing through their veins. But that doesn't mean you need Irish ancestry to make new friends and fully appreciate the quality of life here. Whatever your own background, you'll find the phrase *Céad Míle Fáilte* (a hundred thousand welcomes) applies to you too.

2 An Emerald Overview

What makes Ireland tick? This chapter aims to tell you something about the places and faces—the land, its climate, its people, and their civil structures and social lifestyle.

The Land

Comprising a total area of 27,137 square miles (84,421 square kilometers), the island of Ireland is a little larger than West Virginia. It lies in the Atlantic Ocean at the extreme edge of northwestern Europe. A highland fringe of hills and mountains hems the interior of fertile rolling plains, loughs (lakes), and river valleys. The western Atlantic coast is especially inviting with sandy coves tucked away between cliffs and rocky headlands. Hills march in an almost continuous chain from Donegal to West Cork, the highest pinnacles clustered in the southwest. County Kerry's dramatic landscapes include Carrantuohill, at 3,405 feet (1,038 meters) Ireland's highest mountain.

Ireland's longest river is the Shannon, a 155-mile (259-kilometer) water highway that forms a glittering necklace of loughs as it meanders in a southwesterly direction from its source, the Shannon Pot, in county Cavan. Other notable rivers include the Liffey, which runs through Dublin, and Cork's river Lee. In the northeast, the banks of the Boyne River witnessed a bloody battle between Catholic and Protestant forces in 1690.

Almost 17 percent of the country is covered by peat bogs. Mainly found in the west and midlands, peat bogs consist of water and decayed vegetation and formed around 8,000 to 10,000 years ago. Two types of bogs, raised bogs and blanket bogs, provide fuel for domestic and industrial usage. Peat—or turf, as it is usually called in Ireland—is harvested mostly by machine nowadays, but in some communities it continues to be cut by hand.

From its limpid loughs to its encircling seas, Ireland is a world of water. Rivers and loughs are the habitats of wild salmon, brown trout, char, eel, pike, and bream—and also the haunt of the reclusive otter that feasts upon them. Seals bask along rocky coasts, and Dingle boasts a famous resident wild dolphin. Of Ireland's 31 mammal species, the ones you're most likely to spot are rabbit, fox, and badger. Hares, stoats, and squirrels are also common; smaller species include hedgehogs, field mice, and shrews. Elusive pine martens are found in forests, and the country also supports herds of red deer, notably in Kerry and Donegal. As for reptiles, the legend is true: There are no snakes. The single reptilian denizen of Ireland is the common lizard. The island's only amphibians are a solitary species each of toad, frog, and newt.

Some 380 species of wild birds have been recorded, with 135 breeding here. Year-round residents that feed in gardens include various types of finches and tits, blackbirds, songthrushes, and red-breasted robins. Walk by a lough and you'll often glimpse the turquoise flash of a kingfisher or a solitary gray heron flapping towards its reedbed hideaway. Summer migrants include swallows, swifts, and various kinds of woodland warblers; winter visitors include fieldfares from Scandinavia and white-fronted geese from Greenland; about half the world's population overwinters around Wexford.

Seaside Baltimore, county Cork, is always jumping on summer weekends.

© Steenie Harvey

The thousands of miles of unspoiled coastline offer excellent opportunities for viewing seabirds such as cormorants, stormy petrels, and puffins.

The Weather

Ireland knows little about typhoons, ice storms, or killer heat waves. Influenced by the Gulf Stream, the mild maritime climate is remarkably consistent with few extremes. Seasonal temperatures hardly vary throughout the entire country, and April in Dublin feels much the same as April in Galway. Although it occasionally gets hot, it's never too hot. Winter sometimes brings a few chilly days, but heavy snowfalls are rare except in mountainous areas.

> *From its limpid loughs to its encircling seas, Ireland is a world of water.*

The coldest months are usually January and February with mean daily temperatures hovering between 39 and 44 degrees Fahrenheit (between 4 and 7 Celsius). July and August tend to be warmest: 57 to 60 degrees Farenheit (14 to 16 degrees Celsius) on average, though the mercury has risen to 85 degrees Farenheit (30 degrees Celsius) on rare occasions. May and June usually produce the most sunshine, averaging five to seven hours per day.

The driest months are April, May, and June, but rainfall levels should not be underestimated. The west's picture-postcard landscapes get it in bucketfuls! You may find yourself opening an umbrella on as many as 270 days per year. In 2000, the small town of Crossmolina in county Mayo endured three and a half *months* of continuous rainfall. The likeliest place to escape a drenching is the southeast, where cloudbursts shed only an average annual 30 inches (750 mm). In low-lying midland areas, average rainfall usually amounts to between 31 and 47 inches (800 and 1,200 mm). Parts of the west typically receive an annual 59 inches (1,500 mm) while the mountainous southwest often experiences a monsoon-like 79 inches (2,000 mm) or more.

Ireland's Weather

County/Station	Total annual rainfall in inches (mm)	Mean temperature in °F (°C)	Daily mean sunshine in hours
Shannon Airport	35 (886)	51 (10.5)	3.59
Cork Airport	56 (1,433)	49 (9.6)	4.06
Malin Head	36 (926)	49 (9.6)	3.75
Dublin Airport	31 (787)	48 (9.1)	3.71
Valentia (Kerry)	61 (1,567)	51 (10.5)	3.58
Kilkenny	37 (951)	49 (9.6)	3.67
Belmullet (Mayo)	45 (1,136)	50 (10.0)	3.81
Rosslare	38 (961)	50.5 (10.3)	4.47

The People

The Republic's population officially stands at 3.62 million with 41 percent under the age of 25. Those are the figures from the last census. Since then, the population is believed to have risen to 3.8 million. Over a third live in the Greater Dublin area, whose boundaries encroach farther into the countryside with each passing year. Census figures for principal cities break down as follows: Dublin, 953,000; Cork, 180,000; Limerick, 79,000; Galway, 57,000; and Waterford, 44,000. Urban households account for 56 percent of the population; the remainder is made up of rural households, 16 percent of them family farms.

The last census delivered some curious statistics. If you are seeking a partner, for instance, head to Maynooth in county Kildare, where 53 percent of the adult population is single, or to the city of Galway, where half the adult residents live in unwedded bliss. In the nation as a whole, only 49 percent of citizens of marriageable age have tied the knot. Although Ireland has long tended toward late marriages, it's a sign of changing times that around a quarter of all births are now to single mothers. The birth rate itself also suggests a rebellion against traditional values: It has been falling since the 1980s, and the average number of children per family is a mere 1.8.

Ireland's spiritual power plant: Knock shrine, county Mayo

© Steenie Harvey

Of the citizens residing in the Republic, 93 percent were born in Ireland, and three out of every four still live in the county of their birth. The majority of the remaining 7 percent were born in European Union (EU) member states. Only 42,000 Irish citizens originate from other points on the globe.

People aged 65 and over account for 11 percent of the total population with a slight majority of seniors living in rural rather than urban locations. The town with most senior citizens is Kanturk in county Cork, where they number 22 percent of the total population.

Approximately 92 percent of Irish citizens are Roman Catholic. Steeped in ancient values, this truly is a land of holy wells, visions, moving statues and pilgrim paths. Each year thousands of people climb to the summit of Croagh Patrick, Ireland's "holy mountain" on the shores of county Mayo. Another famous pilgrimage is to St. Patrick's Purgatory in county Donegal, where the ritual involves fasting, sleeplessness and going barefoot.

Although Church attendance remains high in rural areas, recent scandals have reduced the Catholic hierarchy's ability to command the unquestioning respect and political influence it enjoyed in decades past. And while the Church remains closely involved in health and education services, Ireland's new generation is less awed by authority than its forbears were.

> *Steeped in ancient values, this truly is a land of holy wells, visions, moving statues and pilgrim paths.*

Of Ireland's minority faiths, the largest is Protestantism, which accounts for around 3 percent of worshippers. Church of Ireland members account for 2.35 percent of the population, Presbyterians 0.37 percent and Methodists 0.14 percent. There are also small communities of Muslims (0.11%), Jehovah's Witnesses (0.1%) and Jews (0.04%). In Northern Ireland, the religious breakdown is approximately 60 percent Protestant and 40 percent Catholic.

MINORITY GROUPS

Formerly Ireland's biggest export was its people. That is no longer true: The recent economic boom has meant more people are immigrating *to* Ireland than are leaving its shores. Even so, Ireland remains one of the EU's most ethnically homogenous countries—a whopping 99 percent are white. Some older people in rural areas have never met anyone with a different-colored skin.

Despite the Irish reputation for friendliness, racial prejudice occasionally surfaces. In recent years, certain marginalized peoples from throughout the world have targeted Ireland as a country with fairly lax asylum laws. Often arriving hidden in container lorries, around 7,000 refugees have managed to reach Ireland on ferries from France. Most originate from Eastern Europe, Turkey and sub-Saharan Africa. Their arrival has sparked racial resentment, particularly against Romanian gypsies, who are regarded as economic migrants rather than genuine refugees. Some commentators feel it's wrong that such migrants are readily offered accommodation while little is done for homeless Irish people. African refugees have also reported incidents of racial abuse, especially in inner-city Dublin. For refugees who do encounter racism, it must seem ironic that so many past generations of Irish people emigrated themselves to create better lives overseas.

The Irish also marginalize a section of their own society: the tinkers, or

Ireland's Culinary Delights

herb-encrusted Connemara lamb and wild asparagus; goujons of monkfish served in olives and oranges; a *fricassée* of clams, shrimps, scallops and mussels along with organic artichokes in a herb sauce. It all sound delicious, doesn't it? But so does venison pâté and roast Barberry duck with turnip buttons and sautéed *foie gras* in a raspberry vinegar *jus*. Or should you go for baked rock oysters with crunchy samphire followed by turbot garnished with shrimps and leeks in a wine-and-lobster butter sauce?

Irish cuisine has emerged from the Dark Ages with top restaurants and country-house hotels that produce a mouthwatering range of innovative dishes based on fresh local produce. Even in simpler seaside restaurants, seafood is almost always guaranteed to be a joy. Between seafish and shellfish, the number of edible species netted off Ireland's coast numbers well over 60. The country is renowned for salmon, but the annual fishing catch of 340,000 tonnes also includes cod, haddock, plaice and sole as well as unusual fish such as gurnard and John Dory. For a simple lunch, nothing beats a salad with a serving of smoked mackerel or rollmopp herrings, coiled silvery slivers of pickled herring filets that soak up their vinegary juices like a mop soaks up water. Follow up your fishy lunchtime treat with a plate of scrumptiously fresh Wexford strawberries or a pie made of apples grown in the famous orchards of Armagh.

Or how about some tasty brown soda bread with goat cheese? The country larder delivers top-quality meat, poultry, vegetables and dairy products; what's created from the original ingredients is up to you. At least in rural areas, most Irish families still prefer good, plain cooking of the meat-and-two-veggies variety; pork, potato and cabbage are staples. One popular family dish is Irish stew in which neck of lamb, onions, carrots and potatoes are gently simmered together. At Christmastime, butcher shops are unusually aromatic with the scent of cloves, nutmeg and other spices; it comes from joints of spiced beef, a traditional meal often complemented by roast potatoes and a dish of apples and red cabbage.

Most food items in Ireland will be familiar to Americans. As for the unfamiliar, even ice cream flavored with dulsk—seaweed!—isn't as bad as it sounds. If, however, you have a queasy stomach, avoid the following: *Crubeens* are pigs' trotters, often jokingly tagged as "low-mileage." Black pudding, appearing on many a breakfast menu, is *not* a delicious chocolate concoction, but rather a dish made from congealed pigs' blood, studded with fat, and encased in a sausage. *Drisheen*, a similar sausage, is made from sheeps' blood.

Other foods with curious names are more savory. *Boxty* is a potato pancake, usually fried with bacon, eggs and sausage. *Colcannon* is a tasty winter supper dish of mashed potatoes, onions and leftover cabbage, cooked in butter and milk. *Barm brack* is a chewy, spiced tea-bread, traditionally baked at Hallowe'en.

Irish beers and whiskeys are afforded a status that other countries usually reserve for wine. Creamy-topped stout is a delicious black beer; along with the famous Guinness brand, you can also weigh up the merits of Murphy's and Beamish. Harp lager is sold in most pubs, as is a British-style bitter called Smithwicks (pronounced Smithicks, with a silent "w"). Popular brands of Irish whiskey are Jameson's, Paddy, Powers and Blackbush. The notorious *poitín* is illicitly distilled moonshine liquor, often made from potatoes. Production is illegal so *poitín* is only likely to be available from "a man who knows the cousin of a man who knows."

"traveling people," as they prefer to be called. Journeying between halting sites and litter-strewn roadside rest stops, few tinkers wander the roads in horse-drawn caravans any longer. The barrel-shaped Romany *vado* wagons have long since been replaced by unromantic modern trailer homes. There are 10,800 or so travelers within the country, and few "settled" Irish people have a good word to say about them. Prejudice runs high, and whether justified or not, any outbreak of petty crime is invariably put down to tinkers.

Some say the tinkers are descended from orphans cast out on the roads during the Famine; others believe they share a distant kinship with European gypsies. Members of close-knit communities who still produce large families, tinkers' average lifespan is shockingly low. Census figures suggest only 1 percent of travelers can expect to live past age 65. Tinkers once made a living by tinsmithing and horse dealing, but, although they still congregate at horse fairs, no housewife requires her pots and pans to be mended by nomads anymore. Most menfolk now deal in scrap metal and used car parts, and it's not uncommon to see traveler children begging. At festivals, some women make money by telling fortunes.

Education

Education within the Republic of Ireland is compulsory between the ages of 6 and 15. While schooling is free, the cost of books and most extracurricular activities is not, though poorer families do receive book grants and school uniform allowances. Until around the age of 12, most children attend National Schools. Serving around 500,000 children, the primary system incorporates 3,200 mainstream schools staffed by around 20,000 teachers. In Gaeltacht areas, the entire curriculum (excluding English and foreign-language lessons) is conducted in Irish.

Second-level education consists of a three-year Junior Cycle followed by a two- or three-year Senior Cycle. Most post-primary schools are run by religious organizations or are vocational schools with boards of governors. Over 95 percent of funding is met by the State, but again, students' families pay for books and extras. Some 370,000 students are currently being educated at a total of 775 publicly aided schools.

Going to college or university depends on how well students do in the Leaving Certificate exam, which they take at 17 or 18. Competition for college admission, allocated on a points system, is fierce, particularly at prestigious universities such as Dublin's Trinity College. With tuition fees recently abolished, college has become a lot more accessible; about 90,000 students are now enrolled in higher education. However, putting your kids through college is still an expensive business as student maintenance grants are means-tested against parental income.

Crime and Safety

Crime and personal safety issues are important considerations when contemplating relocation. How many murders were there in your own home town or city last year? Over the past few years, murders in the Irish Republic have numbered less than 50 annually. But although Ireland's crime rate is one of the lowest in the EU, Dublin does have drug problems. Addicts require funds and aren't too fussy about who provides them. Just as you would in any city, lock your car and keep an eye open for pickpockets, bag snatchers and other shady characters.

In rural areas, the crime problem is minimal. Leaf through the provincial papers and you'll see that the "criminals" who have appeared in court are likely to be speeding motorists, the odd feuding neighbor and pub landlords caught serving drinks at 3 o'clock in the morning—or their customers. It is actually an offense to be found on licensed premises after closing time.

Politics

In 1920, Britain's Government of Ireland Act partitioned Ireland. Understanding how to refer to the two different parts of the island can be baffling. Over 75 percent of the landmass, 43,926 square miles (70,282 square kilometers), forms the Republic of Ireland (southern Ireland). This book focuses on the Republic, and its residents usually call it "Ireland." Official documents often refer to the Republic as "the State." You've probably also seen the word *Éire*, the Irish-language name for the island of Ireland. Rarely used in everyday speech, *Éire* is normally restricted to texts in the Irish language.

Before plunging into the morass of the Republic's politics, it's worth clarifying the situation in neighboring Northern Ireland. Often referred to by its citizens as "the Province," it is part of the United Kingdom of Great Britain and Northern Ireland. Although many people regard its problems as solely sectarian, recent struggles have been about political power. The majority of Northern Ireland Protestants vote the Unionist ticket and both David Trimble's Ulster Unionist Party (UUP) and Ian Paisley's Democratic Unionist Party (DUP) want to maintain strong links with Britain and its monarchy. Most Catholics vote for Nationalist or Republican parties such as John Hume's SDLP or Sinn Féin, both of which support the concept of a united Ireland.

Until the formation of the new Northern Ireland Assembly in 1998, which delegated greater power to local politicians, the Province came under Westminster's jurisdiction. Its legal and political framework is separate from that of the Irish Republic, and Queen Elizabeth II is head of state. Although Northern Ireland's "Troubles" never really affected the economy or day-to-day lives of Irish people in the south, happenings across the border have always been headline news. When the Irish Republic's Constitution was drawn up, it laid claim to the entire island of Ireland, which didn't help to foster good relations with the North's Unionist majority. However, in a referendum following 1998's Good Friday Agreement between Northern Ireland's Unionists and Nationalists, the Republic's citizens voted by an overwhelming majority to rescind Constitutional claims to their neighbors' territory.

To further muddy the waters, the island of Ireland is divided into the same four provinces as before Partition. Roughly corresponding to north, south, east and west, these provinces are called Ulster, Munster, Leinster and Connacht. Although Ulster is often used as a synonym for Northern Ireland, parts of this province lie within the Republic's territory, that is, counties Donegal, Cavan and Monaghan.

The four provinces are subdivided into 32 counties: 26 in the Republic of Ireland and six in Northern Ireland. The Republic's largest county is Cork, the smallest Louth. The capital of the Irish Republic is Dublin, also the country's main commercial port. Northern Ireland's principal city is Belfast.

Waltzing Matilda: Australian busker with didgeridoo on Grafton Street, Dublin

© Steenie Harvey

A PARLIAMENTARY DEMOCRACY

With a legal system based on the Constitution of 1937, the Republic of Ireland is a parliamentary democracy. The Oireachtas, or national parliament, consists of the office of the President along with a House of Representatives (Dáil Éireann) and Senate (Seanad Éireann). The main political power rests with Dáil Éireann, whose 166 members are elected by the people for a maximum term of five years. Elected members to the Dáil are called Teachtaí Dála (TDs). The Prime Minister holds the title An Taoiseach.

The Republic's 26 counties are divided into 41 Dáil constituencies, each returning between three and five TDs. Known as proportional representation by single transferable vote, the voting method (PRSTV) is fairly complicated and based on a quota system.

The electoral system invariably produces coalition governments. Under Taoiseach Bertie Ahern, the present government is a power-sharing arrangement between the centrist Fianna Fáil party, the smaller but more right-wing Progressive Democrats and various Independents. The previous administration (the Rainbow Coalition) consisted of some curious bedfellows: the right-of-center Fine Gael party, the soft-left Labour Party and the solidly socialistic Democratic Left. As Fine Gael or Fianna Fáil always make up the largest party in whatever coalition is formed, the governance of the country remains on a fairly even keel with few major policy swings. Other political parties attracting limited amounts of support within the Republic include Sinn Féin, the Workers' Party and the Green Party.

The Seanad's 60 senators are either nominated directly by the Taoiseach or indirectly elected from within five panels with particular expertise. More a discussion forum than a body with political clout, the Seanad can, however, petition the President to refuse to sign a bill until the matter is put before the people in a referendum. No bill can become law without the President's signature.

Like TDs, the President (an Uachtarán) is elected by popular vote. The current incumbent is Mary McAleese, who suceeded Mary Robinson. The President's term of office is seven years, and he or she can only stand for re-election once. Although the office is largely ceremonial, the President takes on the role of guardian of the Constitution, which lays down the fundamental rights of citizens.

Guaranteeing a swathe of rights, the Constitution covers personal rights, the family, education, private property and religion. Amendments can take place only if the people give their say-so in a referendum. Social change recently resulted in one important amendment: Divorce is now allowed through the Irish courts. And while the rights of the unborn child were designed to be protected by the Constitution, abortion remains a thorny issue.

Modern-day Ireland

In the early 1990s, a case in which a young rape victim was prevented by the courts from traveling to Britain for an abortion resulted in a hotly contested public debate. Were Irish women to be subjected to pregnancy tests at ports and airports before being given leave to travel? In the subsequent 1992 referendum, the people voted to clarify the matter by allowing all citizens freedom of movement. Even so, abortion for any reason whatsoever—including rape, incest or a severely malformed fetus—remains outlawed.

On the defense front, Ireland is not a member of NATO and, like Switzerland, maintains a neutral stance. Enrollment in the defense force is voluntary. Of the 11,500 members of the permanent defense force, around 9,500 men and women serve in the Army, 1,000 in the Air Corps and 1,000 in the Naval Service. It is not unusual to see soldiers guarding bank premises when large amounts of cash are being transferred. As well as defending the State against any foreign aggression, another of the Army's duties is to aid the civil powers. Because the Gardaí (police) are mainly unarmed, Army-backed bank security was increased following IRA bank raids during the 1970s.

Some 800 Army personnel are also active in United Nations peacekeeping missions. Their involvement ranges from monitoring and observation duties to a humanitarian role. The Air Corps' brief includes search-and-rescue operations, air ambulance missions and fishery protection patrols. The Naval Service is also involved in fishery protection.

Money

Now that you've got your head around the island's political geography, a word about the currency. Recent visitors to Ireland will have been used to getting punts in exchange for their dollars. However, January 1, 2002, was E-day. This was when euro bank notes and coins were put into circulation, and Irish notes and coins started to be withdrawn. Each euro is divided into 100 cents. The largest coin is worth 2 euros; smaller coins come in values of 1 euro, 50 cents, 20, 10, 5, 2 and 1 cents. One side of the euro coins

Symbolic of the sun, cartwheels of hay dot the summertime pastures.

© Steenie Harvey

depicts a national design. The Irish design consists of a harp, the word *Éire* and the year of issue, surrounded by the stars of the EU flag.

Carrying designs of bridges, euro bank notes come in denominations of 500, 200, 100, 50, 20, 10 and 5. If you still have old Irish money stashed away from previous visits, Ireland's Central Bank will exchange them for euros. However, if you travel across the border into Northern Ireland, you'll need to change your euros into pounds sterling.

All prices given throughout the book have been calculated on an exchange rate of 1 euro = US $0.87.

Although the setting of interest rates is now decided by the European Central Bank, any plans for European federalism still have a long way to go. Despite Europe's monetary marriage, Irish politicians aren't entirely toothless when it comes to fiscal policies. For example, the Finance Minister still juggles the country's budget.

3 Planning Your Fact-Finding Trip

If the Emerald Isle is new to you, don't "over-egg the pudding" by trying to cram too much in. Independent travelers often think they'll be able to see everything in less than a week. Yes, Ireland is a small country, but clocking up the distances takes much longer than almost every first-time visitor imagines.

It's easy to look at a map and plan a weeklong trip with overnight stays in Dublin, Cork, Kerry, Clare, Galway, Mayo and Sligo. Such an itinerary would be utterly senseless. Where's the joy in spending most of your precious travel time on the road, seeing nothing but snapshot views and fleeing like hunted refugees from one overnight stop to another? Yes, you'll have the joy of bragging to friends that you covered the entire west of Ireland, but you could have saved your money and bought a video. A jaunt like that is strictly for the demented and won't even give you an inkling of what makes Ireland so special.

How are you going to make time to feel the pulse of a strange town or absorb the local history and folklore? Or to walk along a silver strand to a little fishing village and watch the nets and lobster pots being mended? A frantic itinerary certainly affords no chance to go exploring off the beaten track, along narrow byways and pilgrim paths where the attractions range from tumbledown medieval towerhouses to holy wells dedicated to obscure saints. And where will you find opportunities to visit realtors' offices and pick up property listings?

"But I don't have time for a lengthy trip," you may be saying. "Not this year." Maybe you haven't, but that doesn't mean you have to tick off every major tourist destination mentioned in the guidebooks. Take your time and get to know one or two areas really well. Everything else will still be here on your next trip.

Forget those plans to leave Cork City after breakfast, have the Ring of Kerry done by tea time, and be in Dingle by nightfall. You'll be left with no time at all to discover the endless pleasures of harbor town Kinsale, with its clifftop fortresses and higgledy-piggledy laneways, its brightly painted shops and flower-laden windowboxes; no energy to explore the color-washed cottages and old-fashioned shopfronts of Clonakilty; no peace of mind to bring to the beautiful coves and clifftop walks that stud Cork's coast all the way to Mizen Head. Do you really want to forgo all those delights just to follow the same breakneck speed as the tour buses?

The first thing to determine is what you hope to get from an Irish vacation. What is enticing you across the Atlantic in the first place? Ireland's scenery and historical heritage? The quirky pubs, colorful festivals and traditional music culture? Or perhaps the chance to trace your roots and get to know the people in the area your ancestors came from? With a bit of preliminary planning, it won't be difficult to devise an itinerary to cover your own particular interests. And even if your traveling companion has a different agenda, that needn't present a problem. Wherever you travel in Ireland, golf fiends and fishing addicts are well cared for!

Package Tour versus Solo Travel

To be honest, for me there's no contest: I'll opt for solo travel every time. On most coach tour vacations, you are entirely in the company of people of your own nationality. That's fine if you like your compatriots, but not so great if you're hoping to meet actual Irish people.

By and large, the tour companies travel the same routes, stay in similar hotels and offer the same kind of options: a whistle-stop tour around postcard destinations interspersed with endless opportunities for buying gifts and souvenirs. Kissing the Blarney Stone, attending some pseudo-medieval banquet, and shopping for leprechaun soap-on-a-rope at Bunratty Folk Park does not mean you will have touched the real Ireland. I recently spoke with an American visitor who told me about a trip to Howth's Abbey Tavern near Dublin, an establishment that caters to coach parties. He was enjoying himself until something suddenly clicked. Apart from the waiting staff and singers, he realized that every last person there was a foreign tourist.

The trouble with high-profile tourist areas is the great preponderance of other tourists—not just Americans but crowds of Brits, Italians, Japanese

top tips

- Passport in order? You'll need it to enter Ireland. Just in case, ensure that it's valid for longer than your intended stay. U.S. citizens don't need visas.
- If you take medication, carry a doctor's letter detailing why you need it and naming any generic brand that could be a substitute.
- Take advantage of duty-free shopping. Despite the EU's single market, visitors from North America can still avail themselves of duty-free allowances. Current regulations let you import 200 cigarettes, one liter of liquor, two liters of wine, 60 mls of perfume, 250 mls of eau de toilette and dutiable goods to the value of approximately $40.
- Try planning your visit outside of July and August. Transatlantic fares are lower, and driving around Ireland will be much more leisurely.
- Change currency and traveler's checks in banks, normally open on weekdays between 10 A.M. and 3 P.M. Hotels, bureaux de change and post offices offer less favorable rates.
- When buying gifts, watch for stores displaying "Tax Free Shopping" signs. Non-EU citizens can reclaim VAT (sales tax) on purchases. You'll be given a voucher that can then be cashed at Dublin or Shannon Airport.
- Don't forget comfy walking shoes and raingear. And leave room in the suitcase for those bulky Aran sweaters you'll be taking back.
- Guard against pickpockets, particularly at Dublin's bus and railway stations.
- Don't barge to the front of the queue at taxi ranks. It's not appreciated!

and just about any other nationality you could mention. Like it or not, when you visit Killarney and Bunratty you're destined to be just another faceless unit on the great tourism conveyor belt. That said, a packaged coach tour allows you to see a fair bit of the country if time is very limited and you don't want to rent a car.

Of course, there's a world of difference if you choose a small tour company catering to specialty interests. Like-minded fellow travelers make for good company, especially if you're single. If you enjoy history and culture, it's hard to imagine anything worse than a general coach tour accompanied by traveling companions who jabber endlessly about shopping. Thankfully, any archaeology tour—or, indeed, any golf or fishing tour—will avoid delivering its participants to the doors of Blarney Woolen Mills, Avoca Handweavers and various crystal outlets. A browse through travel sections of major newspapers will give you an idea of what U.S. tour companies offer in the way of specialty tours of Ireland.

GOING IT ALONE

Once you're in Ireland, my recommendation, depending on your time, is to spend a couple of days getting acquainted with Dublin first. From the Liffey Quays to its elegant Georgian squares, the city is compact enough to explore on foot. Those legendary pubs aside, there's plenty in Dublin to keep you busy. Visit Trinity College and see the Book of Kells, spend some time in the art galleries and museums, plunge into the stores around Grafton Street, and wander the cobbled lanes of bohemian Temple Bar with its numerous bars and restaurants.

One unmissable side trip from the capital is to the prehistoric passage tombs at Newgrange and Knowth in county Meath. Built over 5,000 years ago by Neolithic farmers, these mysterious tombs are older than both the Egyptian pyramids and Stonehenge. Situated on a loop of the river Boyne, Newgrange is famous throughout the world for its connection with the winter solstice, when a shaft of sunlight penetrates the pitch-black central chamber at dawn on December 21. If you don't have a rental car, Bus Éireann offer a Boyne Valley and Newgrange tour from Dublin for $19. You can book direct from the Busaras office on Store Street, tel +353 (0)1 836 6111.

Another fascinating excursion from Dublin is into the "Garden County," Wicklow. While you're traveling through the Wicklow Mountains, two places that definitely merit a visit are the magnificent formal gardens of Powerscourt and the ancient monastic site of Glendalough. You could combine both with Mary Gibbons Coach Tours, which offers a number of day trips from the capital. The Wicklow trip costs $20 with pick-ups from many main hotels. Contact the company at 12 St. Catherine's Court, Newgrove Avenue, Sandymount, Dublin 4; tel +353 (0)1 283 9973.

Galway's Eyre Square

© Steenie Harvey

FINDING SOMEWHERE TO STAY

In Dublin there's no shortage of hotels, guesthouses, and bed-and-breakfast establishments. If you arrive without accommodation, tourist offices at the airport and within the city offer a booking service for a fee of around $3. If you're staying for more than one night (and most people will), many hotels offer special weekend and midweek rates. These are definitely worth inquiring about as they're a lot more affordable than rack rates.

For example, if you want to treat yourself to a swanky five-star hotel, the most famous is the Shelbourne, overlooking St.

Stephen's Green, ideally located in the heart of southside Dublin. This legendary hotel has been in business since 1824. Weekend rates (two nights) are $275 per person, sharing, and include full Irish breakfast. Tel +353 (0)1 6634500, fax +353 (0)1 6616006, email: shelbourneinfo@forte-hotels.com.

In the heart of Georgian Dublin, Buswells Hotel on Molesworth Street is an 18th-century townhouse. Just across the road from the Parliament Buildings, it offers a special midweek rate of $177 to $195 (three nights bed and breakfast per person). Tel +353 (0)1 614 6500. Email: buswells@quinn-hotels.com. If you want to spend all night in a pub, O'Neills (36/37 Pearse St., Dublin 2, tel +353 (0)1 671 4074) is the place for you. Including breakfast, a twin room in this Victorian pub costs from $36 to $42 per person sharing.

> *One unmissable side trip from the capital is to the prehistoric passage tombs at Newgrange and Knowth in county Meath.*

For more information about Dublin accommodations, contact Dublin Tourism, Suffolk Street, Dublin 2. Once in Ireland, call the special Callsave number, tel 1850 230330, or email: information@dublintourism.ie, or visit the website: www.visitdublin.ie.

Follow your trip to the capital with a stay in just one or two areas that particularly appeal. Rather than hop around, base yourself in a central location and then explore the surrounding area on day trips. Renting a car affords more freedom, but daily coach excursions are readily available during summer from main tourist centers. Look at what you could do on days out from a base in Galway City:

- Head west towards Clifden and explore the landscapes of Connemara and its coastal villages.
- Take the ferry to one of the Aran Islands, rocky bastions of Gaelic civilization where Irish is the day-to-day language.
- Walk part of the Burren Way in Clare, looking for rare wildflowers and plotting a course past Neolithic stone settlements and abandoned famine villages. After a lunchtime picnic, head to the Cliffs of Moher then call in for refreshments at Doolin village, renowned for traditional music.
- Sample oysters and seafood at Moran's of the Weir, a quaint thatched pub and restaurant near the oyster village of Clarinbridge. Then continue to Kinvara, a pretty fishing village in south county Galway.
- Take a pleasure cruise up island-studded Lough Corrib to fairytale Ashford Castle in county Mayo. Then walk through the castle's woods to Cong village with its ruined abbey, market cross and stone bridges.

One of the best places to stay in Galway is the five-star Glenlo Abbey Hotel, just five minutes by taxi from the city center. A charmingly restored 18th-century manor house at Bushy Park, it boasts its own golf course beside Lough Corrib and an excellent restaurant. Special weekend break rates (two nights B&B + one dinner) are from $177 to $283 per person, sharing. Tel +353 (0)91 526666, email: glenlo@iol.ie.

If you prefer city bustle, Eyre Square is only a short stroll from the countless stores, pubs and restaurants around Shop Street and Quay Street. Looking over Eyre Square, the Great Southern hotel offers a raft of special deals: two-night weekend breaks from $130 pps; five-night midweek breaks from $260 pps. This is good value—the rack rate for a single overnight stay is $87 to $104. Tel +353 (0)91 564041, email: res@galway.gsh.ie.

Mostly charging between $24 and $30 per person per night, there's a plethora of B&B establishments in Galway's seaside suburb, Salthill. It's only a 10-minute bus ride to the heart of the city, and you can watch the sun set over Galway Bay. Try Mrs. O'Hare at Rose Villa, 10 Cashelnara, Knocknacarra Cross, Salthill, Galway (tel +353 (0)91 584200); or Mrs. Lydon, Carraig Beag, 1 Burren View Heights, Knocknacarra Road, Salthill, Galway (tel +353 (0)91 521696).

For something a little different, stay in a two-bedroom luxury apartment in a converted old grain mill beside the Corrib River in Galway city center. Apartments sleep four and cost $307 per week low season, rising to $590 per week during July and August. Sometimes one is available for a two-night weekend stay (though not in high summer), in which case the cost is $189. Contact Granary Hall, 58 Dominick St., Galway; tel +353 (0)91 562595, email: arantvl@iol.ie.

Explore West Cork and Kerry

Spare at least four or five days for this spectacularly scenic region, drifting slowly westwards from Kinsale to Clonakilty and the pretty harbor villages of Glandore, Baltimore and Schull.

There's no shortage of restaurants and good music pubs in any of these places, but when it comes to gourmet cuisine, Kinsale offers the widest choice of top-notch restaurants. Attractions include taking a boat trip across Roaringwater Bay to Cape Clear Island, or hiking along shady lanes and discovering the mysterious Druidic stone circle at Drombeg. And though they're a bleak and emotionally upsetting reminder of Ireland's troubled past, the famine sites around Skibbereen shouldn't be missed.

For one of West Cork's best beaches, continue west from Schull along the Mizen Peninsula and watch for signs for Barleycove. If the sea temperature is warm enough, it's safe to swim at this sheltered spot, an enchanted place where the light turns the ocean into an entrancing swirl of sapphire, jade and turquoise. During summer, the colors of the West Cork coast are simply delectable: purple heather blanketing the mountains, gardens overflowing with pink and blue hydrangea bushes, and hedgerows ablaze with blood-red fuchsias, orange montbretias, lacy white cow parsley and the mauve spires of foxgloves.

From Bantry, head north through the Caha Mountains of the Beara Peninsula that is shared by counties Cork and Kerry. The winding road dips down into the garden village of Glengarriff before continuing to Kenmare, a stopping point on the famous Ring of Kerry. A bustling town of brightly painted houses, many of which date back to the 17th century, Kenmare's name in Irish is *Neidín* (the little nest). One of its best-known crafts is lace making, a business originally set up by the nuns of the Poor Clare Convent to create employment after the great famine of 1845.

Whizzing around the 112-mile length of the Ring of Kerry takes a mini-mum of six hours and that's allowing only for cursory stops at the main highlights. Summer traffic over the mountain passes that link Kenmare to the main tourism hub, Killarney town, moves at the speed of molasses—you've been warned! Around the Ring of Kerry itself, the attractions are almost endless. You can take a pleasure cruise on the Lakes of Killarney, walk the old coach roads and nature trails of Killarney National Park, or take a boat trip out to the remote pinnacle of Skellig Michael, where anchorite monks once lived out a lonely, storm-tossed existence.

If you have a penchant for archaeological sites, Kerry's Irish-speaking Dingle Peninsula has more than 2,000—everything from monastic beehive huts to prehistoric forts. A drive around the peninsula delivers up magical views of the deserted Blasket Islands, and the silver strand at Inch is one of the country's best. Dingle town's music pubs provide lively entertainment,

Kinsale, county Cork, is a bustling harbor town and port resort.

© Steenie Harvey

FISHERIES BOARD PATROL

tipping

When dining out, it's customary to tip around 10 percent of the bill, though this doesn't apply in fast food places or eateries with counter service where patrons help themselves. Some restaurants add the tip as a "service charge" to your bill, so check it carefully—it's not necessary to tip again. If you have received bad service, stand up for your rights and refuse to pay the service charge.

Don't tip bartenders unless drinks are brought to a table. As few establishments offer table service anyway, it's not something you'll encounter much. However, if you get into conversation with a friendly bartender, you may want to ask him to join you for a drink.

It's not obligatory to tip porters, but most people give a few coins to avoid feeling uncomfortable. Nor is it obligatory to tip taxi drivers, but few enjoy being deprived of their expected 10 percent. Some Dublin cabbies are quick to treat ungrateful customers to rather colorful language. As for hairdressers, it's customary for women to tip around 10 percent. Barbers shops and unisex salons don't really expect a man to leave anything. On coach tour vacations, it's usual to tip both the guide and driver around $12 apiece. Your tour company will explain whether this is already included in the package price.

and many serve evening meals for $7 to $10. I enjoyed a piece of freshly caught sole the size of a dinner plate at Murphy's, one of a string of cozy inns along Strand Street near the harbor. Fishermen here supplement their income by taking visitors on sea-angling excursions and trips to see Fungie, the Dingle Dolphin. Dolphin trips cost $7 ($3.50 for kids), and if he fails to show you'll get your money back. You can also take a two-hour dolphin swim for $12; renting full wetsuit gear costs $28.

Scarlet ribbons—the laneways of Kerry and Cork are banked with wild fuchsia hedgerows.

© Steenie Harvey

ACCOMMODATION IN WEST CORK AND KERRY

Bed-and-breakfast accommodation is excellent value. Why pay for expensive hotel rooms when you'll be spending most of your time seeing the sights? And there's no need to worry about advance booking. Any tourist office in the area can book you accommodation in another part of the southwest for a $3 fee, no matter how many phone calls it takes. I walked into the tourist office in Kenmare in county Kerry at 4:30 in the afternoon, and they booked me a B&B in Bantry in county Cork for that same August night. The elderly couple who ran the Bantry B&B where I stayed have now retired, but two other southwest B&Bs I can definitely recommend are:

- Mrs. Sheila O'Regan, Riverside B&B, 5 Millgrove, Fernhill Road, Clonakilty, county Cork. Tel +353 (0)23 35221. A 10-minute walk from the town center, all rooms are en-suite with TV and tea/coffee making facilities. The full Irish breakfast includes the famous (or infamous) Clonakilty Black Pudding. A nice touch was tea and homemade cakes in the kitchen on arrival. Price per person: $24.
- Mrs. Mary Sheehy, Sheehy's B&B, Milltown, Dingle, county Kerry. Tel +353 (0)66 9152104. Opposite St. Brendan's Creek and a wildflower meadow, this pink B&B is a 15-minute stroll from Dingle town center. Rooms are en-suite, there's a comfy guest lounge, and the chatty owners let you borrow walking and cycling maps. Price per person: $21.50.

If you intend to treat yourself to a top-class hotel, do it in Killarney and contemplate the splendor of the lakes from your window. The pampered luxury offered by Hotel Europe (Lakeshore Road, Killarney; tel +353 (0)64 31900) is just heaven. Guests can go boating on the lake, horseback riding, or work off excess energy in the leisure center, which includes a gym,

Sightseeing Savings

It won't cost a penny to visit Dublin's National Museum, where you can marvel at the wonderful stash of Celtic gold artifacts. If you're interested in art, another free treat awaits at the National Gallery on Dublin's Merrion Square. The museum boasts solid collections of works by renowned Irish artists such as Jack B. Yeats and Paul Henry as well as works by Rembrandt, El Greco, Goya and Picasso.

Of course, not everything is free. Visiting Irish castles and monasteries can be quite costly, for example. Anyone planning a serious assault on Ireland's historical trail should pick up a Heritage Card, good for an entire year. Costing $18 ($12 for seniors, $7 for students), it allows unlimited access to numerous historical sites under the care of Dúchas, the public body that cares for ancient monuments. Sites include the Rock of Cashel, Trim Castle and Boyle Abbey. Check out the website at www.heritageireland.ie. For more information, contact Dúchas, Department of Arts, Heritage, Gaeltacht and the Islands, 6 Upper Ely Place, Dublin 2; tel +353 (0)1 6472461, email: heritagecard@ealga.ie.

saunas and an indoor swimming pool. The price of a Summer Special (three nights B&B plus two dinners) is $230 pps.

Special Interest Vacations

If you want to do more than tour and explore, it's easy to put together your own special interest vacation. Many Irish hotels and guesthouses arrange activities for a reasonable price. The per-person costs below were current as of summer 2001. For more ideas, contact any Bord Fáilte office for the latest "Holiday Breaks" brochure.

Golf: (Dingle Skellig Hotel, Dingle, county Kerry; tel +353 (0)66 9150200, email: reservations@dingleskellig.com) Four-star hotel on Dingle Bay with links golf at Ceann Sibeal, Dingle's Par 72 championship course. Non-golfing partners could go horseback riding, sea fishing, dolphin watching or take a boat trip to the Blasket Islands. Weekend (two nights B&B plus one dinner) plus one round of golf: $157 low season, $253 in July or August.

Painting, Bog Craft or Fly Fishing: (Pontoon Bridge Hotel, Pontoon, county Mayo; tel +353 (0)94 56120) Best known as a fishing hotel, you can also learn to paint landscapes in oils and watercolors, on location or in studio. Bog craft courses include field trips collecting mosses, lichens and other materials to create models or scenes from the bog landscape. Special deal (two nights B&B plus one dinner) and two-day chosen activity course: from $118 per person.

Walking: (Hanora's Cottage Guesthouse, Nire Valley, Ballymacarberry,

County fair day—sheep sold by the penfold

© Steenie Harvey

county Waterford; tel + 353 (0)52 36134) Walking in the Comeragh mountains. The hosts provide packed lunches, maps, walking sticks and, if needed, a guide. When you come down from the hills, Jacuzzis and tempting dinners await. The chef trained at the famous Ballymaloe cookery school. A weekend (two nights B&B plus one dinner) and two days walking: $110 to $133. Guide extra.

Romance: (Tinakilly Country House Hotel, Rathnew, county Wicklow; tel + 353 (0)404 69274) Go on, spoil yourself. Victorian Tinakilly is a four-star luxury hotel not far from Dublin. If you have a taste for champagne breakfast in bed, log fires and candlelit dinners, you'll be in heaven. Weekend (two nights B&B plus one dinner): $218 to $236.

Island Hopping: (Brian Hughes, Connemara Safaris, Sky Road, Clifden, county Galway; tel + 353 (0)95 21071) Easygoing walks discovering the archaeology and botany of rarely visited western isles like Inishbofin, Clare, Turk and Shark. The $471 price includes five nights dinner and B&B, picnics, guides, luggage transfers and, if needed, rain gear.

Part II

Irish Culture

4 An Labhraíonn tú Gaeilge?

*C*éad Míle Fáilte. Ceol agus Craic. Sláinte is Saol. If you believe the Irish language is merely English spoken with a soft brogue, you're in for a surprise. For starters, Ireland doesn't have a Prime Minister, it has a *Taoiseach*. The biggest political party is called *Fianna Fáil*, the Soldiers of Destiny. Ever received an Irish Christmas card? Look at the special seasonal stamps; they say not "Christmas" but "Nollaig."

If you haven't already guessed, the title of this chapter asks, "Do you speak Irish?" Not everybody realizes that the Republic's first official language is Irish, or, to give it its proper title, Gaeilge. Often also referred to as Gaelic, it bears little resemblance to English. Like Scots Gaelic, Breton and Welsh, it belongs to the Celtic language group. Until the 17th century, nearly all the population spoke Irish, but English rule undermined most aspects of Ireland's traditional culture, including teaching of the native language. The situation was further exacerbated by the Great Famine and the long decades of mass emigration that drained the country of countless native speakers. Although Irish has been a language in slow decline ever since, there has been an enthusiastic revival in recent years. Every effort is being made to keep it alive: All schoolchildren study Irish as part of the curriculum. Proficiency in the language is a requirement for careers in professions such as teaching, banking and the civil service.

Learning the Language

Despite its official status, newcomers aren't pressured to learn Irish. While Gaeilge is regarded as a cornerstone of the cultural heritage, most people use English as their preferred tongue. Latest census figures showed that although around 1.4 million people describe themselves as having an understanding of Irish, nearly two thirds either never speak the language at all or use it less than once a week.

Even so, you'll soon be using odd Irish words in everyday conversation. Many of your new friends will have names like Niamh (pronounced Neev) or Blaithin (pronounced Bloheen). You may want to visit the Fleadh (literally, "the feast"), Ireland's biggest traditional music festival, or even learn how to play the *bodhrán*, the Irish drum.

You'll soon notice that place names and street signs are invariably given in both Irish and English. Galway is also Gaillimhe; Cork doubles as Corcaigh; Sligo as Sligeach. Baile Átha Cliath isn't so easy to guess: Any bus bound for what translates as "the town at the ford of the hurdles" is actually taking passengers to Dublin.

Follow a direction sign pointing to *An Lár* and it will lead you to a town center. You may also see signs for *an Scoil* (a school), *an Leabharlann* (a library) or *an Ospidéal* (a hospital). A stroll down *Sráid Padraig* (Patrick Street) could take you past the *Oifig an Phoist* (post office). If you get lost you can always ask a *Garda* for directions. Colloquially called "the guards," the Garda Síochána is the official title of Ireland's police force.

There are a few places in the remoter parts of Ireland where even

a lazy afternoon in West Cork

© Steenie Harvey

Dubliners feel like strangers in a strange land. Counties Donegal, Kerry, Cork, Waterford, Mayo and Galway all possess little enclaves known as Gaeltacht areas. The inhabitants of the Gaeltacht only number around 8,000, but more than 60 percent of the residents speak Irish within the home and on the street. During summer-time, many city kids are sent here to board with local families for a thorough immersion course in Gaeilge as preparation for forth-coming exams.

> *Despite its official status, newcomers aren't pressured to learn Irish.*

Gaeltacht roads are not for the faint-hearted. When exploring the country's Irish-speaking pockets, it's well worth knowing a smattering of the language as here direction signs are not bilingual. Yes, your map book says "Carraroe," but the signposts confusingly point to *An Cheathrú Rua*. Although every-body in the Gaeltacht does speak English, few concessions are made to the linguistically challenged visitor. If you're seeking the restroom in some little pub, it's handy to know the difference between the doors that read *Mná* (women) and *Fir* or Fear (men). It could save you some embarrassment!

Ireland's best-known bilingual town is Dingle, a color-washed harbor town on county Kerry's wild and witchy Dingle Peninsula. East of Dingle town, the language is English; head west and you'll soon be deep in Irish-speaking territory. In Dingle, head for An Café Litearta, Ireland's first liter-ary coffeeshop, where you can puzzle over the Irish menu and browse for books on *Tír na nÓg* (the land of everlasting youth). Rumor has it that this fairytale land lies somewhere off the Dingle Peninsula, out in the Atlantic beyond the misty hummocks of the Blasket Islands. However, if you go to the Irish-speaking Aran Islands off the county Galway coast, you'll proba-bly hear that it lies somewhere in that part of the western ocean!

Fairy folklore delivers an interesting example of how many Irish words became anglicized over the centuries. Take the Bean Sidhe, for example, whose name translates as "spirit" or "fairy woman." She is, of course, much better known to the English-speaking world as the fearsome Ban-shee. How do you pronounce a tongue-twister like Bean Sidhe? Exactly as you do "banshee."

Should you wish to learn Irish, plenty of summer schools and evening classes offer adults the opportunity to study this intriguing ancient lan-guage. Radio programs and an Irish-language television station, Telefís na Gaelige, also broadcast into the country's living rooms. The majority of TnaG's programming is in Irish, but it occasionally carries programs from our Celtic neighbors, Scotland and Wales, too. Just to baffle the novice Irish learner, the station's output sometimes includes Gaelic ballads from the Scottish Hebrides and—don't ask me why—Australian rules football.

Where to Learn Gaeilge

The Bord na Gaeilge website at www.bnag.ie has extensive links. Principal course providers for adults wishing to learn Irish include Gael Linn and Oideas Gael.

- Gael Linn, 26-27 Merrion Square, Dublin 2. Tel +353 1 6767283. E-mail: info@gael-linn.iol.ie.
- Oideas Gael, Gleann Cholm Cille, co Donegal. Tel +353 73 30248. (That's how Irish speakers write "Glencolmcille, county Donegal," and postmen need to recognize both forms of address.) Email: oidsgael@iol.ie.

Probably the most enjoyable introduction to the Irish language is to attend a course that combines class work in the morning with activities in the afternoon. Oideas Gael has summer schools in county Donegal's

Irish Place Names

Many place names are anglicized renderings of original names in the Irish language. Taken down by map makers and 19th-century ordnance survey teams, their meanings often describe the landscape, ancient monuments or important local happenings. Common prefixes are the words *dún* (fort); *cill* (church), often written as Kill or Kil; *cnoc* (hill), which usually became Knock; and Bally, which takes its roots from *baile* (town). *Clon* derives from *cluain*, meaning "meadow." Signposts pointing to Drum this and Drom that are all linked to the Irish word *druim*, a ridge.

The original name of Killarney, the well-known tourist town, was Cill Áirne, the Church of the Sloes. Donegal derives its name from Viking times when it became known as Dún na nGall, the fort of the foreigner. The fascination in tracing names back to some misty past can be endless—a place such as Gortahork (Gorta Coirce), initially an incomprehensible mouthful, becomes meaningful when you learn that *gort* signifies "field" and *coirce*, "oats." Thus it's fairly reasonable to assume that Gortahork was once renowned for its oatfields. Knockcroghery, a village in county Roscommon, has a darker derivation—that of a place of execution. *Cnoc* innocuously means "hill," but *crochaire* is the Irish word for "hangman." Anyone with a smattering of Irish knows that Knockcroghery translates as Hangman's Hill.

The word *tobar* within a place name usually signifies a healing well dating back to pre-Christian times. Map makers often wrote it down as *tubber* or *tober*, and in county Mayo you'll come across Ballintober (Baile-an-tobar), the town of the well. Tubbercurry in county Sligo takes its name from Tobar-an-choire, the well of the cauldron. Interestingly, magic cauldrons commonly appear in Celtic mythology, and it's also in county Sligo that you find Knocknashee (Cnoc na Sidhe), the hill of the fairies. One of the most malevolent creatures of the Celtic Otherworld was the *púca*, a shape-changing goblin that haunted lonely places and often appeared to travelers in the form of a black horse. On the boundary of counties Limerick and Cork, the bridge at Ahaphuca takes its name from *ath* and *púca*, the goblin's ford. *Poll* signifies "hole," "cavern" or a deep pool of water; in the wild glens of county Wicklow, the Liffey River spills over a ledge into Pollaphuca—the goblin's hole.

Gaeltacht where you can also take workshops in subjects ranging from Irish dancing to tapestry weaving, hill walking, archaeology and bodhrán playing. The morning language classes are designed to give beginners the basics— stating your likes and dislikes, chatting about the weather and so on. Alternatively you could skip the activities and opt for a more intensive language course. Prices for a weeklong language course (45 hours of study) are $136; language and culture, $113 to $147; and three-day weekend courses, $68. You can also opt for room and board (bed, breakfast and dinner) with a local family, which costs an additional $153 weekly or $68 for the three-day weekend. If you prefer self-catering, you can share a modern house with other course participants at a cost of $79 for the week, $34 for a long weekend.

In the Galway area, contact Áras Mháirtín uí Chadain (the Irish Language Center of University College Galway), An Cheathrú Rua, Co na Gaillimhe; tel +353 (0)91 595101. Their summer courses, more intensive, often draw foreign students wishing to gain university credit. U.S. students would receive six semester credits. Fees for the monthlong beginner's and intermediate courses are $875, plus accommodation costs. Staying with a local family, full board costs $725/$1,075 depending on whether you require a single or a double room.

Each course covers intensive instruction in the spoken Irish language, special classes in traditional Irish dancing and singing, and lectures on history, folklore, literature and society. Excursions and visits are arranged to several Irish-speaking locations, such as the fishing villages of Carna and Rossaveal; inland Clonbur, the birthplace of Thomas Lynch, one of the signatories to the U.S. Declaration of Independence; and the arts-and-crafty village of Spiddal.

Common Irish Expressions

You may hear the expressions below spoken slightly differently as there are three distinct varieties of pronunciation: Ulster Irish, Connacht Irish and Munster Irish.

Dia duit (pronounced jeea ditch)—Good day, Hello. Its literal meaning is "God be with you."

Conas tá tú? (kunas taw too)—How are you?

Fáilte (fawlcha)—Welcome!

Tá go maith, go raibh maith agat (taw gu mah, gura mah ugut)—I'm fine, thankyou.

Cad é an t-ainm atá ort? (kajay in tanyim ataw urt)—What's your name?

atá orm (ataw orim)—My name is ... (Jim, Sadie, etc.)

Slán leat (slawn lyat)—Goodbye (if *you* are staying).

Slán agat (slawn ugut)—Goodbye (if *you* are leaving).

Literature

Ireland always seems to have had more writers, poets and playwrights than there are sheep in the fields. When you consider the country's size, its literary achievements are tremendous. You could say that it all began with the unknown monks of the Celtic Church. Not only did they create illuminated gospels such as the Book of Kells and Book of Durrow, they recorded the ancient myths and heroic sagas that had been thrilling listeners since pagan times. It is these early Irish monks you can thank for timeless stories such as *The Children of Lir*, in which four children are bewitched into swans by a jealous stepmother. The most famous ancient epic is *The Cattle Raid of Cooley (Táin Bó Cuailnge)*, whose hero Cúchulainn uses a frightening array of otherworldly powers to aid the warriors of Ulster in battle against Queen Maeve of Connacht.

Dublin's streets alone have spawned an incredible number of literary greats, not only James Joyce but also George Bernard Shaw, William Butler Yeats and Samuel Beckett, all winners of the Nobel prize for literature. Sean O'Casey told of a tenement world of poverty and revolution in dramas such as *The Plough and the Stars, Juno and the Paycock* and *Shadow of a Gunman*, classics still produced today. Jonathan Swift, who became dean of St. Patrick's Cathedral, has delighted generations of youngsters with *Gulliver's Travels*. Then there was the witty Oscar Wilde, who once informed customs officials, "I have nothing to declare but my genius."

Other acclaimed names include the Wicklow wordsmith John Millington Synge, who wrote of the vagrants who tramped the empty white lanes of county Wicklow and told of village humor and cruelties in the western islands. One of Synge's best-known works, *The Playboy of the Western World*, incited riots when it was first performed at Dublin's Abbey

legends in the park—mythic sculpture at Ardagh, county Longford

© Steenie Harvey

Theater in 1907. Add Brendan Behan, author of *The Borstal Boy,* and Bram Stoker, master of the macabre and author of *Dracula,* and the litany is staggering.

The entire country brims with literary associations: The bleak hills of Monaghan provided Patrick Kavanagh with poetic inspiration; the now-unpopulated Blasket Islands are brought back to life in works such as Maurice O'Sullivan's *Twenty Years A-Growing* and Peig Sayers' *Peig.* Sligo will forever be linked to W. B. Yeats; Edgeworthstown in county Longford was the home of Georgian novelist Maria Edgeworth, of *Castle Rackrent* fame; and county Westmeath is associated with Oliver Goldsmith, who lived here during the 1740s.

Dublin now boasts a Writers' Museum on Parnell Square to complement its literary pub crawls and James Joyce Trail. On "Bloomsday," June 16, James Joyce admirers don Edwardian dress and retrace the odyssey of *Ulysses*' Leopold Bloom around the city's landmarks. Yet Irish literature isn't solely devoted to past glories. The country continues to produce an endless stream of talented writers and poets. John McGahern, John Banville and Edna O'Brien are just a few contemporary novelists whose books are well regarded by critics.

> *If you're seeking the restroom in some little pub, it's handy to know the difference between the doors that read Mná (women) and Fir or Fear (men).*

For a glimpse into the trials and tribulations of working-class life on Dublin's sprawling council estates, read Roddy Doyle; his most memorable books include *The Van, The Snapper, Paddy Clarke Ha Ha Ha* and *The*

Bookshops abound in the literary city of Dublin.

© Steenie Harvey

Woman Who Walked into Doors. If you like romantic weepies, Maeve Binchy never disappoints. Of her numerous novels three of my own favorites are *Light a Penny Candle, Circle of Friends* and *Tara Road*. One of the most unlikely recent bestsellers was *Angela's Ashes*, a grim autobiography by retired New York schoolteacher Frank McCourt about his impoverished Limerick childhood. The work won the 1997 Pulitzer Prize.

The poet Seamus Heaney scooped another Nobel Prize for Ireland in 1995. His collection of poems, *The Spirit Level*, encompasses both the hopes and disappointments of the Peace Process. If you enjoy poetry, I can promise you Ireland still has plenty of it. Éigse Éireann, the national poetry organization, organizes competitions and also arranges a program of readings and festivals throughout the 32 counties, north and south, by Irish and international poets. To find out what's going on where, check their website at www.poetryireland.ie or contact them for their newsletter at Bermingham Tower, Upper Yard, Dublin Castle, Dublin 2. Tel +353 (0)1 6714632.

5 Ireland's People and Culture

Someone once said that the Irish are really a Mediterranean people who got stranded much farther north than they should have been. It's true that most people are extremely convivial, with an unflagging appetite for music and chat. But where does the blarney end and reality start? Not every Irish woman is a red-haired beauty wrapped in a long green cloak, wandering the hillsides with an Irish wolfhound. Nor is every Irish man a silver-tongued charmer. Remember, movies such as *The Quiet Man* were made for a mostly American audience. Those Hollywood images often still color foreign ideas about Irish identity.

You certainly will not encounter the kind of stage Irishman who spends his days making moonshine and gazing out at the ocean muttering "Ah, Begorrah, the shores of Americay...." And you'll get some strange looks if you insist on greeting people with "Top o' the morning to ye." Within Ireland itself, such phrases are mockingly dismissed as "Oirishisms" or "Paddywhackery," so please don't use them unless you want to be laughed at behind your back.

How the Irish View Americans

As an American, maybe you're wondering how your countrymen and women are regarded in Ireland. In general, pretty favorably, but you'll have

the Shamrock

anybody can be Irish on St. Patrick's Day; all you need to do is wear a sprig of shamrock. But although many people imagine that this unofficial symbol of Irishness must be something really unique and special, the truth is rather mundane. Shamrock is nothing other than young clover.

Seamróg in the Irish language, it derives its name from *seamair* (clover) and *óg* (young). The expression "drowning the shamrock" comes from the custom of dropping a sprig of clover into the last pint you swallow on St. Patrick's Day. Once the glass is drained, toss the soggy shamrock over your shoulder. This should ensure a full year's good luck!

to get used to being known as "a Yank," even if you hail from deepest Alabama. Cultural stereotyping cuts both ways, and whether you have $10,000 or $100,000 in the bank, some people will describe you and your fellow Americans as "those wealthy Yanks."

Although some occasional grouse about the creeping Americanization of Irish life (the march of McDonalds, TV schedules crammed with ghastly soaps and chat shows), it's almost impossible for anyone to think too harshly of a country that acted so generously to their ancestors. Centuries of emigration means many Irish families have American relatives somewhere in the background.

That said, Ireland is a highly politicized society and not everyone agrees with American foreign policy. When it comes to global affairs, Ireland instinctively sympathizes with the perceived underdog, and invariably advocates diplomacy rather than military action. As throughout much of Europe, "green" issues are of great importance to most Irish people. President George W. Bush's decision to turn his back on the Kyoto global warming protocols stirred vociferous *vox pop* condemnation.

One sure way of offending Irish sensibilities is by jabbering about how things are bigger/faster/better in America. Do it too long and too loud and someone is likely to tell you to "f— off!" Yes, many Irish people swear at the drop of a hat, and colorful cursing can come from the most unexpected quarters. Usually it's not meant to be offensive, but simply part of the conversation.

Getting to Know the Irish

It's difficult to package the Irish lifestyle into a neat little box, but do note that most people abhor pretentiousness. Classism and delusions of grandeur do not go down well. The Republic of Ireland's rebirth as a nation state sounded the death knell for its former masters, the Anglo-Irish Ascendancy. With its demise went any notions of cap-doffing or perceived inferiority; most people have peasant forebears and feel no need to apologize for it.

Unlike in neighboring Britain, Irish people are not categorized into that ludicrous system of working class, lower middle class, upper middle class and so on.

Today the aristocratic "Big Houses" with their courtyards, coach houses and servants' quarters belong to wealthy business people and rock stars rather than lordlings with obscure titles. On the other end of the lifestyle scale, the country's fairly recent history of high unemployment removed any real social stigma from joblessness and welfare. Ireland most definitely does not use that cruel American expression, "trailer trash."

> *Centuries of emigration means many Irish families have American relatives somewhere in the background.*

Not everybody you will meet will be university educated, but never presume that just because somebody has a modest job, they have a stunted intellect. In no other country have I encountered such a thirst for knowledge or interest in the wider world. I once met a house painter whose favorite author was Dostoevsky—and he was teaching himself to read it in the original Russian.

Of course, people are people the world over, and money always creates its own kind of social gulf. For example, you will rarely come across professionals such as doctors, lawyers and accountants socializing with the hoi polloi who live in rented accommodation on local authority council estates.

County Donegal, St. Patrick's Purgatory — nowadays pilgrims undergo the night watches of their 24-hour vigil inside the island's Basilica. In medieval times they were shut in the cave.

© Steenie Harvey

Ireland's Flag

Sent as a gift by French revolutionaries in 1848, the Republic of Ireland's flag is a tricolor of vertical bands: green, white and orange. The green and the orange represent the island's Catholic and Protestant traditions. White, the color of peace, symbolizes what should be the unity between them.

Nor are the unemployed likely to be found at prestigious golf clubs like Mount Juliet and Druids' Glen.

In the cities it's patently obvious which are the posh sections, but in rural areas the neighborhood mix is usually far more diverse. My neighbors include a telephone engineer, a plumber, a schoolteacher, a retired civil servant, a 90-year-old bachelor, three farming families, an Englishwoman involved in flowercraft designs, and a wildlife warden. Until fairly recently the former Church of Ireland rectory was owned by a German artist, but it has since been bought by two Dublin families as a weekend holiday home.

Although most Irish families enjoy a decent standard of living—over 80 percent own their own homes—shopping for what Americans might consider to be vital consumer goods does not seem to be a huge priority. According to data from the Central Statistics Office, 75.9 percent of households have a telephone, 64.9 percent own a video recorder, but only 16 percent own a home computer. Dishwashers aren't exactly objects of desire either; only 18 percent of households have one. And 53 percent of Irish families feel they can live without the ubiquitous microwave oven.

Choosing Where You Should Live

Ireland is a small country with no distinct regional variations in attitude and lifestyle. However, there is indeed something of an urban/rural divide. People tend to be more conservative on the so-called "moral issues" outside the cities and well-known tourist areas. The 1995 referendum allowing divorce passed by a mere 9,000 votes, and a majority of voters in six rural constituencies actually voted "No" by margins of more than 25 percent. Yet this did not reflect a regional pattern. The six constituencies registering the strongest opposition were scattered throughout the entire country: Cork North-West, Limerick West, Galway East, Mayo East, Cavan-Monaghan and Longford-Roscommon. If the undiluted family values of "holy Ireland" appeal to you, you'll be cheered to know they still hold sway in these deeply traditional rural strongholds.

Whether you choose to live in urban or rural Ireland, you'll find much less urgent time-keeping than you're probably used to. Tradesmen promise to do work on a certain day and then don't appear until two weeks later. Letters sometimes stay unanswered, phone calls go unreturned. You may even make an appointment with a realtor and then find he's neglected to inform you that he'll be out of the office all afternoon. Of course, it's possible that you'll experience no problems whatsoever, but it's good to be forewarned.

Bottom line, people still count in Ireland. Perhaps the realtor didn't show because he was at a neighbor's funeral. Provincial Ireland's strong sense of community means that it's not uncommon for hundreds (and sometimes thousands) of people to pay their respects to the surviving family by attending the graveyard ceremony. It doesn't matter if you knew the person only slightly or even if it was a neighbor's mother whom you had never met. Being part of a village community means attending neighborhood funerals, even if it means closing down your business for an hour or two. What faith you belong to doesn't matter. Most of my own neighbors are Catholic, but almost 3,000 people attended the funeral of a young local Protestant boy who tragically died in a house fire.

Ireland's symbol is the harp, a wonderful motif for a land of music, dance and storytelling.

Daily Life

Although money is important to Irish people, the grab-it-all attitude so common in the United States is rare in Ireland. Want to do business on Saturday? Tough. Few business people will work weekends for something that can wait until Mondays. Nor are employees prepared to give up their social life to work long hours of overtime, let alone take a second job.

Without a doubt, the pub plays a major part in Ireland's social life, but it's a complete fallacy that the entire country is drink-mad. Many people don't drink at all, but the pub is where they gather to play cards, trade gossip or meet up with their local political representative. A number of Western Ireland TDs (Members of Parliament) actually hold "surgeries" for their electoral constituents in the pub! Not to be confused with doctors' offices, which are also called "surgeries," these political forums allow folks to ask their representative what he (and it's usually a "he") plans to do about the state of the roads or improving farm incomes.

Another curiosity is that it's still common in the west of Ireland to give up drinking for Lent. Yet neighbors will still meet friends in the pub, but conversation will be oiled with glasses of lemonade rather than pints of the black stuff.

Central to Irish society is "the Family." Older people are treated with tremendous respect, and there isn't the same emphasis on youth culture that exists in many other western countries. Visitors often comment on

Sport in Ireland

*W*ith more horses per capita than any place in Europe, Ireland is the Equine Isle. Thanks to generous tax concessions, many top European racehorses are at stud here, and there are pony-trekking facilities and riding stables in every part of the country. Even if you don't ride yourself, one of the most enjoyable events is a day at the races, whether it be at a little local course or one of the major classic meetings at the Curragh in county Kildare.

Leaving aside skiing, baseball and American football, most sporting interests are represented. Ireland's 350-plus golf courses are world-renowned and range from parkland courses to breezy seaside links where the hazards often include dry-stone walls and mad-eyed sheep who've gone walkabout. There are sailing clubs in many maritime counties, loughs and rivers provide tremendous fishing, and almost every community has a gun club. The traditional rural pursuits of fox hunting and beagling are particularly strong in counties Limerick, Tipperary and Cork. As for spectator sports, Ireland's soccer team reached the World Cup Finals in 1990 and 1994, and the rugby team takes part in the annual Six Nations Championship along with England, Scotland, Wales, Italy and France. And although rugby can be violent and bloody, it seems like a game for namby-pambies once you've encountered Gaelic games.

Gaelic games are almost exclusive to Ireland, and both Gaelic football and hurling have huge followings. Gaelic football is a field game of 15 players who use a round ball played with either hands or feet and a goal similar to that on a rugby pitch. Depending on whether the ball goes over or under the bar, scoring is a mix of points and goals. Dating back to Celtic times and mentioned in epic sagas, hurling has a similar scoring system, but in this case the game involves a hurley stick and a smaller ball. And regardless of what you'll see, hurley sticks are meant to whack the ball—not opponents' heads. Teams from the 32 counties, north and south, annually compete in the All-Ireland Championships; fans flutter the county flag from windows, gateposts and anywhere else they can proclaim their allegiance. Watched by enthusiastic crowds of around 70,000, hurling and Gaelic football finals take place at Croke Park in Dublin.

how Irish youngsters seem so polite and well mannered. It's not unusual to find three generations of an Irish family sharing the same house, especially if Mammy or Daddy has been widowed.

Compared to neighboring Britain, social change has been slow in coming to Ireland. As mentioned earlier, the country was only very recently offered the option for divorce along with legislation to decriminalize homosexuality. The liberal agenda has its strongest support in the Dublin area, but when it comes to the abortion issue, even Dublin lobbyists come up against a brick wall in the shape of the church-backed Society for the Protection of the Unborn Child (SPUC). Abortion remains outlawed in all cases. Even pregnant women at grave medical risk have to travel to England for the procedure. Some 5,300 Irish women made the journey last year, but those are only the ones who felt confident enough to give Irish addresses.

Mary Robinson's appointment as Ireland's first woman President (since succeeded by Mary McAleese) gave women's self-esteem a big boost, but as yet there are few other women who have achieved top positions in business or day-to-day politics. Although women make up around 40 percent of the work force, only 5 percent of Ireland's business executives are female. When it comes to managing directors and departmental heads, the numbers fall to under 3 percent. Women still tend to gravitate towards the "caring" professions such as nursing, teaching and the social services. Until the early 1970s, women had to give up civil service jobs when they married, and even today in rural Ireland the attitude that a woman's place is in the home is common. For career-minded Irish women, "tradition" sometimes has negative aspects.

Contemporary Culture

Although Ireland's cultural reputation is founded on its Celtic traditions and huge body of literature, many people in today's arts world have achieved a high international standing. Irish playwrights such as Brian Friel (*Dancing at Lughnasa*) are well known on Broadway, and the Druid Theater company's production of Martin McDonagh's *The Beauty Queen of Leenane* garnered four Tony awards. Many Irish films meet with widespread acclaim. Even if you have never heard of home-grown directors such as Neil Jordan and Jim Sheridan, you are undoubtedly familiar with silver screen celebrities like Liam Neeson, Gabriel Byrne, Brenda Fricker and Pierce Brosnan. Irish films of the 1990s that successfully transferred to an international audience include *The Field, The Crying Game, The Snapper, In the Name of the Father* and *Circle of Friends*.

Contemporary Irish music encompasses everything from rock giants U2 to teen heartthrobs Westlife and Granny's favorite crooner, Daniel O'Donnell. Country and western bands attract a big following, especially in the midlands. If you're a jazz

Home ground: the gravestone of the famous poet W.B. Yeats carries an epitaph he penned himself.

Cast a cold Eye
On Life, on Death.
Horseman, pass by.

W.B. YEATS

June 13th 1865
January 28th 1939

© Steenie Harvey

aficionado, don't miss the annual fall festival in Cork; if you're an Enya fan get yourself to Leo Brennan's Tavern near Crolly in county Donegal. Enya is Leo's daughter and customers are occasionally treated to a free performance when she's back home. By now a musical institution, the Eurovision Song Contest has been won by Ireland more times than anyone can remember.

Traditional Culture

Ireland's symbol is the harp, a wonderful motif for a land of music, dance and storytelling. Nowhere else in Europe does the folk tradition carry quite as much impact, burst with quite so much dynamism. Wherever you settle, you won't be very far away from the tinkle of the penny whistle, the droning lament of the uillean pipes, or the unmistakable thump of the bodhrán, the Irish drum.

Music and dance have overlapped and woven themselves into the very fabric of society. More than just cultural pastimes, these are art forms accessible to everyone. The fellow who comes to fix your plumbing or plant your garden may well be an accomplished fiddle player or flautist who learned his skill in a farmhouse kitchen. And all over the country you'll notice little girls skipping along in what look like Celtic party frocks, intricately embroidered with the kind of patterns usually associated with the Book of Kells and other illuminated manuscripts. The youngsters are off to their Irish dancing class, heads filled with dreams of traveling the world as part of the Riverdance troupe.

The bastion of the traditional music scene is, of course, the pub. Inns in tourist towns such as Killarney have *seisiúns* (sessions) of music scheduled on a nightly basis, usually at regular times. Much of the instrumental music that's played is actually dance music and includes everything from jigs to reels to the hornpipe. Sessions also often include ballads, rebel songs and the lone voice of a *sean-nós* singer. Unaccompanied by any instrument and usually sung in Irish, their throbbing songs are the stories of thwarted love, sad farewells and heart-wrenching yearning for a faraway homeland.

In quieter areas tourists rarely frequent, *seisiúns* are more impromptu. Someone whips out a fiddle, an accordion appears, and before you know it the entire bar is tapping its feet and raising the rafters with a rousing rendition of *The Fields of Athenry*. Once underway, the entertainment can roll on until way past closing time.

County Clare is especially good for tuning into traditional melodies that have been passed down like heirlooms through the generations. Folk music enthusiasts from all over the world embark on a kind of pilgrimage to the fishing village of Doolin and its three "singing pubs": McGann's, O'Connor's and McDermott's. Some come to listen, others to join in. Another Clare village, Miltown Malbay, is the venue for the Willie Clancy Summer School, Ireland's largest musical summer school, attracting beginners and local masters every year. As much social event as musical academy, there are classes for most instruments, as well as set-dancing and singing.

MUSIC, DANCE, AND THE ART OF STORYTELLING

Pronounced "fesh," *feis* is the Irish word for a traditional music festival. There are dozens of them. The biggest, the *Fleadh Cheoil* (pronounced "flah kol," it means "feast of music"), it takes place in a different Irish town each year at the end of August. Offering 10 days of non-stop competition and entertainment, it's an unmissable chance to see the country's top step, set and *ceili* dancers.

In step-dancing, the dancers' arms and upper bodies stay rigid while the feet perform the mazy magic of slip jigs, triple jigs and the hornpipe. Step-dancing is as rigorous as it looks, and you really need to learn it as a child to reach competition standard. *Feis* rules require "authentic Gaelic dress," but, although today's costumes look fabulous, they're hardly authentic. After all, these dances used to take place at country crossroads and were performed by peasant villagers dressed in shawls, petticoats and homespun breeches!

Like *ceili* dancing, which developed from the French *quadrille*, set-dancing is a form of social dancing bearing some resemblance to English and Scottish country dancing. It generally involves four couples who follow the intricate turns, steps and patterns of a series of figures—the set. It often takes 15 to 20 minutes to dance an entire set, so participants need plenty of stamina.

Competitively danced sets at a *feis* come from an approved repertoire of

Fiddlers three—music takes to the street in Sligo town.

© Steenie Harvey

dances with evocative names such as the Siege of Ennis, the Blackthorn Stick, the King of the Fairies and Hurry the Jug. Some dances are more than 250 years old. A dance known as the Blackbird actually doubled as a secret code for Irish supporters of the ill-fated Bonnie Prince Charlie, who tried to wrest back the Scottish throne for the Catholic Stuart dynasty.

Many set dances originated during the 18th century, the heyday of the Irish Dance Master. Circuiting a county's villages, he passed on his latest stock of dances to local people, devising new steps and sets with each visit. It was considered a great honor to have a Dance Master board with you, even though he was likely to be eating you out of house and home for a period of up to six weeks.

Another mainstay of the *feis* is the *seannachie*, or storyteller. The art of storytelling, as old as humanity itself, was a revered profession during Celtic times. Journeying from fireside to fireside, the ancient bards and poets thrilled their audiences with elaborate creation myths and stories of heroic victories achieved with the aid of magical weapons. They told of doomed love affairs, of lone warriors battling against the shadowy supernatural forces, of severed heads that could prophesy and provide wondrous entertainment. Like his or her poetic forebears, the *seannachie* too relies on memory alone. Some of the best hail from the Kingdom of Kerry, a county where stories are apt to grow very long legs indeed.

For forthcoming events, contact Comhaltas Ceoltoiri Éireann (Belgrave Square, Monkstown, county Dublin; tel + 353 (0)1 280 0295). Pronounced "Coal-tis Kyol-tory Air-in," its name loosely translates as "a gathering of Irish musicians," though it exists to promote all aspects of traditional culture. The organization has branches all over Ireland, and you don't have to be Irish-born or Irish-speaking to join.

Throughout the country, activities generally mirror what happens in county Cork, where a CCE branch meets up for a Monday night seisiún in Collins Bar at Carrigaline. Other nights are given over to teaching ceili and set-dancing; fees are just over $1 per person per night. And, if you have a basic level of competence in your chosen instrument, they'll teach you traditional tunes and how to play with other musicians. Fees are $45 per term for an individual, with reductions for members of the same family. Concerts are regular events with performances given in local churches at Epiphany and on St. Patrick's Day.

Celebrating St. Stephen's Day

Another big day in their social calendar is St. Stephen's Day, December 26. As part of the celebrations, musicians and dancers dress up as Wren Boys and roam Carrigaline's streets and pubs, collecting money for local charities. It's always a colorful occasion with the Wren Boys giving a cheery send-off to the horses and hounds of the South Union Hunt, its riders dressed in hunting pink. Preparations actually start around August, when oats are cut to make the straw skirts worn by the Wren Boys. (There are craft workshops in how to make these skirts, by the way.)

"Hunting the Wran" (the wren) was more common in previous years than it is today, but groups of colorfully disguised revelers still appear on St. Stephen's Day as part of Christmastime festivities. Although costumes sometimes differ from county to county, most Wren Boys wear white tunics and conical straw hats, and paint their faces black and red. A century ago, they would have rambled across open fields to call on neighbors. In return for a money donation and some food and drink, the odd-looking visitors entertained the household with music, dancing, poetry and drama.

Mean householders often got more than they bargained for. Along with their musical instruments, the Wren Boys carried a holly bush or pole decorated with the slain bodies of harmless little birds called wrens. Any house or farm making an inadequate donation could later expect to find a wren buried near the doorstep. As well as a dire insult, this unneighborly act supposedly ensured that the stingy family suffered a full year's bad luck.

Today it's illegal to hunt wrens, so revelers top their poles with a papier-mâché effigy. And instead of making house calls, most Wren Boys center their activities on pubs and clubs. Besides Carrigaline, two other places where you're certain to see Wren Boys are Woodford in county Galway and Dingle in county Kerry. Led by the colorfully disguised Lord Mayor, Wren Boys also parade through Dublin on December 26.

6 Ireland's History

Ireland's history has been shaped by invasions. Can any other country have been battled over so fiercely for so long? Headhunting Celts were later followed by marauding Vikings; land-hungry Anglo-Norman knights by armies of the British Crown. For good or ill, each successive wave of invaders left their mark.

Celtic Ireland

One of Ireland's most fascinating historical chapters is that of those early invaders, the Celts. Evoking dreams of a glorious heritage, their legacy never fails to kindle the imagination. Yet much of what we *think* we know about the Celts is based on guesswork. Theirs was an oral tradition; they left no written records.

It's generally assumed they were Iron Age warrior tribes from central Europe who migrated northwest, reaching Ireland around 500 BCE. However, folklore clouds the issue with some tales insisting the Celts originated from Spain. Wackier myths hold the theory that Ireland's Celtic forebears sprang from doomed Atlantis, whose people had migrated to Mediterranean and Middle Eastern regions several millennia before.

Like their origins, the customs of Ireland's early Celts are shrouded in historical mist. Their stories were not recorded until centuries later, when

Prehistory

Ireland's turbulent tale begins soon after the Ice Age, some 10,000 years ago. The first inhabitants, who may have came via Scotland, were hunter-gatherers who left little evidence of their ways. Small communities developed only after the arrival of Neolithic tribes around 5000 BCE. Raising cattle in stonewalled fields, building hill forts, Ireland's Stone Age farmers also practiced elaborate funerary rites. The island's thousands of Neolithic sites include the chambered passage tombs at Newgrange in county Meath, mysteriously decorated with cosmic symbols.

One of Europe's most famous prehistoric centers, Newgrange existed long before the Celts invaded. When dawn breaks on the morning of the Winter Solstice, December 21, a pencil-thin ray of sunlight creeps along the passageway and illuminates the lightless inner chamber. On the shortest day of the northern year, was this perhaps a symbol of rebirth? Nobody knows the real explanation why Newgrange was built, but it remains a remarkable feat of Stone Age engineering.

Christianity had eclipsed old pagan beliefs. What is indisputable is that they brought with them a new language, a tremendous appetite for feasting and drinking, and an ability to fashion native gold into highly decorative jewelry and weapons. Their bloodthirsty Earth gods took their place in the existing pantheon of Irish deities, becoming part of the mysterious Otherworld.

Neolithic artifacts dot the Irish countryside.

© Steenie Harvey

Tantalizing glimpses of that Otherworld appear in folklore, place names and symbolic carvings such as the lasciviously grinning fertility figures known as *sheila-na-gigs*. The Celts had a great veneration for the forces of nature; other stone figures portray the guardian spirits of wells, rivers and sacred trees. One winter's afternoon, in an overgrown graveyard on Fermanagh's Boa Island, I gazed upon the implacable features of a two-faced January God. Definitely no Christian figure, his exaggerated eyes stared both forward into the realm of men and backward into some unknown twilight. It was an uncanny sensation, realizing that this cross-limbed idol had watched the sun go down long before St. Patrick ever reached these shores.

Although the observations of classical writers relate only to mainland Europe, Ireland's Celts probably had customs similar to their Continental cousins. According to Julius Caesar, their Druid priests taught that souls were immortal and passed after death into another body. They also believed that all men were descended from the god of the underworld. To Irish Celts this was Donn, the Dark One.

> *Like their origins, the customs of Ireland's early Celts are shrouded in historical mist.*

Common to the entire Celtic world was the Cult of the Head. Much as crucifixes represent Christianity, the Celts' foremost religious symbol was the human head. Even when parted from the body, heads possessed numerous mystical powers. In Irish myths, severed heads sing, prophesy, tell stories and preside over warriors' banquets. Most importantly of all, these grisly trophies also protected against the dangerous forces of the Otherworld. It's not only literature that suggests Celtic Ireland enthusiastically collected human heads: Skulls excavated from hill forts have shown the marks of nails where they were suspended from gateways.

the Celtic CalenoaR

The Celts dated the beginning of their year from *Samhain*. Pronounced "sow-an," this was the most important of the annual festivals. Not only did it mark the passing of the old year and the end of the grazing season, it was also a symbolic occasion of death and rebirth. Surplus livestock were brought down from mountain pastures to be slaughtered; hearth fires died and didn't blaze again until the great ritual bonfires of the Druids had been lit. *Samhain* was a time to be close to home for this was when the invisible veil between the mortal world and the Otherworld got torn asunder. Who could say what supernatural dangers lurked in the lengthening shadows? The Christian church rechristened the feast All Hallows, and All Hallows' Eve (October 31) lives on today as Hallowe'en.

Imbolc corresponds to February 1, St. Brigid's Day. A pastoral festival, it marked the start of the lambing season and the first lactation of the ewes. It was dedicated to the pagan fire-goddess Brigid, who was associated with fertility and crafts. Made from straw, the St. Brigid's crosses often seen in Irish homes may have more of a pagan than a Christian origin.

Beltaine (pronounced "beltanny") falls on May Day. May 1 heralded the advent of summer in the Celtic lands and was a frolicsome festival of regeneration. May bushes were decorated with spring flowers to appease the spirits of the land; cattle were driven through the charmed smoke of the *Beltaine* bonfires to give them protection in their summer pastures.

August 1 is *Lughnasa*, a celebration of harvest and home. Pronounced "loo-nasa," it was dedicated to the god Lugh and a symbolic loaf was baked for him from the first corn. The Christian calendar transformed *Lughnasa* into Lammas, but it remains an auspicious day for digging up the first potatoes. On Ulster's north Antrim coast, the Ould Lammas Fair at Ballycastle is one of Ireland's oldest-known harvest gatherings.

Christians and Vikings

Ireland's Celts escaped the acquisitive clutches of the Roman Empire, but their animistic world began to disintegrate once Christianity arrived. This was a bloodless invasion and conversion came slowly. By the time St. Patrick was brought to Ireland as a slave (circa 405), most inhabitants remained faithful to pagan religions. To convert the pagans, the early monks of what became known as the Celtic Church built places of worship on sites sacred to the Druids: in woodland groves or beside healing springs and wells. One pagan goddess, Brigid, even found herself Christianized and elevated to sainthood.

By 563, monastic settlements had grown sufficiently in size and numbers to export missionaries. Columba's Hebridean foundation on Iona is well known, but other Irish monks established centers in mainland Europe. Within Ireland itself, monastic communities at sites such as Clonmacnoise, Kildare and Clonard became major seats of learning in a period tagged "the Golden Age." It was in such monasteries that gospels were elaborately illuminated and tales about the old heroes and gods recorded.

Despite Christian teachings, Celtic magic and mystery hadn't fled Ireland's landscape. News from the annals claims showers of honey and blood rained down in the year 717. In 752, a whale came ashore bearing three teeth of solid gold, each weighing 50 ounces. And the fiery ships seen in the air in 784 were perhaps a dire portent of a new invasion force. Many of the fledgling abbeys and churches were soon to be rededicated into temples to Odin; prayers and plainsong replaced by lusty drinking bouts and sagas about Valhalla and its shieldmaidens.

Dancing at Lughnasa? stone circle, Drombeg, county Cork

© Steenie Harvey

"The wind is fierce tonight, it tosses the sea's white hair. I fear no wild Vikings sailing the main," penned one optimistic monk. But come the mighty dragon ships did. From 795, Ireland was subjected to sporadic Viking attacks, and by 823 the Norsemen had rounded the coastline. Vikings craved booty like vampires crave blood, and Ireland's great rivers served as watery highways to fabulous prizes: the wealthy inland monasteries. In 842, Clonmacnoise was burnt and pillaged by a Viking named Turgesius. His wife apparently used one of the altars to give out oracles.

The Viking Age lasted until the 11th century. Early raiders returned to Scandinavia with their treasures, but they quickly began settling in Ireland, first in winter quarters and then more permanently. Alliances with local chiefs and intermarriages gave the invaders a secure footing to establish trading posts: Dublin, Limerick, Waterford and Wexford all have Viking origins.

Along with European trade, Ireland inherited its first coinage from the Vikings. Who knows, one day you may dig up a 1,000-year-old King Sitric silver penny. And although the Celtic Church was never to recapture its glory days, many of the invaders eventually embraced Christianity. The ancient cathedral in the Shannonside town of Killaloe is worth a visit as it's home to Thorgrim's cross, which carries a blessing in Norse runic script.

The 9th century Book of Kells *is kept in Trinity College, Dublin.*

The Middle Ages

For centuries Ireland's petty kingdoms, some 80 to 100, had battled over territory, cattle and women. Now control of trade meant control of wealth, and a powerful dynasty under the kingship of Brian Boru emerged. Brian set out to win High Kingship and by 1011 had achieved his goal. However, "the Emperor of the Irish" did not enjoy his lofty position for long. A Viking-aided revolt against the king ended with the Battle of Clontarf in 1014. Brian's side won, but he himself was killed.

With Brian's death, Ireland returned to tribal squabbling. In 1166, control of Dublin was

THE BOOK OF KELLS

© Steenie Harvey

St. Patrick

Ireland's patron saint is popularly credited with securing Christianity in fifth-century Ireland. But although St. Patrick is a worldwide symbol of Irish identity, you may be surprised to learn that he wasn't Irish at all. In his own *Confessio* (a type of spiritual biography), the saint tells us he was born in Britain, in a Roman settlement called Bannavem Taburniae. Where exactly this village was is a bit of a mystery. Guesses range from Wales up to the Scottish borders. What is clear is that Patrick came from a wealthy family of priests and minor officials; his father, the deacon Calpurnius, owned a villa.

Imagine coming from such a background only to find yourself kidnapped and sold to an uncouth Irish chieftain. That's what happened to the 16-year-old Patrick. Instead of continuing his studies, he was forced to tend his new master's pigs and sheep in the bitter winds of a northern winter. Snatched from his home by marauding pirates, the youth lived as a slave in Ireland until escaping to France,

and then home, on another pagan ship. He later returned to France and entered the priesthood. Believed to have been ordained as a bishop by the pope, he returned to Ireland as a missionary in 432, landing at Saul in Northern Ireland's county Down. There he made his first convert: a local chieftain named Díchú.

Numerous places, north and south, have links with St. Patrick. Legend tells that he lit a Paschal (Easter) fire on the Hill of Slane in county Meath as a challenge to the pagan king of Tara. He also apparently visited the Rock of Cashel in county Tipperary for a conversion ceremony where he accidentally pierced the local king's foot with his crosier. Thinking this was an important part of Christian ritual, the king suffered his pain in silence!

Both Slane and Cashel claim to be the place where St. Patrick plucked a shamrock leaf to explain the concept of the Holy Trinity. As most people know, St. Patrick's Day is March 17.

wrested from a very aggrieved Dermot MacMurrough. Dermot fled to Britain in search of mercenaries to help him gain back his kingdom, a move that was to have far-reaching consequences.

Ireland's next invaders entered with the clink of chain-mail and clash of broadswords. The first Anglo-Norman knights arrived in 1169, and, after recapturing Dermot's territories, they quickly began invading adjoining kingdoms. This was Ireland's first taste of English Rule. Although nobody could have guessed it at the time, it was to endure for more than seven centuries.

As the 13th century progressed, the Anglo-Normans imposed themselves on about three-quarters of the land, building castles and fortified towns such as those at Limerick, Trim and Waterford. Like the Vikings before them, many secured their position by marrying into Irish clans. But by the mid-1300s, both natives and newcomers were being terrorized by a new and very sinister invasion: bubonic plague. Carried by rats, the "Black Death" decimated about half the population, some 750,000 people. England's writ of authority shrank to a small area around Dublin that became known as "the Pale." In case you've ever wondered, that's how the term "beyond the pale" originated.

Early Modern Period

Ireland's fortunes plummeted when England's Henry VIII (the one with the six wives) broke with the Catholic Church. He also declared himself King of Ireland, a title successive monarchs resolutely hung on to. Under the Tudor and Stuart dynasties of the 16th and 17th centuries, Ireland was subjected to a new kind of "invasion": colonization. These were confusing times, with a dizzy array of Protestant monarchs succeeding Catholic monarchs and vice versa. Religion became a major factor in Ireland's colonization process. Previous generations of English settlers were often uprooted to make way for new royal favorites.

The seeds of Ulster's troubles were sown in 1607, when it was opened up for expansion by England's new Protestant king, James I. In an episode known as the Plantation of Ulster, it was decreed that settlers should outnumber the Irish, who mostly remained loyal to the Roman Catholic religion.

"Undertakers," new arrivals from England and Scotland who guaranteed to bring 10 Protestant families with them, were given land completely cleared of natives. "Servitors," who had served the Crown in some fashion, were allowed to retain some native labor for a 50 percent increase in rent. Finally, any "deserving Irish" were allowed to rent land for double the normal rate. Areas remained segregated: Scots here, English there, Irish somewhere else. Around 100,000 Protestant settlers arrived between 1610 and 1640. Unlike the Celts, Vikings and Normans, this new batch of invaders rarely integrated.

In 1641, as the English parliament vied with its monarchy for absolute power, Ulster's native Irish took up arms. Around 2,000 Protestant settlers were murdered, but civil war raging in England prevented any large-scale measures against the rebels. It was 1649 before action could be taken against Ireland's unruly dispossessed.

bibles in stone—a high Celtic cross at Drumcliffe, county Sligo

© Steenie Harvey

Cromwell and the Penal Times

Retribution came courtesy of England's Lord Protector, Oliver Cromwell, the villainous bogeyman of Irish history. With England's civil war over, his victorious Parliamentary Army set sail for Ireland. Heading a 20,000-strong invasion force, Cromwell quickly crushed the rebellion, butchering the citizens of Drogheda and Wexford in the process. Widespread confiscation of estates was accompanied by the banishment of thousands of Irish citizens to the country's poorest lands. Like Cromwell himself, the infamous cry of "To hell or Connacht" still arouses bitterness.

Catholicism in the form of public worship became illegal as Cromwell considered demands for the right to celebrate Mass "abominable." Yet the Mass continued in secret, often held in places sacred to the old Celtic religion: remote woodland glades or mountain areas where large boulders made for improvised altars. In memory of those times, an annual outdoor Mass is still celebrated at many such sites today.

In 1685, after more than a century of unbroken Protestant rule, Britain and Ireland found themselves with a new Catholic king, James II. Although the contrary-minded James had quite lawfully succeeded his brother (Charles II), who died without legitimate offspring, the English establishment was staunchly opposed to "Popery." They decided the best way to keep the Protestant flag flying was by deposing James and depriving his own son of any succession rights.

The throne was offered to a Dutchman, William of Orange. Backing his claim with force, William's troops inflicted rapid defeats on the king's loyal forces in England. The conflict moved to Ireland where the deposed monarch again lost crucial battles including the decisive Battle of the Boyne in 1690. That victory by Protestant King Billy (William of Orange) over Catholic James Stuart is still celebrated by many Ulstermen every July 12.

Even though he died nigh on 300 years ago, William of Orange's name still echoes. An icon within Northern Ireland's Unionist culture, Dutch William appears on countless banners during the Easter-to-July marching season. It explains why Ulster Protestants are known as Orangemen and their meeting places as Orange Lodges.

Penal laws for the governance of Ireland were quickly enacted. Catholics could not enter Parliament, buy land, or own a horse worth more than £5. Nor could they marry Protestants without first converting. The purpose of the draconian legislation was to ensure a Protestant Ascendancy within Ireland. It succeeded, but the Irish Parliament remained subordinate to its English counterpart at Westminster: Any bill of law for the governance of Ireland had to first receive approval from English politicians. This was much to the chagrin of Ireland's new ruling class, who were mostly descended from Norman knights and Protestant settlers who had arrived during Tudor and Cromwellian times.

Towards the end of the 18th century, rebellion simmered once again. America's War of Independence and the French Revolution had engendered radical ideas of establishing an Irish Republic. In 1791, two years after the storming of the Bastille, the Society of United Irishmen was formed. The Society's most illustrious member was Wolfe Tone, but (somewhat ironically) the founding fathers were predominately Belfast Presbyterians—today probably the staunchest opponents of a united Ireland and Republican aims.

Wolfe Tone managed to enlist French support for his fellow Republicans, and an invasion force was sent to Ireland in 1796. Yet despite all the patriot games, Ireland never experienced any glorious Revolution and no aristocratic necks bowed to Madame Guillotine's kiss. Ireland's weather conspired against the plotters: Severe storms broke up the French fleet, preventing the landing.

When rebellion finally erupted in 1798, it was badly organized and speedily suppressed. Following this latest revolt, the London government decided the troublesome Irish were best dealt with through the union of both Parliaments. Although many of Dublin's ruling class stubbornly opposed the idea, bribery won the day. Ireland's Parliament voted itself out of existence, and the Union came into force on January 1, 1801.

Ireland in the Union

Few towns lack a street named after Daniel O'Connell, a Kerry lawyer and an important figure in Ireland's long struggle against sectarianism. In the opening decades of the 19th century, Irish Catholics remained in a political wilderness. Attempts to introduce Catholic Emancipation were continuously blocked in London's Westminster Parliament, where all Irish matters were now decided. However, the arrival on the scene of O'Connell gave Catholics hope of gaining some form of political representation.

O'Connell began the Catholic Association in 1823 "to further the interests of Catholics in all areas of life." Fearing a mass political party had been born, the authorities unsuccessfully attempted to indict him for inciting rebellion. Despite the Association's suppression, O'Connell was elected Member of Parliament for Clare in 1828.

Because of his Catholicism, the law forbade O'Connell from taking his Westminster seat. However, the government was alarmed at the possibility of numerous democratically elected Irish Catholics seceding. Forced to counter this, a Catholic Emancipation Act passed in 1829. The victory was not without cost. Freehold property ownership was the deciding factor as to whether citizens were entitled to a vote. Known as "the franchise qualification," the entry level of property value was immediately increased five-fold from 40 shillings to £10. As most Irish Catholics were impoverished tenant farmers who didn't own property anyway, ordinary people were consequently still denied voting rights. It was only the Catholic owners of grander properties who retained the franchise.

Even so, O'Connell was hailed as "the Liberator" and began campaigning for the repeal of the Act of Union. Huge crowds attended his rallies, often held on famous Irish sites. In 1843 a vast gathering took place on the Hill of Tara, the centuries-old seat of Ireland's High Kings. The satirical magazine *Punch* nicknamed O'Connell "King of the Beggars," but an agitated British government made it plain the Union would be defended. When another monster rally was planned for Clontarf (site of Brian Boru's famous victory in 1014), the government banned the meeting, threatening to send in troops if it proceeded. Not wanting to subject his countrymen to a full-scale military invasion, O'Connell accepted the ban and the Repeal Association's campaign petered out.

Famine and the Push for Home Rule

In 1845, an old invader returned to haunt Ireland: famine. Throughout the centuries the country had experienced disastrous harvests and widespread starvation. Crop failure in the 1740s may have killed an equivalent proportion of Ireland's populace but the Great Hunger of the 1840s was better documented and thus had a greater historical impact. The potato crop failed again in 1846, '47 and '48 with horrific and devastating consequences: one million people died from hunger. Another million people were lost to disease or to emigration aboard the coffin ships that carried them away from their homeland forever. By 1851, Ireland's population had fallen from over 8 million in 1841 to a little over 6 million.

The crazy thing is that Ireland continued to export food during the famine years, which may have given rise to rumors that mass starvation never happened or was greatly exaggerated. Certainly there were abundant harvests of wheat and oats, but grain crops do not thrive in Ireland's rock-strewn west, the part of the country that suffered an almost apocalyptic devastation. Here the potato really was the staple foodstuff. If the poor wanted grain then somehow they had to find the wherewithal to pay the market price for it. Very few could. Nor was there much in the way of charitable handouts, though some landlords did set up soup kitchens. However, for the people of Mayo's Achill Island, accepting famine aid brought with it the risk of excommunication and thus eternal damnation. Under the supervision of the Reverend Edward Nangle, a kind of missionary outpost was established on the island. Catholic families were indeed fed and clothed—providing they worshipped at the Church Mission Society's newly founded Protestant church and the island children attended its school.

Pro-Independence activists decided the time for rhetoric alone was past. Despite the very real threat of transportation to Australia's Botany Bay, secret societies proliferated and sectarian violence became commonplace. In 1858, the Irish Republican Brotherhood was established, followed the next year in America by the Fenian Brotherhood. Both aimed to achieve an Independent Republic by means of violent revolution.

> In 1845, an old invader returned to haunt Ireland: famine.

A Home Government Association, founded in 1870, again signaled that the majority of Irish people yearned to follow a more peaceful route to self-determination. In Britain's (and thus Ireland's) first secret ballot election, Alliance of Home Rule candidates won 60 percent of the Irish seats in 1874. The Alliance's leader was Charles Stewart Parnell, whose name is also honored by numerous street signs within the Republic. A skillful politician, he even persuaded the Fenians to travel the parliamentary road to reform with him.

But Ireland still wasn't about to witness an invasion of democratic ideals. The passing of the Victorian Age saw Ulster's politicians uncompromisingly saying no to the notion of autonomy and a Dublin government. However, British Prime Minister Gladstone indicated his awareness of Ulster's opposition and that an amendment to exclude the Province from any Irish Home Rule bill was a possibility. For the first time, the specter of partition raised its head.

Scandal erupted in 1890 when it became public knowledge that Parnell was living with Kitty O'Shea, a colleague's wife. Gladstone refused to continue negotiations with someone who was "morally tainted," and the disgraced Parnell died the following year. The year 1893 saw Gladstone successfully steer an Irish Home Rule bill through Parliament, but the non-elected aristocrats of the House of Lords rejected it. Not entirely surprising, considering that many of them owned Irish estates.

The 20th Century

After 1910's general election, the Irish National Party's 84 members held the balance of power at Westminster. However, the Ulster Unionist Party and its leader, Sir Edward Carson, still fiercely opposed any change in the status quo. When a new Irish Home Rule bill was passed by Westminster's parliament, Carson formed what was effectively a private army, the Ulster Volunteer Force (UVF).

Although the Lords again rejected the bill, delaying its implementation, Ulster sensed the times they were a-changing—and from a Unionist standpoint, not for the better. Determined to remain British at all costs, the UVF's early paramilitaries quickly acquired arms from Germany and began drilling. On the Nationalist side, the Irish Republican Brotherhood formed the Irish Volunteers.

Ireland's Home Rule bill received royal assent in 1914, but the outbreak of World War I moved the knotty Irish problem once again to the governmental back burner. Continuously thwarted in their attempts to achieve any form of autonomy by parliamentary methods, a number of Nationalists weren't prepared to wait for British agreement any longer.

Why was Britain so reluctant to let Ireland go? Well, it has been suggested that Ireland was seen as the linchpin of that Empire on which the sun proverbially never set. Remember, in those days Dublin was the "second city" of the Empire, Britain a major power, and more than a fifth of the global map colored red. To British eyes, removing the linchpin opened up the horrendous possibility of other colonies demanding independence.

On Easter Monday 1916, the Irish Volunteers and the smaller Irish Citizen Army finally rebelled against British rule. With a force of under 2,000, they occupied the General Post Office and other buildings in central Dublin. Patrick Pearse, elected by the IRB as President, emerged from the post office to declare a Republic.

But the Easter Rising generated little public support, and after six days of holding out against superior numbers and heavy artillery, the Volunteers surrendered. However, the British government's response soon changed popular opinion when martial law was declared and rebel leaders were court-martialed. Fourteen faced the firing squad in May that year, and many others would be shot before American pressure stopped the executions.

By now the public's general mood had changed, and a small group formed in 1905 by Arthur Griffith called Sinn Féin began attracting support. In 1918's general election, Sinn Féin swept the boards. Pledging not to go to Westminster, they formed the first Dáil, or independent parliament, under Eamon De Valera as President. Britain's attempt to suppress the new parliament led to more conflict. The Irish Volunteers became the Irish Republican Army (IRA) and fought a guerrilla war against British troops and Police.

In today's Ireland most people shun terrorism. Yet the fact remains that violence and bloodshed served as midwives to the birth of what became known as the Irish Free State. Were the original IRA bad guys or good guys? Terrorists or patriotic freedom fighters? It's still hotly debated whether the people of southern Ireland would have cast off the shackles of imperialism without the gunmen.

But if nationalist Ireland were to be given autonomy, what was to be done about Ulster, whose majority Protestant community insisted on remaining part of the Union? In agreement with the Ulster Unionists, British Prime Minister Lloyd George came up with new legislation: Ireland was to be divided. The 1920 Government of Ireland Act partitioned the island the following year.

Negotiations to end the war of independence in the south took place later in 1921 with Arthur Griffith and Michael Collins representing the Dáil. Offered much less than hoped for, they nevertheless signed the Anglo-Irish Treaty. An Irish Free State of 26 counties was given Dominion status with six Ulster counties remaining British and outside the new State authority. The British Parliament's satisfaction with the deal was not mirrored in Dublin; bitter divisions arose in the Dáil. Having to swear allegiance to the British monarch was an especially contentious issue, but in January 1922, the Dáil voted to accept the treaty. De Valera, trenchantly opposed, resigned. Civil war followed within months, with the country splitting into pro- and anti-treaty factions. Friends and neighbors who had fought as comrades-in-arms against the British now started slaughtering each other. The brutal conflict finally ended with a truce in May 1923.

Slowly and by degrees, southern Ireland continued to break with Britain and the monarchy. In 1937 the Irish Free State declared complete independence and changed its name to Éire. Finally, on Easter Monday 1949, Éire became the newly inaugurated Irish Republic and said farewell to the British Commonwealth.

In 1972 the country elected to join the European Community, which effectively resulted in an influx of financial help from wealthier neighbors such as Germany. Not only did this set the scene for today's economic success, it gave Ireland newfound confidence. As a member state on equal terms with its European neighbors, Ireland's national psyche has been transformed. Most Irish people fully embrace the European ideal, and it could be that the country has at last emerged from the shadows of its ancient struggle with Britain.

PART III

Daily Life

7 Keeping In Touch

Forget all those old jokes you hear about the Pony Express and pigeon post. Ireland now has a modern and efficient communications system.

Mail

Ireland's state-owned postal service is run by An Post. According to their own figures, more than 560 million letters are delivered annually with over 90 percent achieving next-day delivery. Main post offices are generally open weekdays from 8:30 A.M. to 5:30 P.M., Saturdays 9 A.M. to noon. Along with handling mail, they pay out State pensions and unemployment benefits; sell TV licenses, lottery tickets and prize bonds; stock travel pass and passport application forms; and operate currency exchange facilities and various savings schemes.

Village post offices do not offer as extensive a range of services and most close for lunch. However, as the local post office is often the village grocery store too, it's usually possible to buy stamps after the mail counter has officially closed. To catch the last post you'll need to check locally as every postbox has its own particular collection time.

Within Ireland itself, postcards and standard letters under 25 grams cost an equivalent of $0.33 to mail. Heavier items are charged by weight. A flat package weighing between 250 and 500 grams costs $1.27; a 2-kilogram package $5.75.

Airmail deliveries to the United States generally take between five and seven days. Letters under 25 grams cost $0.50 and are again then scaled by weight. A 300-gram package costs $5.30; a 900-gram one $15.90. Economy surface rates are far cheaper than airmail—that same 900-gram package costs only $5.53 by surface. The major drawback is that it could take as long as 15 weeks to reach its destination.

If you are mailing important documents or valuables within Ireland, you can send them by registered mail for an additional fee. There are three minimum rates for letters: $2.54, $3.16 and $3.73, depending on weight. A 2-kilogram package costs a minimum of $7.95 to register. Should a package get lost, you can claim compensation of up to $1,412 depending on registration cover chosen. It's also possible to register mail destined for the United States, but the maximum compensation allowed falls to a paltry $22.50.

A Poste Restante service allows visitors to have mail sent to a local post office. Free of charge, it can be had for up to three months. You can also rent a private box number at head post offices, delivery depots and certain other post offices around the country. In towns, An Post charges $78 per year for letters, $155 to receive parcels as well. In rural districts the $78 fee includes both parcels and letters.

The range of options for business customers includes pre-paid response mail, on-site collection services and direct mail. Should you wish to shower a locality with leaflets, rates per thousand items start at $67 and fall to $45 per thousand for a target market of 500,000 householders. For more information, contact An Post Customer Services, GPO, FREEPOST, Dublin 1. (Outside Ireland you'll need a stamp on the letter.) Within Ireland you can call the special Callsave number, 1850 575859.

Most major international courier services are represented in Ireland and have collection depots around the country. Quotes for sending a 50-gram package to the States were $37 with FedEx and $40 with DHL. However, I've found the cheapest to be SDS; you'll pay $26 for the same package, and you can send packages via SDS at main post offices. For local offices look under Courier Services in the telephone directory's Golden Pages. Most have freephone numbers connecting to a central call center. For FedEx, call 1800 725725; for DHL, 1800 535800. The national number for SDS is (0)1 459 1133.

Telephone

The Republic's main domestic service is provided by Eircom, a former state-owned company with one of the world's most up-to-date digital systems. Like most monopolies it's fairly expensive, but deregulation in telecoms is opening the market to competition.

Today it rarely takes longer than 10 days to get a telephone installed. Costs of connection depend upon whether it's a first-time installation or if the line is already in place. If you are an existing customer moving to a new residence, the reconnection service is free. A first-time connection costs $109; this fee includes both line connection and a telephone set with features such as call-waiting and three-way calling. The price includes VAT (sales tax).

There are 18 telesales centers around the country. Simply dial 1901 within Ireland for more information about getting connected, or contact the head office: Eircom, St. Stephen's Green, Dublin 2; tel + 353 (0)1 671 4444.

Bills arrive every two months, each one carrying a line charge of approximately $25. That's $150 per year before you've even made a single call. And I'm afraid there's some more unwelcome news: In Ireland there's no such thing as a free call. Unlike in the States, gossiping to new friends and neighbors down the road will cost you. The number of units used determines the actual cost of calls. Each unit buys a certain amount of time; how much depends upon the time of day, whether it's a weekday or a weekend and also the destination of the call. Prices have come down in recent months, and for some strange reason it's cheaper to phone North America than Europe. Calls at different times of the day from private phones are charged by the following method:

Calls within Ireland

BAND	RATE	PRICE PER MINUTE
Local calls	Daytime	$0.045
	Evening	$0.01
	Weekend	$0.01
National calls	Daytime	$0.84
	Evening	$0.55
	Weekend	$0.01
Calls to national cell phones	Daytime	$0.26
	Evening	$0.17
	Weekend	$0.14

International Calls

BAND	RATE	PRICE PER MINUTE
U.S. & Canada	Daytime	$0.17
	Evening	$0.14
	Weekend	$0.14
Britain	Daytime	$0.14
	Evening	$0.13
	Weekend	$0.11
Near Europe	Daytime	$0.34
	Evening	$0.29
	Weekend	$0.26

Making international calls from a public pay phone is very costly. Charges per minute to the United States and Canada are $1.60 standard (noon to 6 P.M., Monday through Friday), $1.37 reduced (8 A.M. to noon and 6 to 10 P.M., Monday through Friday), and $1.23 economy (10 P.M. to 8 A.M. Monday through Friday, and all day on Saturdays, Sundays and public holidays). To call the Middle East or South Africa costs a staggering $3.35 per minute.

How to Make Calls

Within Ireland, telephone numbers are quoted with subscriber trunk dialing (STD) codes given first in brackets. These are the equivalent of area codes. For example, the STD code for Dublin is 01; for Galway it's 091. Say you were in Dublin and wished to call Galway's tourist office (tel 091 537700). The digits given are those you would dial. If, however, you were calling from within Galway itself, simply ring 537700.

When phoning from the States, you first need to dial the international access code (011) followed by the country code for Ireland (353). And although Galway's STD code is 091, that initial 0 is dropped when phoning from abroad. Thus, to reach Galway's tourist office, dial 011 353 91 537700.

As another example, say you want to call the Revenue Commissioners at Dublin Castle (tel 01 878 0000). That's the number you call if phoning on an Irish phone from outside Dublin. Within Dublin you ring 878 0000. If calling from the United States, you dial 011 353 1 878 0000.

To call the United States from Ireland, first dial the access code (00) followed by the country code (1), followed by the area code and then the local number. The Irish Embassy's number in Washington, D.C., is (202) 462 3939. To call from Ireland dial 00 1 202 462 3939.

PAY PHONES

Public pay phones accept either coins or call cards, which are sold at post offices, gas stations, newsstands and most grocery stores. Call cards are available in units of 10 ($2.26), 20 ($3.96), 50 ($9.05) and 100 ($18.10). Units are charged at different rates depending on whether a coin phone or card phone is used. A $0.20 coin buys a three-minute local call, but the cost is fractionally reduced if using a 50-unit call card. Operator-assisted calls cost $0.80 minimum. To call the operator dial 10.

EMERGENCY CALLS

In an emergency, dial either 999 or 112. Calls are free and you must ask the operator for the service you want: fire brigade, Gardái (police), ambulance, lifeboat or mountain rescue. When the emergency service answers, state the address or location where help is required.

DIRECTORY INQUIRIES

Can't find the number you're seeking? Call 1190 for numbers within Ireland and Northern Ireland, 1197 for numbers in Britain, and 1198 for all other international inquiries. Customers are allowed four free directory inquiry calls per bill. Otherwise the charge is $0.39 per call for a maximum of three inquiries. If you're a real pennypincher, inquiries from public pay phones are free of charge.

When the going gets tough...

© Steenie Harvey

Mobile Phones

The mobile phone revolution has taken off in Ireland in a big way. Some 1.5 million people now own a cell phone, and most towns have at least one mobile phone store. At present, three main companies within Ireland provide access to mobile phone technology. Eircell, Esat Digifone and Meteor operate digital networks. Two capacity re-sellers, Imagine and Spirit, offer cut-rate mobile calls.

Mobile phones range in price from $33 to $170, but calls are far more expensive than on a fixed land-line phone. With Esat's Digilite service it costs $0.17 to $0.48 per minute to call a fixed phone number at peak time. Monthly rental costs are between $13.50 and $41. Eircell offers broadly similar pay-later packages. You can also choose what's called the ready-to-go option: mobile phone, $22.50 "Go" card and a charger. You can add to the credit on your Go card as you wish and thus avoid monthly bills. Meteor didn't launch services in Ireland until March 2001, and as yet covers only the major cities of Dublin, Cork, Galway and Limerick.

> *The mobile phone revolution has taken off in Ireland in a big way.*

Both Esat and Eircell claim to cover roughly 98 percent of the population, and both have roaming agreements with over 100 countries including the United States. Sounds good, but population isn't territory, and mountains tend to have an unfortunate effect on mobile phone transmissions. Technology meets its match in west Kerry, Connemara and parts of Donegal. You may even encounter problems around Dublin because of the Wicklow Mountains.

Contact Eircell Customer Service at the Ramparts, Dundalk, county Louth. Within Ireland, call their freephone number, 1907.

Esat Digifone can be reached at the National Technological Park, Limerick on +353 (0)61 203501. Once in Ireland call their freephone number, 1909. Contact Meteor Mobile Communications at Kingwood Avenue, Citywest Business Park, Naas Road, Dublin 24; tel +353 (0)1 430 7000.

Passing souvenir shops and stands may make you miss home just a tad.

© Steenie Harvey

Email and the Internet

Ireland has a number of Internet service providers if you're keen on traveling the information superhighway. You can choose from free service providers such as Oceanfree, though the disadvantage with these is that sometimes you cannot get connected because the lines are busy. If you're willing to pay for premium service, the average yearly subscription fee is $135; installation software costs between $5.65 and $14. Costs of telephone calls connecting you to the Internet or your POP email service are charged at the local rate. Thus it will cost $0.135 per three minutes during peak weekday hours; $0.60 per hour during the evenings and weekends.

Eircom.net is one of the main providers. Contact your local Eircom sales center or call their Callsave number, 1850 203204. Ireland On-Line is another big player. They can be reached at Alexandra House, Earlsfort Terrace, Dublin 2; tel +353 (0)1 604 6800. Business users may find it worthwhile to contact the Irish Internet Association, P.O. Box 6118, Dublin 2; tel +353 (0)1 668 8108.

If you don't yet own a computer, you can log on to the Internet in one of the growing number of cybercafés popping up in most sizable Irish towns, or at some public libraries. Charges are around $5.50 per hour, though in some cases there's limited free access if you become a library member.

Ireland on the Web

For those who already have computers with an Internet connection, you'll find an amazing amount of information on the Web on all things Irish. For example, ask a search engine to come up with details on Irish travel and you'll be overwhelmed with a choice of thousands of sites ranging from corporate golfing vacations to cottages for rent in county Clare. Many Irish-interest websites are actually based in the United States, but there are some interesting homegrown ones too.

USEFUL WEBSITES

www.irlgov.ie The Irish government's official website links to various departments such as Foreign Affairs, Health, Justice, the Revenue Commissioners, etc. Although visiting the tax man isn't exactly an entertaining experience, you can download comprehensive files on everything from vehicle registration tax to self-employment requirements.

www.luminarium.org/mythology/ireland An absolutely fascinating site of myth, folklore and stories containing heaps of esoteric material. Did you know that caisean uchad was a kind of Celtic pass-the-parcel game in which a burning sheep's head was passed around a group of revelers?

www.mayo-ireland.ie Where you'll find Comhaltas Ceoltori Éireann,

Ireland's main organization for keeping the flame of traditional culture alight. Plenty of information on festivals, music teaching, music publications and local branches.

www.ceolas.org Another Irish music site with sound clips and a wealth of information on traditional music and dance.

www.macnas.com All about Galway's community-based arts and street theater group with clips of the annual madcap parade during Arts Week.

www.iavi.ie Real estate through members of the Irish Auctioneers and Valuers Institute. Some members are better at keeping their listings current than others, but the site provides a good overview of countrywide properties available and prices. You'll find everything from cottages to farmhouses, pubs to hotels, Georgian mansions to urban apartments.

> *If you don't yet own a computer, you can log on to the Internet in one of the growing number of cybercafés popping up in most sizable Irish towns.*

www.ireland.travel.ie The official site of Bord Fáilte, the Irish Tourist Board. All the basic need-to-know information about hotels, restaurants, sights to see and things to do. Plus, if you're seeking a special interest vacation, check out its searchable database. It came up with 148 suggestions for an equestrian vacation.

www.irish-times.com All the daily news and views from one of Ireland's top newspapers. The site includes a genealogical gateway where you can discover the history behind many Irish surnames or embark upon a search for your own Irish ancestors.

www.finfacts.ie Extremely useful site for current information on economic indicators, savings options, best airfares, etc.

www.hookemacdonald.ie If you're looking for a house or apartment to rent in the Dublin area, check out Hooke & MacDonald's Let on the Net site. When I investigated, these realtors offered a good range of available properties including a furnished one-bedroom apartment in the Rathmines area for $735 per month.

www.wow.ie WOW means What's on Where. If you want nationwide listings of films, music, theater and gallery openings throughout Ireland, this site should fit the bill.

www.jesuit.ie Need some spiritual guidance? Although not everyone will want to pray in front of a computer screen, Ireland's Jesuit priests are now online. Their website includes a Sacred Space with a daily prayer.

www.nationalarchives.ie Ireland's National Archives now has a searchable database. It includes the Ireland-Australia transportation index complete with names, trial dates and crime descriptions. I discovered numerous Harvey namesakes who made the journey "Down Under" on convict ships. In 1838, an unfortunate 22-year-old named Thomas

Harvey from Louth was sentenced to seven years transportation for stealing a plate.

www.rte.ie Up-to-date Irish news, radio programs plus daily TV and radio listings from RTE, the state-owned broadcaster.

http://foxleap.fortunecity.com/irishlyrics Who will plow the fields all day and who will thresh the corn? That's the first line of "The Bantry Girl's Lament." Or maybe you want to know the words to "The Wild Colonial Boy"? You'll find the lyrics to more than 100 traditional Irish folk songs here.

www.iha.ie Irish racehorses: an investment or a gamble? Run by the Irish Horseracing Authority, this is an informative site for those who want to buy a thoroughbred or simply check out the fixture list calendar for race meetings.

www.golfclubireland.com Golf enthusiasts will want to experience the rub of the Irish green. This site includes pars for various Irish golf courses, green fees, club memberships and much more besides.

www.ostlan.com Go to Ostlan for a guide to pubs and restaurants. The site includes a review section—you can write your own review or see what previous happy (or disgruntled) diners have said about Irish establishments.

www.ireland.com All the daily news and views from the *Irish Times*, one of Ireland's top newspapers. The site includes a genealogical gateway where you can discover the history behind many Irish surnames or embark upon a search for your own Irish ancestors.

Though you might miss home cooking, seafood pubs and restaurants are a joy.

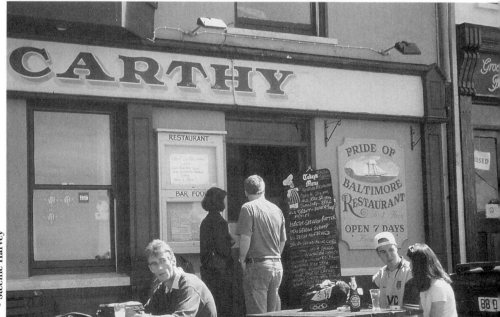

© Steenie Harvey

Newspapers and the Media

The Republic's two main dailies are the *Irish Times* and the *Irish Independent*; both currently cost $1.13 per issue. The *Irish Times* has quite a serious point of view; the *Irish Independent* carries more gossipy lifestyle features. Both have good business coverage and special weekly property supplements (Thursdays for the *Times*, Fridays for the *Independent*.)

Published in Cork, the *Examiner* is another daily, but its sale outside the southern half of the Republic is not that widespread. If your taste runs to tabloids, there are special Irish versions of British dailies such as the *Sun, Mirror* and *Star*. All carry a relentless cavalcade of celebrity gossip and scandal and not very much in the way of news.

On Sundays you can choose from the *Sunday Independent, Sunday Business Post, Tribune* and an Irish edition of Britain's *Sunday Times*. The *Sunday World* is rather more downmarket and celebrity oriented, but undeniably popular. There are also a substantial number of provincial newspapers, which are published on a weekly basis and concentrate mainly on local issues and events.

As far as U.S. publications are concerned, *Time, Newsweek* and the *International Herald Tribune* are usually on sale at larger newsstands. If you want regular copies your local newsagent will be able to order them for you. Don't, however, expect to find any papers or magazines in your mail box or on your front porch; there's no newspaper delivery in Ireland.

Many of Ireland's local newspapers are available in U.S. cities with sizable populations of Irish Americans. You'll certainly be able to buy the *Sligo Champion* or the *Longford Leader* in New York and Boston. It's also worth looking at magazines such as *World of Hibernia* or *Ireland of the Welcomes*, both of which carry plenty of travel and general interest features.

One of the best reads for potential new residents is the quarterly subscription magazine *Inside Ireland*. Most of its readership is American, and it contains lots of valuable practical advice along with quirky features and lifestyle articles by folks who have already bought a home here. You can obtain a sample copy by sending $2 postage and handling ($4 airmail) to Inside Ireland, P.O. Box 1886, Dublin 16; tel +353 (0)1 493 1906.

The public television service currently consists of RTE 1, RTE 2 and an Irish-language station, TG4. An independent station, TV 3, also broadcasts. Home-produced programs that are very popular include *Glenroe*, a soap opera about farming families, and *The Late, Late Show*, claimed to be the world's longest-running talk show. Many other programs, about 60 percent of the total, are brought in from Britain, Australia and the States, so if you're pining for familiar fare, you'll be able to keep up with what's happening on *Frasier*, find out who Oprah is chatting with, and even tune in to the U.S. Masters Golf Tournament. Sports coverage is good. Although you'll rarely catch baseball, there's more than enough in Gaelic games, soccer, golf, tennis, snooker, horseracing and Formula One to keep even the most fanatical sports fan satisfied. If you want more, there's cable TV and satellite channels such as Sky Sports and Eurosport.

An important point to note is that you need a license to watch TV. It costs $79 annually, obtained from the post office. If a detector van comes around and you cannot produce a license, you will be taken to court and fined as much as $565 for a first offense. The money garnered from TV licenses goes to fund the RTE programs.

Ireland's three national radio stations are supplemented by a plethora of regional independents. Like everywhere else in the western world, some offer wall-to-wall pop; others a mix of music, chat and call-in programs. One of the most entertaining call-ins, where everything and anything is up for discussion, is the *Gerry Ryan Show*. It broadcasts weekdays between 9 A.M. and noon on RTE 2FM (FM 90.4—97MHz; MW 612, 1278 kHz). Opera, including performances from the New York Met, and classical music can be found on Lyric FM (FM 96—99 MHz).

8 Money Matters

A sking how far your money will stretch in Ireland is one of those "how long is a piece of string?" questions. Although there's no escaping the fact that many day-to-day living costs are higher than in the States, other factors help balance the picture. For starters, you won't be paying property taxes or rates (local council taxes). Retirees can take advantage of a valuable free travel concession, and free hospital emergency treatment is available to any resident who needs it. And, if you're on a fixed income, it's reassuring to know that Ireland has a relatively low inflation rate, currently 5.5 percent.

As in any other country, much will depend on where you choose to live, the kind of lifestyle you expect to enjoy, and your hobbies and interests. Theater tickets are astoundingly cheap, for example, but computer and high-quality photographic equipment is exorbitant. With green fees pitched at around $22.50, membership at many of the small midland clubs that form the backbone of Irish golf can be had for $350 to $400 annually. That said, founder members of the prestigious new Kinsale course in county Cork were charged $11,300, and a round of play at Powerscourt Golf Club in county Wicklow costs $68.

Leaving aside the question of rent or mortgage payments, if you're happy with simple country pleasures—a modest home with all the necessary comforts, a small fuel-efficient car, adequate health coverage and occasional treats—then $2,000 per month should prove more than ample. Obviously if you're the type of person who expects to dine out regularly in top-class Dublin restaurants, drive a Mercedes, belong to an exclusive gym, and own a huge Georgian mansion with equally huge heating bills, you're going to need significantly more in the way of funds.

To put the income question into some kind of context, the basic State Pension for Irish couples under 80 years of age currently stands at $842 per month, $479 for single pensioners. The most recent figures issued by the Central Statistics Office put the average monthly wage at $1,566 for males and $1,037 for females, figures that encompass extremely varied salary levels.

To cite a few examples, clothing factory machinists average $760 per month whereas most workers in the gas, electricity and water industries can command monthly salaries of around $2,065. Entry-level positions in the computer technology industries pay around $1,550 monthly; those in telesales around $1,000. Any good Dublin-based brick layer will expect to be making around $3,200 over the same monthly period.

At the time of writing this book, the exchange rate against the dollar was 1 euro = $0.87.

Banking

Do you find articles on banking and savings accounts a source of endless fascination? Or are you like most people: They make your eyes glaze over? Well, my apologies if money matters bore you, but these practicalities need addressing. I'm sure you don't want to come to Ireland and keep your money in a suitcase under the bed.

Opening a bank account in Ireland is straightforward. There are no exchange controls and thus no limit on the amount of money you can bring into or take out of the country. If you are buying property, it will be important to have funds transferred as soon as possible. Even if you've chosen to rent a home, you'll almost certainly want to have a current account with a bank near the town where you plan to live.

A current account is a checkbook account that you'll probably use for day-to-day expenses or to pay off credit card bills. It can be used in conjunction with a cash card, which acts as a check guarantee card and allows holders to draw funds from ATMs (automated teller machines), sometimes known as "hole-in-the-wall" machines. Through a current account, you can also arrange standing orders to pay regular bills such as electricity and telephone.

When opening an account, all banks ask you to show a passport or some other form of identification. This is to comply with government legislation (Criminal Justice Act 1994), introduced to prevent criminal organizations and drug dealers from using Irish banks as laundry baskets. Accounts are largely confidential although the Revenue Commissioners, Ireland's tax authorities, can scrutinize certain types of deposit accounts.

The two largest retail banks are Allied Irish Bank (AIB) and Bank of Ireland; both have branches in small towns. Larger places usually also have branches of National Irish Bank, Ulster Bank and TSB Bank. Irish Permanent and First Active are former building societies (mutuals) that converted to banks and floated their shares on the stock market. Both offer the same kind of financial services as their high-street competitors.

It should come as no surprise to find that banks are out to profit from their customers and most transactions cost a fee. If, however, you keep an equivalent balance of approximately $115 in your current account throughout the fee period, you won't pay for most normal transactions. All banks apply similar charging structures, and their fees shouldn't be a worrying sum for the average spender. Looking at my own recent bank statement, quarterly fees amounted to just over $13.

Banks also handle credit card arrangements, but holding a full deck of cards could prove expensive in more ways than one. The government intends to apply a kind of stealth tax of approximately $17 annually on each credit card held, and it will probably be in place by the time you read this. The main credit cards used in Ireland are Visa, MasterCard and American Express, which are accepted in most large stores, supermarkets and gas stations. Around 30,000 Irish establishments take credit cards, but it's still cash or check in most village shops and definitely cash only in pubs. If you're traveling around the country, be aware that not all B&Bs take credit cards. Charge cards such as Diner's Club are accepted in many places where tourists gather, but you rarely see their signs in more out-of-the-way localities. As you already know, credit cards can prove an expensive way of borrowing if bills aren't settled on time. In Ireland, annual percentage rate (APR) on credit card borrowing is typically twice the standard bank overdraft/personal loan rate of 12 percent.

For more information on bank services, call any local branch or contact the following:

AIB Bank Headquarters, Bankcentre, Ballsbridge, Dublin 4; tel +353 (0)1 660 0311.

Bank of Ireland Head Office, Lower Baggot St., Dublin 2; tel +353 (0)1 661 5933.

First Active, Skehan House, Booterstown, county Dublin; tel +353 (0)1 283 1801.

Irish Permanent, 56/59 St. Stephen's Green, Dublin 2; tel +353 (0)1 661 5577.

National Irish Bank Head Office, 7/8 Wilton Terrace, Dublin 2; tel +353 (0)1 638 5000.

Trustee Savings Bank, Frederick House, South Frederick St., Dublin 2; tel +353 (0)1 679 0444.

Ulster Bank, 33 College Green, Dublin 2; tel +353 (0)1 677 7623.

SAVINGS

As permanent residents, most expatriates will seek a safe Irish home for at least part of their savings. All banks and building societies offer various types of deposit accounts that will give you sleep-easy-at-night security. Unfortunately, Ireland's low-interest-rate environment equates with paltry returns for savers; it would be hard to make Ireland's savings rates seem sexy even if I spoke with a sultry French accent! On ordinary demand deposit accounts, the best rate available is around 4 percent, and that's only if you have at least $280,000 to invest. Under $3,400 and you'll be lucky to get 0.5 percent interest.

Without getting too technical, when a country offers high interest rates on savings deposits, it usually indicates galloping inflation and an unstable economy. Forty-percent interest rates sound brilliant but you just don't get them in Ireland. The only possibility of getting returns like that is by exchanging your hard-earned dollars for dodgy Third World currencies held in even dodgier Third World banks. When the ruble/peso/ringgit or whatever plunges against the dollar (and it always does), you'll come to the sickening realization that hyperinflation has wiped out the value of your savings. That 40 percent return? It's going to take a lot more than *that* to buy back your original sum.

Thankfully Irish punts are not Russian rubles. Nor is Ireland one of those "emerging markets" from which it always seems impossible to emerge. So, where to stash your cash if you don't want keep it all Stateside?

Fixed-term accounts are the best hedge against inflation, but even if you're willing to tie up ordinary deposit savings for six months, current yields average only between 2.75 and 4.75 percent. It will be difficult to find better returns because Irish interest rates need to comply with European Union monetary criteria. To find which institutions are offering the most attractive rates, read a financial publication such as *The Sunday Business Post*. Comparative interest rate tables of all Ireland's banks and building societies are published weekly.

Broadly speaking, most types of savings accounts don't deliver tax-free gains on any interest earned. A tax known as DIRT (Deposit Interest Retention Tax) is deducted at source; the current rate is 20 percent. However, those aged over 65 who are not liable to pay income tax may be able to claim it back from the Revenue Commissioners.

The government has recently given the go-ahead to a new range of savings products known as Special Savings Incentive Accounts (SSIAs). Although these are designed to encourage people with modest incomes to save, they're definitely worth a look. I know of no other country where the government will add on 25 percent to your savings! An SSIA allows you to put away a sum ranging from $13 to $226 a month for five years. This can be in either an approved deposit account or a stock market–based investment fund. For every $4 you save, the government will contribute $1, or 25 percent. If you maintain the account for the full five-year term, the only tax levied is 20 percent on the interest or profit. Most financial institutions offer SSIAs. Under this initial offering you have until the end of April 2002 to sign up.

You can also place your nest egg with An Post, the State-owned postal service. Its savings certificates and bonds deliver totally tax-free returns and are State guaranteed. Although interest rates can only be described as paltry, if you need to get at your money quickly, only seven days' notice is required. With savings certificates, individuals can invest amounts of between $57 and $67,800 over varying terms ranging from six months to five and a half years. If held to maturity, savings certificates currently return 16 percent interest over the full term. Bonds pay 8 percent, again tax-free, over a three-year period. With these, individuals can invest between $113 and $67,800. For more information, contact An Post Investment Services, College House, Townsend St., Dublin 2; tel +353 (0)1 705 7200. Within Ireland, you can call the freephone number, 1800 305060.

It's certainly worth stashing a little money in a building society. These are mutual societies that are theoretically owned by their members—savers and borrowers. Possibly more will change their status to banks and so deliver windfall shares to account holders. This has already happened in the case of First Active (formerly First National) and Irish Permanent when they demutualized and floated on the Irish stock market. Two of the largest remaining mutuals are Educational Building Society, 30 Westmoreland St., Dublin 2, tel +353 (0)1 677 5599; and Irish Nationwide, 1 Lower O'Connell St., Dublin 1; tel +353 (0)1 478 0022. (For more equity-based investments, see Chapter 19, Investing in Ireland.)

BORROWING

Ireland has one of Europe's highest rates of home ownership, with over 80 percent of families having a stake in the property market. Their principal source for home financing is, again, the bank or building society. Subject to income, status and good references from a U.S. bank, American newcomers seeking a mortgage may be able to raise between 50 and 70 percent of a house or business purchase price. Once you've been a resident in Ireland for a while, you may be able to obtain a 90 percent loan if you've established a sound financial relationship with the prospective lender. This 90 percent maximum criterion applies to Irish citizens too.

Ireland doesn't seem to have heard of the "gray power" movement; age plays a big part in whether you'll be considered a suitable borrower. Unless seeking a short-term mortgage (five to 10 years), those over 50 years of age may find it difficult to get finance. And there is no point in me giving you any blarney about arranging a mortgage Stateside. When it comes to foreign home ownership, American banks are just as timid as their Irish counterparts.

Opening a bank account in Ireland is straightforward.

According to the HomeOwners Finance Center, "American lenders have no interest in funding loans where the security is foreign property." Gloomy confirmation came from Chase Manhattan, which "does not finance homes located outside of the United States." Older readers needing to raise capital to fund the purchase of an Irish home may find the only solution lies in selling or remortgaging any property they own Stateside.

In general, Irish lenders take income into consideration when determining the amount you can borrow, though with the high values of property, there has recently been some flexibility. Working individuals can typically borrow two and a half times their annual income; thus someone making $35,000 could borrow $87,500. This sum can be upped if your spouse also has an income, generally by a multiple of one. For example, a couple earning $35,000 and $25,000 should be able to borrow $112,500. You may be able to borrow more, but a lot depends on your banking and employment histories and current circumstances.

Mortgage repayments can either be at a fixed rate for a given number of years or fluctuate with prevailing interest rates. There are dozens of packages on the market; as a ballpark figure the typical one-year fix on a 20-year term annuity mortgage is set at 5.7 percent interest; a 10-year fix at 6.95 percent. Assuming you've borrowed an equivalent of $56,500 over 20 years, a variable rate of 7.1 percent (7.3 percent APR) means monthly repayments of $441.50. If interest rates increased by 1 percent, an additional $35 would be payable monthly.

Inflation

Money loses its purchasing power if inflation is running above the after-tax rate of savings interest. The good news in recent years is that inflation has not decimated the value of Irish savings and investments; the average rate was under 2.5 percent throughout the 1990s. However, it has recently crept up to around the 5.5 percent mark.

The country doesn't have the greatest record of inflation-proofing people's wealth if you go back a little further in time. Within the past 30 years, some damagingly high levels have been scaled, particularly between 1969 and 1983. The peak was 1975, when inflation soared to an astonishing 21 percent.

As indicated by the savers' deposit rates currently available from financial institutions, interest rates are historically low. Once tax has been deducted, savers are only just keeping a step or two ahead of inflation. For those trying to make gains in Ireland's present low-interest-rate environment, the only real solution has been to have part of their portfolios in property and equities. Obviously this requires a willingness to expose your capital to risk factors such as a collapse in house prices or sharp downturns on the stock market.

Comparing the Cost of Living

Throughout the world, countless analysts devote their entire working lives to gleaning cost data from numerous cities. Most recent surveys show that Dublin scores better than New York for home services, utilities, entertainment and, somewhat surprisingly, groceries.

Whether that's correct or not, shopping basket items usually provide worthwhile cost comparisons. Although some towns now have branches of discount European supermarkets such as Lidl, prices within standard chains (Tesco, Supavalu, Londis, Spar) tend to be on a par, although bargain hunters can often snap up special deals: two chickens for the price of one, a pound of sausages given away with a pound of bacon rashers, etc. Figures released by the Central Statistics Office show that an average household (two adults, two children) spends around a fifth of their weekly income on food.

Sharp-eyed readers will have noticed that the shopping list on page 92 indicates weights by both the imperial and metric standards. Although Ireland theoretically went metric over 20 years ago, a dual system still operates. In most butcher shops and greengrocers, foodstuffs continue to be priced by the pound. And while milk is now sold in liters, barmen continue to measure out beer in pint and half-pint glasses.

Smokers may decide to quit when they discover a pack of 20 cigarettes costs almost $4.40. A bottle (750 cl) of white Australian Chardonnay wine

CuRRent costs of Basic foodstuffs:

100-gram jar of Nescafé: $2.50

1lb. of pork chops: $3.39

80 good-quality tea bags: $0.98

Medium-size chicken: $5.64

6 free-range eggs: $0.98

Liter of milk: $0.76

Liter of orange juice: $1.07

225 g of butter: $0.94

Head of lettuce: $0.40

1/2 lb. of sausage: $0.96

7 lbs. of potatoes: $2.25

Standard brown soda bread: $1

1 kg of sugar: $0.94

500 g of cornflakes: $1.86

1lb. of apples: $1.13

1.5 kg of white flour: $1.41

Sirloin steak: $4.50/lb.

500 g of cheddar cheese: $1.70

1.5 kgs of porridge oats: $2.03

1lb. of marmalade: $1.12

341 g of natural honey: $1.52

Medium can Heinz baked beans: $0.49

454 g of frozen haddock filets: $4.50

costs $6.77 minimum in most stores while a decent French red like Crozes Hermitage will set you back around $8.50. A six-pack of beer (Heineken lager or Guinness) costs around $10.20.

Value Added Tax (VAT)

Sales tax is not charged on groceries; nonetheless Ireland does have a general sales tax that applies to numerous goods and services. Known as VAT (Value Added Tax), it's not generally itemized separately, except on utility bills. In all shops, restaurants and other consumer outlets, the amount you see on price tags and menus is the price you'll pay. Aside from groceries, certain other items are VAT-free: these include books and children's footwear and clothing.

Varying rates of VAT apply to different services and sales. The standard 20 percent rate is charged on things such as telephone bills, new vehicles, gas, beer, liquor, most household goods, adults' footwear and clothing, and many professional bills including lawyers' fees. A reduced 12.5 percent rate applies to electricity, fuel for the home, restaurant meals, newspapers and cinema tickets. A rate of 3.6 percent covers the sale of livestock, greyhounds and renting horses. VAT isn't a talking point for most consumers as it's an invisible tax; only if you intend to *provide* any services need it concern you.

Household Goods

Electrical appliances and other household goods are quite expensive, particularly when it comes to good quality furniture. Furthermore, items such as stoves and refrigerators are like dinky doll's house pieces compared to what's available in North America. You'll just have to keep telling yourself "small is beautiful."

Even if you plan to rent rather than buy a property, the cost of furnishings is something you need to budget for. Although vacation rentals and student accommodation almost always provide the basics, not all Irish houses for long-term rental are let as furnished. It isn't possible to rent furniture, though many newer properties will have fitted kitchens and built-in wardrobes. Those on tight budgets should check out local auctions, where you can often find great furniture bargains.

It's not worth bringing electrical items with you as the voltage system here is different: 230 volt AC 50 Hz. Plugs are normally of the flat three-pin variety. For the moment, TVs operate on the 625 line PAL system, although the expected digital explosion will bring myriad changes. Don't bring VCR tapes either as they will be incompatible with Ireland's VHS system.

Light and Heat

Electricity bills, sent every two months, include a standing charge of $7.63. General domestic charges per unit of electricity are charged at $0.84. Costs obviously depend upon usage: including VAT, my own bill for the September-

Costs of new Brand-name items:

Zanussi refrigerator/freezer, 4.9/1.5 cu ft: $298

Zanussi 3.7 cu ft chest freezer: $169

Tricity Bendix dishwasher: $287

Bendix washing machine: $364

Zanussi tumble dryer: $334

Sharp microwave oven: $101

Electrolux single oven stove: $330

Moulinex food processor: $127

Philips 20-inch TV: $177

Panasonic 28-inch TV: $662

Philips video recorder: $132.51

Electrolux vacuum cleaner: $111

Morphy Richards toaster: $22.50

Astral shower unit: $235

5 ft divan bed: $225

Triple wardrobe: $450

Natural wool carpeting: $22.60 per sq yd

Compaq personal computer (64 Mb RAM with DVD and CD re-writer): $1,435

(all prices include VAT)

October billing period was $98. This covered lighting and the usual electrical items as well as bedroom radiators.

Natural gas is only available in Dublin and along parts of the eastern and southern coasts. The rest of the country uses bottled gas, which is sold by most supermarkets, village shops and hardware stores. If you plan to use a gas stove, a bottle of gas should last around five weeks with normal usage and cost around $16.50.

If you want a peat (turf) fire, there are two methods. The easy way is to buy bales of peat briquettes, which are again sold by most general stores. They cost around $2 per bale, which should be sufficient for a roaring blaze in the sitting room all evening. The alternative is to rent a patch of bog from a farmer during summer and cut, foot and dry your own turf. Believe me, it is filthy, backbreaking work and you'll probably only try it the once. Cost depends upon the quality of the turf: I paid $115 for a supply that lasted most of the winter.

While milk is now sold in liters, barmen continue to measure out beer in pint and half-pint glasses.

Coal is mostly Texan or Polish. Ireland's own coalmines have closed down, for they yielded only low-grade "brown" coal suitable for industrial use. A 25-kilogram sack of smokeless coal for domestic fires costs around $5.65. Like peat, coal can also be used in old-fashioned kitchen ranges, many of which provide hot water as well as cooking facilities.

Hiring Help

You shouldn't come to Ireland expecting to find legions of maids, cooks and gardeners seeking live-in positions. Nor are people prepared to work for a pittance. Although it's common to find Dublin's professional classes employing cleaning ladies, this isn't the case in the rest of the country. Although nearly all parish priests still have a housekeeper, ordinary mortals would be considered very odd if they advertised for domestic help nowadays. Most people in rural areas are fiercely independent, and it's only the very elderly or housebound who require assistance, in which case it's classed as a social need and provided by the health authorities.

That's not to say you won't be able to get paid help, though it will come at a price. High living costs apply to Irish people too and a daily "treasure" will expect at least the minimum adult wage of approximately $5 an hour, though you certainly will not find anybody to work for that sum in Dublin. In countryside areas, persuading a man to come and plant the garden or paint the house will cost at least $40 a day plus materials. If it's a case of occasional help to mow the lawn or weed the flowerbeds, you should be able to find plenty of willing schoolboys available for weekend and vacation work at around $3.50 per hour.

Entertainment Costs

Culture is wonderfully accessible in Ireland; ticket prices for most forms of entertainment are very inexpensive. Art exhibitions are generally always free, though the disappointing news is that the Irish keep their livestock in the fields instead of pickling them in formaldehyde. The price of listening to traditional pub music is merely the cost of your drinks. A pint of Guinness costs around $2.80 in most country pubs, though it can be over $3.40 in Dublin. Most tickets for classical music concerts are priced between $5.50 and $18. Sometimes you don't even have to pay that. Dublin's Hugh Lane Gallery often has free recitals—as I write this, I see this week's offering is a performance of Ravel's songs.

Theater is outstanding value, and you don't necessarily have to take a trip to Dublin to catch a good play. Especially during the summer months, theater companies regularly tour the provinces. Two of Dublin's top theaters are the Abbey and the Gaiety; ticket prices are generally $11.50 to $28 and $17 to $19.50, respectively, though you can pay as much as $56 when the Gaiety has an opera performance. There are dozens of smaller performance venues—Bewley's Café Theater, Andrew's Lane Studio, even Mountjoy Prison; the inmates usually put on a performance once a year. The latest was Brian Friel's *Philadelphia, Here I Come*, which must seem rather like wishful thinking to some of the jailbirds. Tickets for Cork's Opera House and Everyman Palace are generally $11.50 to $17. Galway's Town Hall Theatre charges $11.30. Cinema tickets are a real steal. For example, in Dublin's city center Savoy Cinema, tickets go for $4.50 in the afternoons and $6.25 after 6 P.M.

The cost of dining out varies, and choice will very much depend upon population size and whether you're living in a touristy area. Wherever you live, there's never any problem in finding old-fashioned cafés serving tea and scones for $1.70 or tucking into a hearty pub lunch for $6 or $7. Away from larger towns and the better-known tourist routes, it's in the evenings that things can get a bit more difficult. Small-town Ireland does not really have a dining-out culture, and choice is often limited to a hotel dining room, a burger/pizza place or the local Chinese restaurant. Although a three-course meal will cost only around $11, the chef is more likely to have trained in Sligo's catering college rather than Hong Kong.

Country house hotels usually have innovative menus and are often open to nonguests. However, a meal here is generally in the "treat" category as prices hover around $30 a head, wine extra. On the other hand, Dublin never need prove an expensive place to visit. It boasts wonderful ethnic restaurants in the Temple Bar quarter where three-course meals cost less than $15.

Personal Taxation

The question of taxation is horrendously complicated and much will depend on your personal circumstances. For instance, are you planning to become a permanent resident or just spend the summers in Ireland? Are you contemplating self-employment or simply planning to enjoy a well-earned retirement? Do you intend trading on the Irish stock market? The list of financial activities resulting from having to take care of a tax liability is extensive, but the basic rule is that *all* income arising from Irish sources is subject to Irish income tax. That's true unless you are an artist or a writer. Ireland can be a wonderful financial haven for creative types as royalties and sales of works considered worthy of artistic or literary merit are tax-exempt.

As regards income from sources outside Ireland, the State has a double taxation agreement with a number of countries including the United States. In essence, this ensures that you won't be taxed twice on the same income such as funds from a company or social security pension (which can be paid to you in Ireland). You'll receive a credit to cover the tax that's already been paid in your country of origin, which you must produce when submitting tax returns within Ireland. U.S. citizens will obviously have to obtain this proof from the IRS.

To be classed as a resident for tax purposes within Ireland, you need to spend 183 days in the country during the tax year that runs from April 6 to April 5. Spend less than 183 days in Ireland and the Revenue Commissioners deem you a visitor and no part of your income from non-Irish sources is subject to personal taxation. If a visit falls across two separate tax years, the number of days for tax residency purposes is 280.

For more extensive information on the tax residency laws, contact the Revenue Commissioners, Dublin Castle, Dublin 2; tel + 353 (0)1 878 0000. The useful free booklet "RES 1" details the tax liabilities of foreigners residing in Ireland.

INCOME TAX
Income tax provides around 38 percent of the government's total tax revenues. The system covers PAYE (pay as you earn), which employers are obliged to deduct from workers' salaries and also self-assessment. In both

cases, everyone is entitled to certain allowances and reliefs and persons whose income falls below a certain level aren't taxed at all. Current income tax exemption rates for individuals are an equivalent of $6,215 for those under the age of 65, $7,120 for those over. For married couples the exemption rate is doubled. Thus a couple who are both aged 66 are allowed an income of $12,430 before they start paying tax.

After allowances have been deducted, the rates on taxable income for single people are 20 percent for the first $22,600 of earnings and 42 percent on the remainder. A 42 percent top rate of tax may seem shocking, but it has come down from the 65 percent levels of the 1980s. One-parent families are allowed to earn an equivalent $26,160 before entering the top rate tax bracket; a married couple with only one income, $32,770.

If applicable, you can also claim relief on things such as mortgage interest repayments, health insurance premiums, charitable donations and, if employed, contributions to pension schemes. Private health insurance premiums are eligible for tax relief of 20 percent regardless of whether you fall into the 42 percent tax bracket, though this is now deducted at source. Pension plans allow eligible individuals to invest up to 15 percent of their income every year. These qualify for full tax relief and the returns also grow tax-free.

Unless you find paid employment within Ireland, PRSI (Pay Related Social Insurance) contributions won't apply. PRSI is an additional tax on wage earners that goes towards State contributory pensions, unemployment benefits, disability allowances and so on. The PRSI system is complex with differing levy rates, but most workers pay 4.5 percent on their weekly incomes. Again, you can obtain more information from the Revenue Commissioners.

CAPITAL GAINS TAX

The rate of capital gains tax (CGT) stands at 20 percent with an annual exemption of just over $1,100 per individual. Investments that may attract capital gains tax include directly held equities, bonds and certain types of property. The sale of the principal family home is exempt from CGT, as are lottery winnings and bets. A higher rate of 40 percent applies to disposals of development land.

Capital acquisitions tax (CAT), probate tax and inheritance planning are a minefield for the layperson. If you have substantial assets, it's vital to discuss the subject with a lawyer or a financial adviser who specializes in inheritance laws. While the Revenue Commissioners do produce guidance on these taxes, the language is arcane and blood relationships are subject to all kinds of provisos. The situation is especially tricky for cohabitees who are deemed "strangers in law" in the matter of inheritance rights.

Key points are that spouses are exempt from CAT and probate tax, as is the family home. Children can inherit up to approximately $340,000 each before becoming liable to pay CAT. If you die intestate (without a will), your estate gets divided up according to guidelines in what's termed the Succession Act. Although not everybody feels comfortable about making a will, it's the only way of ensuring your wishes will be carried out. A straightforward will costs in the region of $100; legal details that may pertain to your locality can be had from Citizens Advice Bureaux, Law Centers or the Law Society of Ireland, Blackhall Place, Dublin 7; tel +353 (0)1 671 0711.

9 Staying Healthy

Oone of the central issues to consider in moving to a new country is health care. Ireland's standards are high quality for such a small country, though the range of services is nowhere near as high-tech or extensive as in the United States. While most county towns have a good general hospital, patients needing procedures such as specialized heart surgery invariably have to travel to Dublin. However, general health care within rural communities is fairly well served by family doctors, health centers and public health nurses.

For administrative purposes, Ireland's national health service is divided into a regional system of Health Boards. Residents of counties Galway and Roscommon, for instance, come under the Western Health Board. They will provide information on local doctors, dentists and public health centers. To obtain the address of a relevant Board, contact the Department of Health & Children, Hawkins House, Hawkins St., Dublin 2; tel +353 (0)1 635 4000.

Whether you're arriving as a visitor or to establish residency, there are no strange diseases here to be worried about. You won't need shots, though if you're of a very cautious nature you may wish to get inoculated against tetanus. Those working on farms and in the building trade are always advised to have inoculations as the Irish countryside delivers hazards in the shape of barbed-wire fencing and rusty nails. Keen gardeners won't need reminding that a thorny rosebush can also occasionally yield a nasty surprise and an unwelcome stay in the hospital. Tetanus jabs are generally effective for 10 years.

You are not going to tread on snakes, encounter any other poisonous reptiles or meet up with marauding packs of rabid dogs. Rabies is unknown within Ireland, thanks largely to the country's strict quarantine laws. The bug life is pretty harmless too: midge bites are merely an irritant and the stings of wasps and bees aren't life threatening, unless you're really unlucky and suffer from a rare allergy. In rural areas, the nastiest bite you're likely to receive is from a horse-fly, colloquially known as a "cleg." Bites result in angry-looking red lumps, which can be quickly soothed with antihistamine cream and should require no visit to the doctor.

An obvious concern to some people will be Ireland's damp climate, particularly during winter. If you suffer from respiratory ailments or asthma, there's no avoiding the fact that long sojourns in Ireland are unlikely to improve your condition.

On broader health issues, Ireland is a modern country with modern problems. Like everywhere else, we have AIDS and HIV sufferers, the highest incidence being among young heroin addicts in inner city Dublin. Sexually transmitted diseases aren't unknown either, but at least the problem is recognized and condoms are readily available in both pharmacies and public restrooms.

One frequently asked question is, "Is it safe to drink the water?" Yes, it's perfectly safe, whether from taps or spring wells. In parts of the midlands and western Ireland, you may notice water sometimes has a brownish tinge, a bit like very watered-down whiskey. This doesn't indicate contamination; the color results from the high peat content of the ground it flows through.

Another issue is BSE, better known as "mad cow disease." There *were* cases in Ireland, though nothing like the numbers in neighboring Britain. Animal screening measures have been brought in and farm management procedures are subject to rigorous scrutiny by the Department of Agriculture. Nobody wants to take any chances as the country depends heavily on beef export markets. And don't worry about foot and mouth disease either. It affects only livestock, not humans. Ireland had a couple of incidents of foot and mouth in early 2001, but the disease was quickly stamped out and didn't spread outside county Louth's Cooley Peninsula.

Costs of Medical Care

Illness isn't something that most people like to dwell on, but it's vital you make provisions against it happening. You may have heard mention that Irish residents enjoy free medical care. So they do—up to a point. To qualify for the entire range of free services depends on age, status, income level and exactly what level of medical attention is required.

To begin with, those who are coming to Ireland as visitors or on a short fact-finding mission will need private medical insurance. Free or reciprocal emergency care applies only to EU citizens who can produce what's known as an E111 form. As an American citizen you will undoubtedly be familiar with the concept of private health insurance; you will of course need to check if yours covers foreign travel or whether you need to take out a separate policy.

Irrespective of nationality, once you become a resident in Ireland the picture changes. Should you need emergency treatment, you are now entitled to free medical attention in all hospitals and it isn't dependent on income levels. If, however, you and your broken finger simply turn up at a hospital casualty department without a doctor's referral, you will need to pay a charge of $28 for the initial visit. Obviously, common sense should dictate what constitutes an emergency requiring immediate attention.

As an Irish resident, again irrespective of nationality or income, you'll also be entitled to free inpatient and outpatient services in public hospitals. This includes consultancy services, surgeon's fees, and so on, but does not cover the cost of hospital meals and accommodation. The rate charged is $28.50 per day, up to a maximum of $285 in any one year. These rates apply to beds on public wards. People on very low incomes who hold what are called "Medical Cards" don't have to pay any accommodation fee. If, however, you opt for private or semi-private accommodation in a public hospital, current daily charges are $177.50 (private) and $139 (semi-private) in regional hospitals, $146 (private) and $119 (semi-private) in general hospitals. These charges are additional to the daily public hospital accommodation charge.

As free hospital care for residents seems such an attractive proposition, you may well wonder why over 1.5 million people here belong to private health insurance plans. The answer can be summed up in three short words: hospital waiting lists. Treatment and operations for what are described as nonemergencies can sometimes mean very lengthy waits. It isn't unknown for some patients to have spent three years and more waiting for hip replacements.

Private Health Care

Joining an independent health insurance plan means you can effectively leapfrog the waiting list and obtain treatment as required. Furthermore, health-care premiums can be offset against standard rate income tax. Depending on the level of cover chosen, subscriptions allow for anything from semi-private accommodation in a local public hospital to your own room in one of Dublin's private institutions, such as the Mater Hospital or the Blackrock Clinic. You can generally assume that premium-priced plans deliver premium-priced hospital accommodation. On the treatment side, all price bands within these plans cover general medical costs, fees for anesthetists, radiologists, surgeons, consultants and also most outpatient charges. Private health plans are regulated under the government's Health Insurance Act 1994.

Within Ireland, you'll often see Health Insurance Plans referred to as Health Insurance Schemes. Here the word "scheme" is free of the negative connotations it has in the United States.

Ireland's largest independent provider is the Voluntary Health Insurance Board (VHI). Founded as a not-for-profit mutual organization in 1957, it has around 1.4 million members throughout the country. Regardless of your age, if you are already a plan holder with Blue Cross, Blue Shield or any other member of the International Federation of Voluntary Health Service Funds, you'll be able to transfer it to the VHI. Those aged under 65 may join the VHI directly; if you are over 65 you will not be taken on as a member.

Five different plans are offered. Depending on coverage selected, annual adult premiums range from $226 to $999. Costs are not age-linked, and a 30-year-old pays exactly the same as a 60-year-old with the same plan. Although you don't have to undergo a medical examination, there are some initial limitations on coverage if you're joining independently and not transferring a current plan. While benefit is immediately available for treatment due to accidents, for other illnesses and conditions there is a waiting period: 26 weeks for those aged under 55 and a full year for those over 55. Pre-existing medical conditions are subject to a very lengthy restriction period: five years for those under 55; seven years for those aged 55 to 59; 10 years for those aged 60 and over. Note too that routine dental and ophthalmic treatment isn't covered. For more information, contact the Voluntary Health Insurance

new arrival, maternity unit, Sligo General Hospital

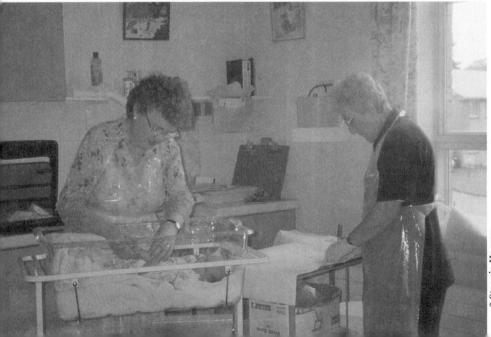

Board, Lower Abbey St., Dublin 1; tel + 353 (0)1 799 7068. You can get an on-line quote from the website, www.vhi.ie.

Competition has recently come to the Irish marketplace in the form of BUPA (British United Provident Association), an international health insurance provider that offers similar coverage. It has a choice of four plans called Essential, Essential Plus, Health Manager and Essential Gold. Annual premiums are $211, $291, $347 and $1,043, respectively. The main difference between BUPA and the VHI is that BUPA covers alternative therapies such as acupuncture and homeopathy. Additionally, patients needing specialized attention can receive treatment at an appropriate hospital in Britain. But again, unless you already hold current medical insurance, BUPA won't take you on if you are over 65. For more information, contact BUPA Ireland, Mill Island, Fermoy, county Cork; tel + 353 (0)25 42121. Quotes are available on the website, www.bupaireland.ie.

> *In rural areas, the nastiest bite you're likely to receive is from a horse-fly, colloquially known as a "cleg."*

Critical Illness Insurance

For a real belt-and-braces approach, pre-retirees can also take out critical illness insurance as extra protection. Although it's not designed to replace health insurance such as that offered by BUPA and VHI, critical illness policies pay out a tax-free cash benefit if you or another named party gets a serious illness or requires surgery. Unlike medical insurance, however, critical illness premiums are not offsetable against a tax bill.

The list of illnesses covered by insurers usually includes heart disease, cancer, kidney failure and so on. Most policies also include a hospital cash plan. This pays an agreed sum per night spent in hospital, regardless of any other claims made on your ordinary medical insurance. Under these type of policies the cost of coverage *is* age-linked and rises sharply as you become older.

With 21 offices across Ireland, New Ireland Assurance is one of a number of companies offering this type of insurance. Premiums for a 30-year-old male would be approximately $19.50 monthly to provide coverage of $84,750 critical illness, $84,750 death benefit, $84,750 permanent or total disability insurance, and $56 per day hospital cash plan. For more information, contact New Ireland Assurance at 11-12 Dawson St., Dublin 2; tel + 353 (0) 1 617 2000. Email: info@newireland.ie.

Personal accident plans provide protection against permanent disability arising from an accident. Again, they usually pay out cash sums in the event of hospitalization and up to $85,000 if an injury causes permanent disability. Bank of Ireland customers can avail themselves of special policies with Royal & Sun Alliance with monthly premiums for standard coverage starting at $11.80 for individuals, $18.75 for couples. Ask in any bank branch or contact Royal & Sun Alliance, 13-17 Dawson St., Dublin 2; tel +353 (0)1 677 1851.

For information on other Irish brokers offering similar policies, contact the Irish Brokers Association, 87 Merrion Square, Dublin 2; tel +353 (0)1 661 3061.

Family Doctors

Wherever you choose to live, you won't be very far away from the services of a GP (General Practitioner), the family doctor. It may come as a surprise to find that Irish GPs are quite prepared to make home visits, even in the middle of the night if need be. Naturally, if you're simply suffering from general aches and pains, he or she will expect you to visit the office, called a "surgery." This may be in the doctor's own home or at a health center.

Most GPs charge between $22.50 and $30 per consultation. If you belong to a private health insurance plan, part of the cost of GP consultations can be reclaimed under your outpatient cover. This isn't quite as generous as it sounds as the first $375 of fees in any one year has to be met by the individual. Insurance companies only refund anything in excess of that amount, normally up to an annual limit of $3,750. Medical Card holders don't have to pay for GP visits or prescribed medicines.

awaiting restoration—quayside buildings in Westport, county Mayo

© Steenie Harvey

írish herb lore

Camphor Plant (*balsamita vulgaris*). Its dried leaves can be used to keep moths out of wardrobes and linen cupboards.

Feverfew (*chrysanthemum parthenium*). A daisy-like cottage garden plant once widely grown to treat fevers, migraine and headaches.

Fleabane (*pulicaria dysenterica*). As the name implies, the burnt foliage can serve to drive away fleas. It was also once employed medicinally against dysentery.

Heartsease (*viola tricolour*). An attractive flower with multicolored white, yellow and purple petals, it's commonly associated with love potions.

Horehound (*marrubium vulgare*). Commonly used by herbalists in syrups for coughs, colds and lung ailments. Before the introduction of hops, it was one of the bitter herbs used in beer making. Black horehound was also once used to treat the bites of mad dogs.

Houseleek (*sempervivum tectorum*). Fleshy and rosette-like, its juice is still sometimes used for skin ailments such as styes on the eyelid. Superstition says that if growing on a roof, the houseleek provides protection against fires.

Mugwort (*artemisia vulgaris*). Traditionally associated with magic and warding off evil spirits on St. John's Eve, its feathery fronds can serve as an insect repellent.

Rue (*ruta gravedens*). One of the most powerful herbs in medieval leechcraft, its best-known use was as a narcotic.

Self-heal (*prunella vulgaris*). Boiled in water, the purple heads were reputedly an effective restringent against internal bleeding.

Speedwell (*veronica chamaedrys*). Low growing with tiny blue flowers, this creeping plant was once used to treat coughs, asthma and catarrh.

Valerian (*valerina officinalis*). A tall, red-flowered plant that's pretty enough for the garden, its roots yield a strong sedative.

Vervain (*verbena officinalis*). Apparently an important plant in Druidic times and later used as a charm against witchcraft, its qualities include the treatment of nervous disorders, staunching blood and easing the pangs of childbirth.

Medical Cards

What are Medical Cards and are you eligible for one? In general, the answer is only if you acquired Irish or other EU citizenship. You would also have to have a very low income or be over the age of 70. Current qualifying rates are a weekly income below $113 for individuals under 66, $123.50 for those between 66 and 70. For couples in the same age brackets, qualifying weekly income rates are $106.50, respectively. Regardless of income, all residents over the age of 70 became eligible for Medical Cards in July 2001. If you think you may qualify for a Medical Card (perhaps through holding dual citizenship), the plan is administered through regional Health Boards.

Medicines and Pharmacies

Unfortunately private health insurers don't cover the cost of medicines prescribed by your GP. To cite one example, it costs around $28 for a short course of antibiotics for a chest infection. There is a safety net, however, and no resident needs to run up massive bills.

Replacing former subsidization arrangements, the Drugs Payment Scheme covers part of the cost of prescribed medicines. Individuals or families have to pay only the first $47.50 of the cost of their prescribed drugs and medicines in any month. Any further prescriptions are made available by the local pharmacy without charge. You do have to register, however. Forms are available from pharmacies, GPs' surgeries and local Health Board offices.

Every small town has at least one pharmacy, better known in Ireland as "the chemist." They are generally open during normal retail hours but within larger towns a rota system allows for late night services too. Along with prescription drugs, cosmetic items and toiletries, they also stock a range of patent medicines—painkillers, cough syrups and the like—many of which are manufactured by international drug companies. Plenty of medicines you're familiar with are to be found in Ireland. In more rural districts, chemists are also the purveyors of animal husbandry products, and it's not uncommon to see remedies for cattle fluke sitting above a shelf stocked with shampoos and hair colorants!

Black and white piebald horses are prized by Ireland's nomadic traveling community.

© Steenie Harvey

Dental Costs

The costs of routine dental care will also have to come out of your own pocket unless you hold a Medical Card. Fees vary considerably. Expect to pay between $28 and $50 for an initial check-up, $28 to $60 for a filling or extraction, $230 to $520 for capping. A course of treatment for gum disease could cost around $950 while a full set of dentures averages $450. It's possible to take some of the pain out of paying for dental treatment by traveling across the border to Northern Ireland. Fees charged by Belfast dentists are lower by about 20 percent, but whether you save may depend on the prevailing exchange rate. You'll see their ads in newspapers such as the *Irish Times and Irish Independent*.

A Healthy Retirement

Specifically on retirement health issues, there's a commitment to develop a national program to promote "healthy aging" among older people. In Ireland's family-oriented society, it's not uncommon to find three generations living under the same roof. Less than 5 percent of seniors reside in nursing homes or other long-stay institutions. Most seniors are completely independent. According to the National Council on Aging and Older People, four out of five of those living in private households were reported as needing no physical help or care.

Even so, geriatric medicine has developed to become the largest sub-specialty of internal medicine with consultants based in most of the country's general hospitals. At present, seniors represent only 11.5 percent of the population, but demographic trends indicate numbers rising to 26 percent by the year 2011.

Other aspects of senior care within the community are as yet centered primarily in large towns and cities, Dublin, Cork and Galway in particular. If you're interested in getting involved as a volunteer with health education

Queue for a barbecue

© Steenie Harvey

projects, there are quite a few opportunities in these areas, especially for retirees. For details of projects currently seeking volunteers, contact Age & Opportunity, St. Joseph's Building, Marino Institute of Education, Griffith Ave., Dublin 9; tel +353 (0)1 837 0570.

Keeping Fit

Ireland annually spends over $75 million on leisure and recreation with sales of fitness equipment alone reaching $23 million. If treadmills, rowing machines and cardiovascular workouts are your idea of bliss, you may want to join a gym. Nowadays you'll find private gyms and fitness clubs in most cities, but the cost of keeping fit can be quite expensive. Furthermore, demand is so high that prospective members may have to join a waiting list.

Before you sign up for a pricy annual membership, ask yourself if you really intend making good use of all the state-of-the-art equipment. Would you be better off with a weekly aerobics class in the village hall ($2.80 to $5 per session) or a free workout on the public tennis courts? The dropout rate of gym members is estimated to be as high as 60 percent, and few clubs give refunds. To help you make your mind up, always call to inquire if any of the local gyms or health clubs offer free trials to prospective members.

In Dublin, one of the largest and best-equipped gyms is the Westwood near Leopardstown racecourse. Individual annual membership costs $845, which includes a joining fee of $184. Before committing to membership, you can buy a $13.50 day pass to try out the facilities. For more information, contact Westwood Club, Leopardstown Racecourse, Foxrock, Dublin 18; tel +353 (0)1 289 3208.

The Shelbourne Club is even more expensive at $1,950 for individuals and $3,630 for couples. This price buys five-star exclusivity; the club has fewer than 500 members as opposed to the Westwood's 5,000. Contact the Shelbourne Club, Shelbourne Hotel, St. Stephen's Green, Dublin 2; tel +353 (0)1 676 6471.

In Galway, the Kingfisher Club charges an annual fee of $560 for individuals and $978 for couples. Facilities include a 25-meter pool, sauna, steam room and gym; you can also try out aerobics, aromatherapy, reflexology and physiotherapy. There is also a nursery, or creche, if you have young children. Contact the Kingfisher Club, Renmore, Galway; tel +353 (0)91 773344.

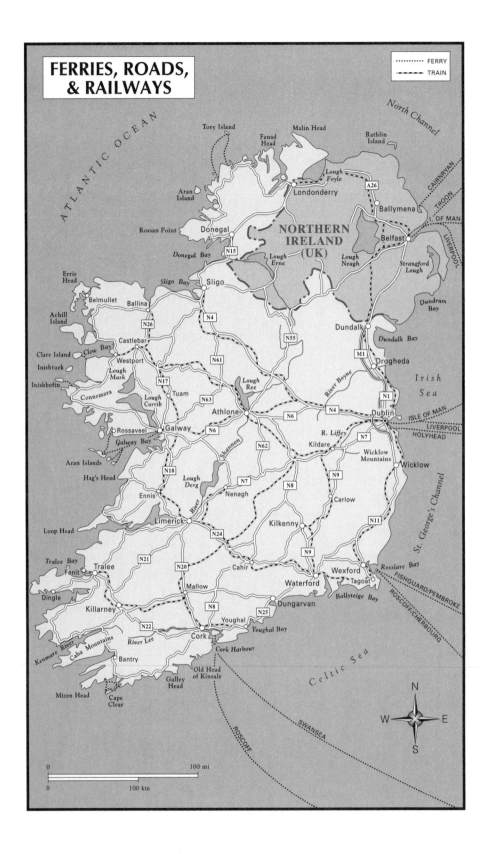

FERRIES, ROADS, & RAILWAYS

······· FERRY
-·-·-· TRAIN

North Channel

ATLANTIC OCEAN

Tory Island
Fanad Head
Malin Head
Rathlin Island

CAIRNRYAN
TROON

Aran Island
Lough Foyle
Londonderry
A26
Ballymena

Rossan Point
Donegal
NORTHERN IRELAND (UK)
Belfast

I. OF MAN

N15
Donegal Bay
Lough Erne
Lough Neagh
Strangford Lough

LIVERPOOL

Erris Head
Belmullet
Ballina
Sligo Bay
Sligo
Dundrum Bay

Achill Island
N26
N4
N55
Dundalk
Dundalk Bay

Castlebar
Clew Bay
Westport
N61
M1
Drogheda

Clare Island
Inishturk
Lough Mask
N17
Tuam
Lough Ree
River Boyne
Irish Sea

Inishbofin
Connemara
Lough Corrib
N63
Athlone
N6
N4
Dublin
N1

ISLE OF MAN
LIVERPOOL
HOLYHEAD

Rossaveel
Galway
N6
N62
R. Liffey
Kildare
N7

Galway Bay
Wicklow Mountains
Wicklow

Aran Islands
Hag's Head
N18
Lough Derg
N7
N8
N9
Carlow

Ennis
Nenagh

Loop Head
River Shannon
Limerick
Kilkenny
N9

St. George's Channel

N24
Tralee Bay
Fenit
Tralee
N21
N20
Cahir
Wexford
Rosslare Bay

Dingle
Mallow
Waterford
Tagoat

FISHGUARD/PEMBROKE

Killarney
N8
N25
Dungarvan
Ballyteige Bay

ROSCOFF/CHERBOURG

N22
Youghal
N22
Cork
Youghal
Youghal Bay

Kenmare River
Caha Mountains
Bantry
River Lee
Cork Harbour

Old Head of Kinsale
Galley Head

Celtic Sea

Mizen Head
Cape Clear

N
W   E
S

ROSCOFF
SWANSEA

0   100 mi
0   100 km

10 Getting Around

You'll have to drive on the other side of the road, and you may have to hop a ferry to get where you're going, but you'll soon find getting around in Ireland is no hassle at all.

Air Travel

Deregulation in the air travel business has brought much-needed competition to the skies above Ireland. Airlines now fly direct to 62 scheduled destinations. Each year sees increasing numbers of vacation charter flights to North America, the Caribbean and popular Mediterranean hot spots.

With 12.8 million passengers annually, the country's main international gateway is Dublin Airport (tel +353 (0)1 814 1111). Shannon Airport (tel +353 (0)61 712000), 10 miles from Limerick, lost much of its business with the abolition of the so-called Shannon stopover, a ruling that all incoming and outgoing transatlantic flights had to touch down there. Although Shannon still offers limited flights to the United States, its only other links are to Dublin and two U.K. cities, London and Manchester.

Overseas flights from Cork (tel +353 (0)21 4313131) are confined to the U.K., Paris, Amsterdam and the Channel Islands. However, Belfast's airport (tel +44 (0)1849 422888) provides another overseas gateway. It's worth considering if you're seeking budget charter fares to Canada; returns to Toronto can sometimes be had for under $350.

Ireland's network of small domestic airports connects Dublin to the provinces and provides limited flights to the U.K. Most are served by the national carrier, Aer Lingus, which flies between Dublin and Cork, Galway, Kerry, Shannon and Belfast. Aer Arann also provides services between Dublin and Sligo, Cork, Galway, Donegal, the Isle of Man, Derry in Northern Ireland and Sheffield in England. Domestic flight times are under 40 minutes, but fares are astonishingly expensive for the relatively short distances covered. For example, return flights between Dublin and Sligo currently cost $87. These services are mainly used by business people whose companies pick up the tab. Note too that it isn't possible to fly direct between provincial airports; all journeys necessitate a changeover in Dublin.

County Mayo's Knock Airport (tel +353 (0)94 67222) is served by Ryanair flights from Dublin and the U.K. It gets quite busy in summer with charter flights of pilgrims bound for the Marian shrine in Knock village. Out in the Atlantic, the Aran Islands are served by Aer Arann from Connemara Regional Airport (tel +353 (0)91 755569) with four daily flights during winter and up to 25 per day in peak season. Return fares are currently $40.

On the transatlantic route, Aer Lingus flies direct to six U.S. destinations: New York, Newark, Chicago, Los Angeles, Baltimore/Washington and Boston. Its North American flying partner is Delta Airlines, which connects Ireland with over 240 U.S. cities through its two gateway airports, New York and Atlanta. As part of its expansion program, Continental Airlines has also entered the Irish marketplace, providing onward connections to a range of U.S. cities through its gateway airport, Newark. Flight times between Ireland and the U.S. eastern seaboard cities average eight hours.

Transatlantic fare structures are in a constant state of flux and invariably subject to seasonal differences. In general, high summer and the Christmas/New Year holiday periods are the most expensive times to book flights to and from the States as there's always increased demand from visiting friends and relatives. Much depends on how flexible you can be and how far in advance you can book. Although cut-price economy returns to New York are advertised from $211, the reality is likely to be in the region of at least $340 for a return over the Easter period.

At the time of writing, Aer Lingus' best available deal was an economy return on its Newark-Shannon route for $358. Tickets needed to be booked at least seven days in advance and required a Saturday night stay. Just like in the States, it pays to shop around and keep your eyes peeled for special promotional offers in the media, travel agents' windows, or on the Internet. Again, if you can be flexible, some good bargains can be had with package tour companies that offer an option of "seat only" deals to independent travelers. Tour America, an Irish-owned company specializing in North

American holidays, has flight-only deals to Boston/New York from $254, Orlando from $298, and Los Angeles/San Francisco from $374. Contact them at 62 Middle Abbey St., Dublin 1; tel +353 (0)1 878 0400. Check their website at www.touramerica.ie.

Another way of shaving costs is by booking through a consolidator or independent flight specialist such as Trailfinders. On their North American menu, round-trip tickets from Dublin to Washington, D.C., start from $277, Chicago from $313, and New Orleans from $368. As always, low-priced seats are subject to availability and fares may be substantially higher if you need to travel at short notice or during the main holiday season. Contact Trailfinders at 4/5 Dawson St., Dublin 2; tel +353 (0)1 677 7888.

The real bonanza for Ireland's air passengers is on the Dublin-Britain routes where competition ensures numerous rock-bottom return fares starting at as little as $44. It's a great opportunity for you to travel further afield, not just to London but also to cities like historic Edinburgh, the Scottish capital. Fly to Leeds/Bradford and you're at the gateway to medieval York and the Yorkshire Moors—remember *Wuthering Heights* and the Brontë sisters? Or, for an authentic glimpse into blue-collar English culture, join the legions of Irish fans who regularly fly to northwest England to watch soccer teams like Liverpool and Manchester United.

As for other European destinations, the most affordable cities to reach are Paris and Brussels; economy returns can be had for $119. Other European cities are not particularly cheap to get to from Ireland, especially when compared to the flight deals available to North American destinations. (The blame is put on high taxes and landing fees.) A sample of the

the Tipperary shore of Lough Derg

© Steenie Harvey

lowest-priced returns with Aer Lingus include Amsterdam ($187), Dusseldorf ($193), Zürich ($221), Madrid ($225), and Rome ($397). However, you may be able to find better offers with competing airlines such as Air France, Lufthansa and Scandinavian Airlines, all of which have Dublin offices.

To cut costs when traveling to Europe, I often fly to Britain first. Sure, traveling via London's Stansted or Gatwick Airport adds time, but it can save you a great deal of money. For example, this summer I'm visiting the Italian island of Sardinia. Total cost for my return ticket Dublin-Stansted-Alghero on Ryanair is $211.

ADDRESS BOOK

Aer Arann (flights to the Aran Islands, domestic), Connemara Regional Airport, Inverin, Galway; tel +353 (0)91 593034. Website: www.aerarann.ie.

Aer Lingus (domestic, European and transatlantic), Dublin Airport, Dublin; tel +353 (0)1 705 3333. Website: www.aerlingus.ie.

Continental Airlines (transatlantic), Level 2, Link Buildings, Dublin Airport; tel +353 (0)1 814 5311.

Delta Airlines (transatlantic), 24 Merrion Square, Dublin 2; tel +353 (0)1 886 2222/886 8888.

Ryanair (domestic and European), Dublin Airport, Dublin; tel +353 (0)1 609 7800. Website: www.ryanair.com.

All travel agents also sell air tickets, but they are now losing quite a bit of their business to agents on the Web. Two of the biggest sites are www.ebookers.com/ie and www.farenet.ie. Although I haven't personally used Ebookers, I had no problems when booking a flight to Cyprus through Farenet.

Ferries

Apart from the Aran Islands, which have their own air-strips, the only way to reach the 18 inhabited islands off Ireland's coastline is by ferry. They are mostly run by small, private concerns with some boats able to take only 12 passengers. Larger vessels are equipped to carry cars, but these aren't superferries; the Arranmore ferry takes only eight cars at a time. Sailing schedules vary and there are always more crossings between Easter and late September to accommodate tourists.

Ferries are the traditional way to reach Inishmore, Inishmaan and Inisheer, the three Aran Islands. Depending on your embarkation point (Galway, Rossaveal or Doolin in county Clare) and eventual destination, journey times take between 30 and 90 minutes. A number of ferry companies serve the islands, though some operate only during summer. Aran Island Ferries runs an all-year service to each island with return fares from

$14.50 (seniors from $13.25). Contact them at Victoria Place, Galway; tel + 353 (0)91 561767/568903. Website: www.aranislandferries.com.

A Gaelic-speaking island off the Donegal coast, Arranmore is a 25-minute crossing from Burtonport village on the mainland. During summer, the resident population swells from 900 to around 1,500. For sailing times, contact the Arranmore Ferry at tel + 353 (0)75 20532. Return fares are $8 for foot passengers, $22.60 for car and driver.

At the opposite end of the country, in county Cork, Cape Clear Island copes with an estimated 20,000 annual visitors. Many come for the birdlife, for this is one of the main passageways for summer migrants. Sailing time from Baltimore village on the mainland is 45 minutes. Contact Coiste Naomh Ciaran for schedules at tel + 353 (0)28 39119. Return fares are $10.20. It makes a nice day trip; you leave Baltimore at 11 A.M. and depart Cape Clear at 4 P.M.

In county Mayo, Clare Island was the old stomping ground of Ireland's infamous pirate queen, Grainne Uaille. Some 150 people live here permanently and it can be reached from Roonagh Quay, 12 miles from Westport town. Fares are $11.30 roundtrip. Contact Westport tourist office for sailings at tel + 353 (0)98 25711. Another island worth exploring is Inishbofin, the "Island of the White Cow" in county Galway. Sailings leave from Cleggan village; fares are $13.60 roundtrip. Call tel + 353 (0)95 44642 for times. There's usually a sailing at 11:30 A.M.

Should you wish to cross the Irish Sea to Britain, there is a reasonable number of day and nighttime ferries. Services to Holyhead in North Wales are operated by Stena Line, tel + 353 (0)1 204 7700, from Dun Laoghaire and Dublin ports, and by Irish Ferries, tel + 353 (0)1 638 3333, from Dublin port. Prices for both are similar and rise dramatically in high season. With Irish Ferries, a five-day return for car and driver costs $132 in low season but $242 in July. Additional passengers are charged $11.50 each way. Depending on whether travel is by high-speed catamaran or traditional ferry, crossing time is between one hour and 40 minutes and three and a half hours.

The main crossing point for ferries to South Wales is Rosslare in county Wexford. Again, Stena and Irish Ferries share the route. With Irish Ferries, returns for foot passengers cost $40–60; if taking a car, prices vary from $110 to $287, depending on season and length of stay. Again, extra passengers are charged $11.50 each way, and the crossing time averages four hours.

If you have the stamina for a 16-hour-minimum sea crossing, bowls of milky coffee and fresh buttery croissants await in France. Irish Ferries sails to both Roscoff and Cherbourg; single tickets cost between $50 and $93 for foot passengers. There is a range of deals if you want to take the car and stock up the trunk with inexpensive wine. Nine-day spring and fall specials start at $242 return.

Buses

In general, all towns of any size are on a bus route with regular links to Dublin or the nearest city. It's possible to travel between most places, though not always by the direct route. Journeys may involve changes and sometimes a lengthy wait in midland transport hubs such as Mullingar and Athlone.

Villages, especially those west of the Shannon River, are not particularly well served. Some rural communities offer only once-a-week service; many don't offer even that. There are numerous localities where catching the bus means first undertaking an 8- or 10-mile trek to the nearest main road.

The country's national bus service is Bus Éireann, tel +353 830 2222, its logo a friendly looking Irish setter. Fares are less expensive than train fares, though purchasing a one-way ticket isn't substantially cheaper than buying a return. If you're planning just a one-day trip, ask about special day return offers as these are usually good value. Ordinary weekday return fares to selected destinations are as follows: Dublin-Cork $20.50, Dublin-Tralee $24.50, Dublin-Galway $12.50, and Dublin-Ballina $14.50. Service is quite frequent; seven buses travel daily to Tralee, for example. Check more fares and timings at www.buseireann.ie.

Competition is provided by numerous local operators whose coaches usually provide services to destinations that Bus Éireann does not. Depending on local need, services generally vary between twice a day to once a week. In the little county Leitrim town of Drumshanbo, for instance, there's one early morning bus every weekday taking workers to Sligo.

Hop aboard a Dublin bus

© Steenie Harvey

Shoppers can use the service, but it means spending all day in Sligo town as the coach doesn't return until after 6 P.M. and all the regulars are on board.

Most buses leaving for the provinces depart from Dublin's central bus station, Busaras. On the north side of the Liffey River, it's less than a five-minute walk from Connolly railway station. Within the capital itself, a fairly comprehensive service is provided by Dublin Bus, tel +353 (0)1 873 4222. As well as linking the city to suburbia and the Greater Dublin area, they run frequent services to the airport, ferry ports and the two main railway stations.

The minimum fare is $0.70, and make sure you have exact change. You can check current fares for all routings at www.dublinbus.ie. What happens if you overpay? You're issued a voucher, redeemable at the Dublin Bus office on Upper O'Connell Street. The fare to the air-

In general, all towns of any size are on a bus route with regular links to Dublin or the nearest city.

port, 10 kilometers north of the city, is just under $4 from Busaras or Heuston Station. In other cities, Bus Éireann provides city-to-suburbs service.

Rail

The Republic's rail service is called Iarnród Éireann, Irish Rail, Connolly Station, Amiens Street, Dublin 1; tel +353 (0)1 836 6222. Although trains are faster than long-distance buses, the network is by no means extensive. For example, you cannot reach any location in counties Donegal, Cavan or Monaghan. Nor can you travel to the seaside towns of West Cork, Kerry's Dingle Peninsula or the far western corners of county Clare.

For journeys originating in Dublin, Connolly Station is the departure point for trains north to Belfast, northwest to Sligo, and down the east coast route passing through Wicklow to Rosslare harbor. Heuston Station is the

Free travel for Retirees

Regardless of citizenship or income, all residents over the age of 66 are entitled to free travel on the road and rail services of Dublin Bus, Bus Éireann, Irish Rail, the DART and certain other private bus and local ferry services. There's no limit to the amount of free travel you can enjoy, though some restrictions apply to city bus services during peak travel times.

The free travel pass can also be used for cross-border journeys to and from Northern Ireland. In addition, Aran Islands residents can claim up to six free return flights to the mainland every year. Another benefit is that your spouse doesn't have to pay when traveling with you, even though he or she may be a pre-retiree. Applications for travel passes can be picked up at post offices or your local Social Welfare office.

the Age of Steam

Steam engine buffs should make tracks for the Shannonside village of Dromod, where enthusiastic volunteers are gradually rebuilding the Cavan & Leitrim Railway. First opened in 1887, it was built to the Irish narrow gauge of three feet. In those early years, transportation of livestock was the backbone of the service as the sparsely populated countryside delivered few human passengers. The line's later traffic mostly consisted of coal from the mines of the Arigna Mountains.

By the time the last trains ran in 1959, the line's locos were virtual museum pieces. Happily, a lifted track was re-laid and a project to restore the railway started in 1993. If you have a taste for nostalgia, short-haul passenger services now run on Saturday and Sunday afternoons between May and October. Kiddies always look forward to the end of the season and the Halloween special when they can ride a "Ghost Train" past a haunted graveyard, Dr. Frankenstein's workshop and all kinds of other spooky places. Volunteer helpers are always needed during winter, the maintenance season. Contact the Cavan & Leitrim Railway, Dromod, county Leitrim; tel +353 (0)78 38599.

place to board for Cork City, Limerick, Galway, Tralee and a number of other towns in the south, southwest and west. (The stations are connected by the No. 90 Dublin Bus service.)

As with buses, day return tickets represent the best value in what is a rather complex fare structure of off-peak returns, weekend specials, midweek returns and so on. Staff are normally very helpful in advising the best-priced ticket to suit your plans. Sample second-class midweek return fares are as follows: Dublin-Athlone $19, Dublin-Galway $24.50, Dublin-Belfast $32.50, Dublin-Cork $46.50, and Dublin-Tralee $49.

Dublin also has the DART, the acronym for Dublin Area Rapid Transport. An electric rail system with several stations within the capital, it plies between Howth on the north county Dublin coast and Bray in county Wicklow. For those catching ferries to Britain, a one-way DART ticket from Pearse Street Station in central Dublin costs $1.30.

Driving in Ireland

Driving in Ireland can be both a pleasure and a penance. Yes, it's true that many roads are blessedly quiet and free of other motorists. It's also true that it's perfectly safe to stop and ask locals for directions if you get lost. Alas, the typical country road is likely to be pitted with potholes, awash in winter floodwater and—just when you want to use it—a private gathering place for beasts of the field.

Not that we country folk envy city motorists. Peak time in Dublin is an abysmal snarl. This was a city built for the horse and carriage trade, not juggernauts, buses and commuter traffic. Even the brand-new motorway link to the west of Ireland is subject to frequent congestion and delays. To add insult to injury, the price of gasoline is enough to make you weep. Most major oil companies are represented here, but there is little variation on prices within cities. However, you can pay a lot more in remote rural areas where there is no competition. Regular unleaded gas currently costs between $0.71 and $0.87 per liter, a few pence more for diesel and LRP. The initials LRP stand for Lead Replacement Petrol, but you are unlikely to use it. Only very old and environmentally unfriendly cars still run on leaded gas.

RULES OF THE ROAD

For first-time visitors from North America, the golden rule to remember is that Ireland drives on the left. Other things to get used to are passing on the right and giving way to traffic approaching on your right at roundabouts. Car rental companies usually recommend that you avoid country roads for the first day or so until you're familiar with the car and the new driving environment.

Their advice makes lots of sense. When you first encounter a boreen—a narrow, rutted track with grass growing up the middle—you may well wonder how you are expected to keep to the left side of the road when it's barely wide enough for one vehicle, let alone two. Panic-stricken at the sight of a tractor hurtling towards them, some foreign motorists head straight for "the soft margin," better known in other countries as the ditch. The trick to driving safely along boreens is to keep your speed down and be constantly on the watch for likely passing places such as farm gateways.

Helped by EU grants, Ireland has made heroic efforts to improve its road network, but there's still a long way to go. While there are short sections of

Yield! Major road ahead.

© Steenie Harvey

motorway around Dublin, they're nothing like the freeways of North America. Unless otherwise indicated, motorway and dual carriageway speed limits are 70 mph (112 km/ph). Direction signs are white print on a blue background. Tolls are payable only at two points within the country, both in the Dublin area. One is on the M50 ring-road between the airport and N4 interchange to the west. The other is on the R131 East Link Bridge. In both cases the toll for cars is $0.90.

you and the Irish Road

1. What does a broken white line along the center of a road signify?
   a) No passing.
   b) You may pass if it's safe to do so.
   c) A dual carriageway.
   d) The paint ran out.

2. What does a single continuous white line along the center of a road mean?
   a) No passing.
   b) You may pass if it's safe to do so.
   c) Nothing in particular.

3. What do double yellow lines along the edge of the road mean?
   a) No parking.
   b) No cycling.
   c) You are allowed to park if displaying a parking disk.
   d) Parking for tractors only.

4. What persons have the authority to halt traffic?
   a) The Gardaí.
   b) People in charge of animals.
   c) School wardens.
   d) Lost tourists.

5. What is the legal minimum tread depth your tires must have?
   a) 1.6 mm
   b) 16 mm
   c) 160 mm
   d) There is no minimum; bald tires are OK.

6. Approaching a crossroads with roads of equal importance, who has right of way,

you or the Massey Ferguson coming down the road to your right?
   a) You do, always.
   b) The Massey Ferguson.
   c) Whoever is quickest.
   d) What's a Massey Ferguson?

7. What is the legal alcohol/blood limit applicable to Irish drivers?
   a) There isn't one.
   b) 800 milligrams per 100 milliliters.
   c) 80 milligrams per 100 milliliters.
   d) You cannot drink and drive at all.

8. Who has right of way at a roundabout?
   a) Traffic approaching from the right.
   b) You do, no matter the circumstances.
   c) Larger vehicles.
   d) Nobody—it's a free for all.

9. If you follow a sign to An Lar, where will it take you?
   a) A hospital.
   b) The coast.
   c) A library.
   d) A town center.

10. What is the principal cause of tractor accidents?
   a) Driving too fast.
   b) Driving too slowly.
   c) Collisions with stray animals and rubber-necking tourists.
   d) Overloaded trailers.

Answers: 1-b; 2-a; 3-a; 4-a, b and c; 5-a; 6-b; 7-c; 8-a; 9-d; 10-a.

Between most towns you're likely to be driving on "N" roads, national primary routes. Here the general speed limit is 60 mph (96 km/ph) until entering a built-up area, where it reduces to 30 mph (48 km/ph). Direction signs have white or yellow lettering on a green background. Unless indicated otherwise, the same speed limit applies to "R" roads, secondary routes where signs have black lettering on a white background. Then, of course, there are the boreens where direction signs of any kind at all are conspicuous by their absence. If you're lucky enough to find a signpost at a country crossroads, it's not an exaggeration to suggest that the fingerpost is likely to be pointing in the wrong direction.

On newer signs, distances are given in kilometers, even though most Irish people continue to think in terms of mileage. Older signs carry distances in miles. To further confuse the visiting motorist there is also such a thing as the "Irish mile," slightly shorter than a conventional mile. Thankfully the Irish mile is a rarity nowadays and usually spotted only on centuries-old stone markers hidden in hedgerows. More confusion awaits in Gaeltacht areas where road signs are entirely in the Irish language. The most important direction sign to watch for is a red-bordered triangle carrying the words "Géill Slí." This indicates a major road ahead and you must give way to traffic on it.

The minimum driving age is 17, and it's compulsory to wear seat belts in both the front and back seats. Children under 12 are not permitted in the front seat. Documents that should be carried when driving are a valid driver's license and the vehicle log book or your rental agreement; insurance and road tax discs also have to be displayed on the front windscreen. If you or another party is involved in an accident, the Garda (police) must be informed.

Driver's Licenses

As a visitor, you're allowed to drive on your American or an International driver's license for up to 12 months. After that, brace yourself for some unwelcome news. Unfortunately for Americans, yours is not one of the licenses that can be exchanged for an Irish license. Residents are required to obtain a provisional license and then take the driving test. It's fairly rigorous and the pass rate remains static at around 50 percent.

Issued by the motor tax offices of local authorities, a provisional license costs $13.50 and is valid for two years. Application forms need to be accompanied by a birth certificate, two passport-sized photos and an eyesight report from your doctor or optician. If you haven't passed the driving test within the two-year time span, you can obtain another provisional license on producing a notice of failure from the driving test center.

The law requires provisional drivers be accompanied by a qualified driver, though this rule is often blatantly ignored. Curiously enough, there are some Irish drivers who have never taken the test yet legally hold a full license. During the late 1970s the wait for driving tests was so lengthy that the government simply gave up and issued full licenses to all and sundry on the list. It's unlikely to happen again as the wait for a test is not as long nowadays—six to eight weeks in the provinces, a little longer in Dublin.

No matter how highly you rate your driving skills, it's advisable to take a few lessons with an instructor before taking the Irish driving test. They'll know the local test routes and what a particular examiner is likely to ask you to do. Driving lessons average around $22 per hour. Most people take lessons in the instructor's car that can also be used for the test.

Taking the driving test costs $33 and the ordeal lasts for 45 minutes. First the examiner tests your eyesight by asking you to read out registration numbers in the parking lot. You'll then be asked a number of questions regarding the rules of the road and also to identify specific road signs from a chart. The actual on-the-road part of the test takes 30 minutes. You'll have to perform tasks such as an emergency stop and a three-point turn, and show you can park safely. Once the test is over you're told immediately whether you've passed or failed.

You then have to buy a full license. These are valid for one, three or 10 years and cost $4.50, $13.50 and $22, respectively. Drivers aged 67 or over are issued only three-year licenses and need to retake an optician's eye test before being issued another one.

For more information on licenses and tests, contact your local motor tax authority or Driver Testing Section, Dept. of Environment, Government Buidings, Ballina, county Mayo; tel +353 (0)96 24200.

Driving schools can be found through your local telephone directory's Golden Pages, but make sure they belong to an accredited body such as the DIR (Driving Instructor Register) or ACDI (Association of Certified Driving Schools).

Buying a Car

Unless you opt for city life, it will be extremely difficult to get by in Ireland without a car. While it's possible to import your own car without paying duty (subject to fulfilling certain conditions such as having owned it for a year), few American newcomers would bother to do so. Due to the width of many Irish roads, driving will be very difficult in the larger U.S. models, and just think of all the gas they guzzle. And where are you going to find spare parts for a Cadillac or a Chevrolet? Furthermore, the driver's controls are on the "wrong" side, which doesn't make for safe driving. If you insist on bringing your own car, further details on the question of importing cars can be had from the Revenue Commissioners, Dublin Castle, Dublin 2; tel +353 (0)1 679 2777.

Although new car sales are currently at an all-time high, prices are very expensive due to the tax regime. One of the smallest cars on the road, the Fiat Seicento, retails for $7,625. Roomier mid-range cars go for around $14,800. Opel Astras and Toyota Corollas start at $15,000, and the Volvo S401.6 at $20,800. The cheapest BMW (316i model) retails for $28,000. A good website for checking out what kind of car you can get for your money is www.motorweb.ie.

Second-hand cars are rather more affordable, but still not cheap. For example, $5,000 buys a 1994 Nissan Sunny. Obviously, price depends on the age and make of car. You can spend anywhere from $1,500 for a 10-year-old Opel Kadett to $11,000 for a two-year-old Toyota Corolla, one of Ireland's most popular cars. Other favorites are the Ford Fiesta and Ford Escort, around $5,650 for a five-year-old model. The vast majority of those who sell second-hand cars are trustworthy, not fly-by-night characters who will sell you an unsound heap of rust. After all, garage owners are part of the local community too, and there's no profit in rooking the people you live with!

It's not worth crossing the border into Northern Ireland and buying a car at British prices. Although prices in the North used to be a lot cheaper, this is no longer the case. Due to currency fluctuations, prices in the Republic of Ireland are more advantageous. And even if the currency situation does change, it still won't be worth it. The Revenue Commissioners will slap you with the Vehicle Registration Tax, an import tax based on the book value of each particular make of car, new or second-hand. It has been carefully crafted to wipe out any savings you make by buying outside the State. It's impossible to avoid this tax as you need to produce the car's log book when buying a road tax disc or renewing your insurance.

Car Tax and Insurance

All cars on the Irish road need to be taxed and insured. Levied annually (or, if you wish, quarterly), the state road tax operates on a sliding scale based on the size of a car's engine. A car with a 950cc engine such as a Ford Fiesta is taxed at $102 annually. A bigger car, say, a Peugeot with a 1400cc engine, attracts a levy of $208. Road tax is paid at your local motor tax office.

The law also compels you to have motor insurance. Get caught without it and you'll be taken to court and given a heavy fine. Persistent offenders are often jailed. Cost varies enormously depending on whether you take out fully comprehensive coverage or opt for just third party insurance. Factors such as age, driving record, type of car and whether you hold a full or provisional license are also taken into account. For example, full insurance coverage on a new or almost-new medium-range car driven by a mature driver who has never sub-mitted a claim is likely to be in the region of $390 to $555, depending on where you live. (Dublin has a growing reputation for car thefts, so premiums for city residents are higher.) If you live in a country area, third party coverage is likely to cost around $250 for a mature driver with a good driving record.

A host of insurance companies operate in Ireland—Hibernian, Irish National, and Guardian PMPA, to name but a few. Instead of spending hours on the phone getting quotes, it's far simpler to call an insurance bro-ker who will do the job for you. You'll find brokers in every town; many are also agents for building societies and auctioneers, so they're easy enough to find. Alternatively, contact the Irish Brokers Association for a list of mem-bers. They're based at 87 Merrion Square, Dublin 2; tel +353 (0)1 661 3061.

Service and maintenance costs also need to be budgeted for. Large garages linked to specific dealerships may charge you as much as $220 for an annual service—new points, spark plugs, oil change, replacement filters, brake pads, etc. In contrast, a one-man-band local garage may charge half that for the exact same work. If you're happy with your local garage, use it.

The NCT Test

January 2000 ushered in bad news for all of us who owned old bangers. Under pressure from Europe, the Irish government decreed that all cars over four years old would have to be mechanically tested and carry proof of roadworthiness: the NCT (National Car Testing) Certificate. Your car now has to pass an NCT competence test every two years. It is an offense to drive an uncertificated car.

There are 43 testing centers around the country. But no need to go look-ing for one—they find you from the registration records at the Motor Taxa-tion Office. When your car is due for its NCT test, you'll be sent an "appointment" six to eight weeks beforehand.

I scrapped my 13-year-old French Peugeot before the appointment date and bought a 10-year-old German Opel that had just passed its NCT. One in five other Irish motorists also opted to exchange their cars. However, even now that the most ancient of old bangers have gone to the breaker's yard, the failure rate is currently clocking up at just over 50 percent. If you're going to buy a second-hand car, *make sure it has a current NCT certificate.*

To add insult to injury, you have to pay a $39 fee to have the car tested. If it fails, you must take it to a garage and get the faults put right, then pay another $22 for a re-test. The only ways of avoiding the NCT test are to own a car that's classed as vintage or keep your car on an island that isn't linked to the mainland by a roadbridge.

Car Rental

Major international rental firms such as Hertz, Avis and Budget are all represented in Ireland. Their desks are often the first things that greet you upon arrival at Dublin and Shannon airports. You'll also find outlets in all major towns; look in the telephone Golden Pages under "car hire."

If you leave booking until you arrive in Ireland, weekly rental rates are punitive: around $350 in high season for a small car such as a Nissan Micra, around $400 for a larger model like a Toyota Corolla. These rates include fully comprehensive insurance cover, VAT and unlimited mileage. Off-season rates are around 25 percent lower, but you'll probably get much better deals if you book from within the States. The cheapest I have been able to identify is Thrifty, at $138 weekly for a Nissan Micra during the low season, which runs until the end of May. The longer you rent a car, the cheaper the fee, though with most firms it still costs around $950 monthly during summer for a medium-sized car like an Opel Astra. Smaller rental firms often have more attractive price deals than the big boys. At Dublin airport, Access Car Rentals offers an off-season special weekly price of $147 for a Daewoo Matiz.

To rent a car, it's essential to have a valid driver's license from your country of origin and it normally must have been held for at least two years. Age requirements are generally from 23 to 70 or 75; you'll find it almost impossible to rent a car if you fall outside these limits. All major credit cards are accepted. With the international firms, you should be able to rent models that have automatic rather than the normal manual transmission.

traffic hazards

© Steenie Harvey

Most Irish rental firms have recovery service agreements with the AA (Automobile Association, not Alcoholics Anonymous!). Unlucky drivers who break down should contact the rental company as soon as possible and call the AA's freephone number, 1800 667788.

ADDRESS BOOK

Avis, 1 East Hanover St., Dublin 2; tel +353 (0)1 605 7555.
Budget, Eyre Square, Galway; tel +353 (0)91 566376.
Hertz, 149 Upper Leeson St., Dublin 2; tel +353 (0)1 660 2255.
Thrifty, Central Reservations, Unit 3B3, Airport Business Park, Cloghran, county Dublin; tel +353 (0)1 8400800.
Access, Suite 201, Forte Posthouse, Dublin Airport; tel +353 (0)1 844 4848.
The Automobile Association (AA), 23 Rock Hill, Blackrock, county Dublin; tel +353 (0)1 260 0388.

Taxis

In Dublin, Cork, Galway and Limerick, taxis are metered. It's rare to come across cabs cruising for passengers. The best places to find them are at official taxi ranks and bus or rail terminals. Alternatively you can call a particular company's central operations depot for a pick-up. In Dublin, taxi charges are $2.11 for the first half-mile then $1 per subsequent mile. Extras include $0.45 for each piece of luggage and extra passenger. The fare from St. Stephen's Green to Heuston Station recently cost four of us $6.50. From Connolly Station to the airport, expect to pay around $16.

From Shannon Airport to either Limerick or Ennis (Clare's county town) you'll pay around $22, and you should have no problem finding a taxi. However, in many small provincial towns there may be only one or two firms, usually family-owned businesses where the sons and nephews do the driving. If you have a train to catch, don't leave phoning until the last minute. You may find somebody else has just booked the last available cab.

Taxis throughout provincial Ireland are not metered, so it's normal to agree on the fare beforehand. As a rule of thumb, average rates are $1.15 to $1.65 per mile. As with city cabs, it's customary to tip around 10 percent. Do beware, though, that long-distance cab rides can be very expensive, as most drivers will calculate a price to compensate for their return trip. Quotes of $200 from Dublin to Cork or $220 from Dublin to Tralee in Kerry are not uncommon.

PART IV

Moving In

11 Making the Move

hen moving to an English-speaking country like Ireland, it's easy to assume the words "culture shock" don't apply. Yes, Irish people use a few weird words and speak with peculiar accents, but day-to-day living will be pretty much the same as it is back home, right? After all, you're simply exchanging a frenetic big city existence for that idyllic life you've been dreaming about for years. You can picture it already: an old-fashioned farmstead on a dozen emerald acres, walking your dogs along the beach, maybe even getting a little part-time job in the local bookstore.

Hmmm. Some clouds are looming over the horizon if that's your plan. Do you realize that your pets will be quarantined? Or that you cannot buy more than five acres of land without obtaining special permission? And there'll be no job in the bookstore or anywhere else for that matter, not unless you buy your own business or you've got claims to Irish or any other European-Union citizenship.

The subject of employment is covered in depth in Chapters 18 and 19, but it's worth pointing out here that all non-EU nationals need work permits to get paid employment within Ireland. This isn't something you can obtain yourself; applications must be made by *employers* before a prospective employee even arrives in Ireland. However, if you have a historical entitlement to Irish or any other EU citizenship, then the door to employment is wide open.

Residency Requirements

No visa is necessary to enter Ireland, but unless you already hold dual citizenship, you'll need to register with the authorities if planning to stay longer than three months. This rule applies to all non-EU nationals. For newcomers living in the Dublin area, registration formalities are handled by the Aliens Registration Office, Garda Síochána, Harcourt Square, Dublin 2; tel +353 (0)1 475 5555.

Elsewhere in the country, local Garda (police) stations issue residency permits. Permission to stay in Ireland is renewable annually and will almost certainly be granted provided you have the means to support yourself. Currently there is no fee for registering. After five years, you can claim permanent resident status, and there's no further requirement to renew your permit. You can also apply for Irish citizenship if you were unable to claim this earlier.

Irish citizenship is a valuable thing to have as it affords a range of economic and social benefits including the right to live and work in any part of the European Union. And maybe one day your grandson may even play for the Irish soccer team; most of our heroes who currently wear the green jersey are in the team through the Irish "granny" rule. More prosaically, as an Irish citizen you'll have the right to vote (and be a candidate for elective office) in elections for both the European Parliament and at national level.

There are a number of ways to obtain Irish nationality: in your own right, by right of a parent's or grandparent's birth in Ireland, by marriage,

On the shores of Lough Derg, in county Clare, Killaloe is popular with summer tourists. A refurbished townhouse could offer letting potential.

© Steenie Harvey

and by naturalization through residence. As you may already be entitled to Irish citizenship, let's look at the different ways you can stake a claim.

Citizenship

CITIZENSHIP BY BIRTH
Regardless of parental nationality, anyone born in the Republic of Ireland after 1921 is considered an Irish citizen. For those born before 1921, the ruling covers the entire island of Ireland, including Northern Ireland.

CITIZENSHIP BY LINEAGE
If either parent was born in Ireland, you're automatically deemed Irish by right of birth (the *jus sanguinis* principle). There is no need to register a claim or even to take up residency to acquire citizenship. To obtain an Irish passport, all you have to do is to submit the necessary documentation to the nearest Irish embassy or consulate. Along with passport photos, you'll be asked to produce your own birth certificate, your parents' birth certificates and their marriage certificate. Within the United States, the current fee for processing passport applications is $77 plus $5 for postage.

Again, you don't have to be resident in Ireland to claim citizenship through a grandparent. However, the procedure is a little different and needs to be undertaken by what is known as "foreign birth registration." Applications are processed through the local Irish embassy or consulate or, once you are in Ireland, through the Department of Foreign Affairs, Consular Section, 72/76 St. Stephen's Green, Dublin 2; tel + 353 (0)1 478 0822.

A great deal of paperwork will need to be produced, both the original certificates and two copies of each document. You'll need your own birth certificate, the birth certificate of the parent through whom you are claiming Irish ancestry, and also that of your Irish-born grandparent. If their birth certificate is unobtainable, a baptismal certificate may be acceptable though this is likely to slow down the process somewhat. You'll also need to produce marriage certificates for yourself (if applicable), parents and grandparents. Death certificates are also required if a grandparent or the relevant parent is deceased.

Along with two passport-sized photos, you must also submit a photocopy of a current passport if you have one, and photocopies of three additional forms of identification such as a driver's license, social security ID card, pay slips or bank statements. Costs depend on the prevailing exchange rate. It's currently $115.50 for adults and $38.50 for those under 18. If you require an Irish passport too, that will cost another $51.

You may have heard that Irish citizenship can be claimed through a great-grandparent. This was so until 1984. Unfortunately the legislation was

genealogy

What were your great-grandparents' names and where did they come from? Quite possibly from the Emerald Isle for it's estimated that 40 million Americans are of Irish descent. If you too have Irish forebears somewhere in your background, why not take the opportunity to find out something about their lives and communities. Just imagine the thrill of glimpsing something of the world they knew—their town or village, the fields the family tilled, maybe even the local school or holy well they visited on the patron saint's day. You may even find distant cousins you never knew existed.

Where do you begin if your Irish background is a bit hazy? Well, you'll certainly need more information than just a family surname, so the more facts you can garner about maiden names and the names of siblings, the better. There are more than 70,000 listed townlands throughout Ireland, and it's vital to be able to pinpoint the county where your ancestor(s) was born. If you're not sure, the best place to begin your research is in the United States. The National Archives (700 Pennsylvania Ave., Washington, D.C. 20408; tel (202) 501-5400) holds an extensive collection of immigration records and passenger lists. Those from 1883 onwards generally include the last place of residence in Ireland. Another source is the Washington National Records Office (4205 Sutland Road, Washington, D.C. 20409; tel (301) 457-7010), which holds naturalization records. These may contain the date and place of birth, occupation, and previous place of residence for each immigrant.

Armed with that sort of information, it will be possible to search through Ireland's census returns, parish records, national school records and many other resources, which will give clues about other family members. You can even search transportation records to discover if any unfortunate relative was shipped away on a convict hull to Australia. Each Irish county has its own computerized genealogic database, though some are more comprehensive than others. Those interested in undertaking research work but unsure about where to start should first contact the Genealogical Office at Kildare Street, Dublin 2 (tel +353 (0)1 661 8811), which runs a general consultancy service.

altered, and it's no longer possible for great-grandchildren to benefit from the *jus sanguinis* principle.

CITIZENSHIP THROUGH MARRIAGE

Marriage is another route to Irish citizenship. A person married to an Irish citizen for three years or more can take up his or her own Irish citizenship simply by registering with an Irish embassy or consulate. If your American-born husband or wife has an Irish parent and you've been married for at least three years, you too are immediately entitled to an Irish passport and citizenship rights. If, however, your spouse's Irish ancestry is through a grandparent but he or she has yet to register a claim, you'll have to wait for a full three years.

CITIZENSHIP THROUGH NATURALIZATION

Ireland's Department of Justice handles applications for naturalization, and citizenship is granted at the Minister's "absolute discretion." It's a slow process, generally taking between 18 and 24 months before a decision is reached. To be considered for Irish citizenship, the following criteria have to be satisfied:

1. The applicant is resident in the State and is 18 years of age or older.
2. During the preceding nine years, the applicant must have resided legally in the State for five of those years. The last year must have been one of continuous residence, though an absence for vacations or business purposes is not generally regarded as a break in residence.

Applicants must satisfy the Minister of their good character and their intention to reside in Ireland after naturalization.

The following documentation has to be submitted with an application, both the originals and a photocopy of each.

- A passport.
- Garda Síochána certificate of registration (green residency permit book).
- Birth certificate with a certified translation if not in English.
- If applicable, a marriage certificate—again, with certified translation if necessary.
- A statement from the Revenue Commissioners that all due taxes have been paid. Depending on circumstances, you must include details of personal tax, company tax, PRSI contributions and VAT payments.
- Documentary proofs of financial status such as bank or building society statements.
- If applicable, pay slips or statements of earnings from an employer.

Should the Minister grant your application, a fee of approximately $565 becomes payable for yourself with additional fees of $113 each for your spouse and any children who are still minors. You will be required to stand

across Toormore Bay to Mount Gabriel, from Spanish Point, West Cork

© Steenie Harvey

in open court before a district court judge and make a declaration of fidelity to the nation and loyalty to the State.

For more information contact the Department of Justice, Immigration and Citizenship Division, 72/76 St. Stephen's Green, Dublin 2; tel +353 (0)1 678 9711 or (0)1 602 8202. (Calls are accepted only on weekdays between 10 A.M. and noon.)

HOLDING DUAL NATIONALITY

Unlike in some European countries, taking up Irish citizenship does not require renouncing another citizenship. Ireland's Department of Foreign Affairs has no objection to anyone holding dual citizenship, but it does advise individuals to clarify the position with home governments first.

Looking at it from the reverse angle, the U.S. government will not consider that you have committed an expatriating act if you become a dual national. To lose your legal status as a U.S. national, you would need to have committed treason or have formally renounced your citizenship.

One specification is that you are required to use your U.S. passport when leaving or entering the United States. However, even if you decide to use your Irish passport when traveling elsewhere, you can still call on the assistance of U.S. embassies and consulates. Another point to note is that the U.S. government still expects its overseas citizens to file tax returns, even if no tax is payable. Even so, one congressional report estimated that around 61 percent of Americans living abroad are flouting this rule. In an attempt to keep track of its wayward citizens, every U.S. national applying for a passport is supposed to file an IRS information report listing foreign residences and other details the tax man may find interesting.

RIGHTS AND OBLIGATIONS

The main obligation for Irish citizens resident in the State is to undertake jury service if called upon to do so. As a citizen you'll also have full voting rights, which, for others, depends on status.

At present, only Irish citizens can vote in presidential elections or on referenda. The only resident foreigners entitled to vote in elections to the Dáil (the Irish Parliament) are U.K. citizens. That's because Irish citizens living in the U.K. also have the right to vote there. Voting in elections to the European Parliament is open to any resident holding citizenship of an EU member state.

However, you don't need to hold Irish or any other kind of EU nationality to vote in local elections; you simply need to be resident here and have your name on the electoral roll. Those who are entitled to vote only in local elections have the letter "L" after their names on the register.

A new register of electors is compiled each year. To get on the register, either contact your local council offices or fill in a form at the post office. The process of compiling the register starts in September/October and comes into effect the following February. To make sure you're on the electoral roll, you can check the draft register that is published on November 1. It's available for inspection in post offices, libraries, Garda stations and local authority offices.

Social Welfare Perks

Depending on income, Irish citizens of retirement age qualify for certain welfare benefits. For those in the 66-to-70 age group, it depends upon income. However, those over 70 are entitled to all of the benefits, regardless of their financial means.

As an American citizen residing in Ireland, you may also be eligible to claim them if you're receiving a social security pension and your weekly income is no more than $45 above the State's Social Welfare Pension rate. On current exchange rates, this stands at $119.50 for individuals and $210.50 for couples. If, however, you are over 70, there is no means test on your income and you will qualify for all the free benefits. These include:

- Free electricity. The concession covers ESB standing charges ($46 per year) and 1,500 units of electricity per year, worth $126. Alternatively you could opt for an equivalent allowance for natural or bottled gas.
- If living alone, a free telephone line rental allowance ($150 per year) plus $2.15 worth of calls in each billing period.
- Winter fuel allowance for 29 weeks between October and May, worth about $6 per week.
- Free TV license worth $79 per year.

All these benefits are administered by the Department of Social, Community and Family Affairs, Pension Services Offices, College Road, Sligo, county Sligo; tel +353 (0)71 48374.

Bringing Pets to Ireland

Sad news. You'll have to bid a tearful farewell to Rex and Tibbykins for a while. Ireland has draconian quarantine laws, and all pets have to spend six months at an approved quarantine station. The only exceptions are racehorses (not considered pets) and pets entering the country from the U.K., another island nation whose own quarantine regulations are just as tough as Ireland's. The reason behind the ruling is to keep both countries rabies-free—the disease still surfaces in parts of continental Europe. Therefore, it won't be possible for you and your pet to fly first to the U.K. and get around the regulations. There's no benefit in your coming to Ireland and your pet having to spend its quarantine in Britain.

Pets arriving without proper documentation will be flown straight back home at your expense—and so will you. And don't even think about trying to smuggle your pet into the country; as well as a stiff financial penalty you'll also be risking a possible jail sentence. This book can tell you many things, but how to adapt to life in Dublin's Mountjoy Prison isn't one of them!

Quarantine fees for the six-month period are charged according to the size of the animal, but expect to pay an average of $1,200 for a cat and $1,350 for a medium-sized dog such as a spaniel. You'll also have to pay any necessary veterinary fees while your pet is in quarantine. As the documentation process may take as long as three months, don't delay in getting forms from either the Irish Embassy or the Department of Agriculture, Veterinary Division, Kildare St., Dublin 2; tel +353 (0)1 607 2862.

Customs and Excise

If you're relocating from outside the European Union (such as from the United States), you're allowed to import, duty-free, any belongings that you have owned for at least six months. You can continue to import your personal possessions for up to one year after relocating. The only proviso is that should you decide to sell any of your imported belongings within the first year of residence, duty becomes liable to be paid. There are some items that you are not allowed to import—handguns, for example.

For information on customs and excise laws, contact the Revenue Commissioners, Customs and Excise Information Office, Castle House, Sth Gt George's St., Dublin 2; tel +353 (0)1 679 2777.

Culture Shock

Things are not going to be the same as back at home. Take the issue of tobacco, for instance. Pubs and restaurants are not smoke-free zones, and many Irish people (teenagers included) puff away like the proverbial chimneys. Nobody is going to take the slightest bit of notice of your exaggerated coughing or any trenchant insistence that you have the right to breathe clean air. And once you're inside the smoky confines of a pub, you may be surprised to find yourself sharing a table with a group of 15-year-olds. It's all quite above board; although the legal age for drinking alcohol is 18, children under the age of 15 are allowed in pubs if in the company of a parent or guardian. So long as they stick to soft drinks, those aged between 15 and 18 can spend all day and night in the pub—even if it's the roughest den in town—without any parental accompaniment whatsoever.

If you've been used to an urban lifestyle, the reality of rural Ireland may provide you with more than you bargained for. The countryside isn't a picture book, it's a working environment. Cows smell, pigs smell, and you'll undoubtedly smell a bit ripe too if your next-door neighbor is a farmer who sprays slurry—a fertile mix of animal dung and urine—on his fields. The joys of rural life include not only roosters crowing at the unearthly hour of 5 A.M., but also the summertime sounds of agricultural machinery grinding away at 2, 3 and 4 o'clock in the morning. Due to the fickle weather, farmers often work through the entire night to get the hay in. You'll just have to put up with a few nights of disturbed sleep.

Countryside properties don't come with quite the same services as in towns or cities. Unless you buy a village house, it's most unlikely there will be any street lamps on the laneway, and everywhere may seem rather spooky on moonless nights. Of course, the great benefit of living in a place with no light pollution means you'll be able

> *Village pubs operate as community centers, and you'll often find they're the venue for quiz nights, charades and card games as well as live music.*

to step outside and look at the stars. When was the last time you did that? Another surprise to city dwellers is the complete absence of sidewalks. A country stroll usually entails leaping into the hedgerow every time a car whizzes past.

No street lamps, no sidewalks and no sewage treatment plants either. Rural Ireland lacks a proper sewage system and even if you've bought a trophy property costing over $1 million, you'll still be in the same position as

A 'DART' train crosses the river Liffey in Dublin.

Weird Words

No parking lots for drivers, no sidewalks for pedestrians. Restrooms? Forget it. Nor are we familiar with gas stations, drugstores or diapers. As a blow-in (foreigner), you'll need to get used to some strange new terminology.

Want to fill your car with gas? No, no, no. You want petrol or diesel. And you put your messages (groceries) in the car boot, not the trunk. The fender is the bumper and the hood is the bonnet.

Shopping too has a language all of its own. You buy medicines at the chemist and stores are always called shops. Minerals are soft drinks such as cola and lemonade, rashers are bacon, and courgettes are what you call zucchini. Babies will need to get used to wearing nappies, not diapers. A new pair of pants? If you mean trousers or slacks, say so. Pants are something you'll find in the mens' underwear department.

Why do you want to go to the bathroom if you don't intend having a bath? The door marked W.C. (Water Closet) is a toilet, lavatory, loo or, if you've fallen into rough company, the jacks. It is not, repeat *not*, a restroom.

Any tool that us culchies (country bumpkins) forget the name of is a yoke as in

"Pass me that yoke." Any person whose name you can't remember is yer man or yer woman. "You know who I mean, yer man beside the lough."

Naughty kids are bold and anybody who seems unwell probably looks well shook. If you're tired, you're banjaxed. However, if your radio or TV is banjaxed it's broken or damaged. (Though cruder people will tell you it's bollixed.)

And if somebody asks if you're enjoying the crack (*craic*), don't be alarmed. It's not a reference to illegal substance abuse, rather a harmless word for sharing a joke or having a fun time.

"Scheme" is another word that sends American eyebrows up. In Ireland you'll see it everywhere: health insurance schemes, drug subsidization schemes, community employment schemes, seaside resort schemes. Scheme never signifies anything dubious, it's simply an alternative word for a plan or project.

You'll also see numerous spelling differences. Words such as colour, sceptic, centre, traveller, theatre, labour and honourable all seem to have been misspelled. Not to us. It's you who spell them wrong!

a buyer with a $50,000 cottage. You'll need a septic tank in which to store all that stuff most people don't talk about in polite society. Connected to the house by a waste pipe, septic tanks are buried in the ground. You'll know if yours needs emptying when the contents start to seep into the garden or back along the outflow pipe. Though it sounds like a bit of a nightmare, it isn't something to fret over. In general, a septic tank needs emptying only once every 10 years, and it isn't something you'll have to do yourself. Neighbors will give you a local contact name; expect to pay in the region of $100.

Thought chimney sweeps only belonged in Dickens' novels? Think again. If you have open fires, chimneys need to be swept free of soot twice a year. For around $40 you can buy rods and brushes and do the task yourself. Alternatively, contact a chimney cleaning service or an old-fashioned local sweep who will charge around $65 for the average-sized cottage or bungalow.

Dressing for the Occasion

Ireland is a jeans and sweaters type of country: casual gear does for almost all occasions. Even in cities such as Dublin and Cork, there are few fashion victims and most people dress very informally. Of course, different standards apply to management and professional people, so you should certainly wear something a bit more formal if you intend on conducting business here. People also generally make an effort to dress up at weddings, special social functions, theater trips and for dinner at a classy restaurant. Otherwise the rule is "come as you are."

Leaving aside Dublin's chattering classes, Ireland doesn't really have a dinner party culture (in rural areas dinner is the meal you eat at midday), and most social contact with neighbors is down at the pub. Village pubs operate as community centers, and you'll often find they're the venue for quiz nights, charades and card games as well as live music. You don't have to drink alcohol if you don't want to. It's quite common to see people with soft drinks, tea or coffee. In the west of Ireland especially, many pub-goers give up alcohol completely for the 40 days of Lent. Well, almost completely. The Church allows a special dispensation to break the Lenten fast on March 17, St. Patrick's Day.

Contact Groups

You are not alone. U.S. expatriates and retirees can touch home base through the Irish-American Society, a support group offering advice, get-togethers, business contacts and so on. One red-letter day in their calendar is Thanksgiving with a dinner hosted by the U.S. ambassador to Ireland. Independence Day is another; the society holds a barbecue, barn dance and fireworks display at Dun Laoghaire, county Dublin. For more information contact Joan Hanley, 16 Dargle Wood, Templeogue, Dublin 16; tel +353 (0)1 494 4091.

Built as a refuge from Viking invaders, Ireland's high, round towers point heavenwards like stone moon rockets.

© Steenie Harvey

Ex-servicemen and -women can join the American Legion, which has branches in Dublin, Claremorris in county Mayo, and Killarney in county Kerry. They'll keep you informed on U.S. government policy towards veterans and pension entitlements and also about various Legion get-togethers. Contact John N. Power, Adjutant, 11 Skiddy's Homes, Pouladuff Road, Cork; tel +353 (0)21 314188.

The American Women's Club of Dublin produces a monthly newsletter for members and organizes lectures, tours and courses on different aspects of Irish culture. Contact them at 40b Dartmouth Square, Dublin 6; tel +353 (0)1 676 6263.

Depending on your business interests, you may want to contact the American Chamber of Commerce Ireland, which promotes cultural and commercial exchange between the two countries. Reach them at Heritage House, 23 St. Stephen's Green, Dublin 2; tel +353 (0)1 661 6201.

A list of affiliated clubs and societies with American links can be had from the American Embassy at 42 Elgin Road, Dublin 4; tel +353 (0)1 668 8777.

12 A Roof Over Your Head

Whether you aim to rent or buy, Irish property comes in a myriad of enticing guises, from traditional farmhouses to cozy modern bungalows and rambling Georgian mansions clad in skeins of ivy. You can even purchase a plot of land in a glorious location and build that dream home you've always had in mind. The Republic's 26 counties offer a treasure chest of beguiling ideas, though some areas are a lot more expensive than others. Like everywhere else, Ireland has its millionaire homes and property hot spots. The east coast in particular has seen a phenomenal rise in house values over the past few years—and prices are still rising. Space is rapidly running out, and 18 percent of all new homes built last year were apartments.

Ireland's Rental Market

Are you a student? A computer expert sent over to Ireland on a year-long assignment? An adventurous spirit who simply wants the experience of living here for a couple of years? If so, you'll probably be thinking of renting a property.

Perhaps you don't fit into those categories at all. It could be that you've long dreamt of owning here and nothing is going to deter you. Well, although you may have already made up your mind that you want to buy,

home sweet home

Some Irish realtors have a passion for purple prose. Others ... well, let's just say a few have been known to be economical with the truth. In short, beware of those enticing descriptions of ideal properties. Here are what they may *really* mean.

"Uninterrupted views"—of the gas-works/abattoir/lunatic asylum.

"Garden requires a little attention"—Welcome to Ireland's version of the Amazon rainforest.

"Oozing with old-fashioned charm"—Plumbing dates from the 1740s.

"Perfect for a handyman"—Completely derelict.

"Must be seen to be believed"—I can't believe this dump costs $100,000 either.

"Wonderfully compact"—Would suit a midget.

"Very secluded location"—25 miles from anywhere.

"Renowned wildlife habitat"—House is infested with mice, cockroaches and death-watch beetles.

"Ready to walk into"—No front door, no back door, cows using the kitchen as a byre.

"Fishing on the doorstep"—Area prone to flooding.

"Awaits a discerning buyer"—Nobody else has been fool enough to make an offer.

"Clifftop cottage, attractively priced for quick sale"—due to fall into the ocean within the next two years.

"Totally unvamped"—Woodwormy floorboards, dry rot behind the plasterwork.

"Tastefully decorated"—if your tastes run to shocking pink decor and mirrors on every ceiling.

"With some unusual features"—such as the gaping holes in the roof.

there are two main reasons why I think you should also take a look at rental options.

The first is financial. No two ways about it, many people are going to find the cost of purchasing a home prohibitive. Unless you've been holed up in a cave for the past few years, you'll know Irish real estate prices have shot into the stratosphere. While the rate of increase has slowed in recent months, that doesn't mean house values are plummeting. You'll find more information about our high value homes in the Buying Property section on pg. 149, but the general consensus is that prices will rise around 10 percent in 2002. The rise in 2000 was 18 percent and during the previous year, values increased by more than 30 percent in some areas.

Another reason I think renting is a good idea is this: There's always the possibility that Ireland and the Irish lifestyle might not meet your expectations. Living in a foreign country is always very different from spending a vacation there. If Ireland is completely new to you, it certainly makes sense to rent a property for an initial six or 12 months so you can get to know the country and its people.

Even if you do eventually intend to buy or build a home, renting allows ample time to visit different counties and find the right property at—hopefully—a reasonable price. You don't want to be rushed into a hasty decision you might later regret. It's all too easy to do if you're here on a two-week summer vacation trip when skies are that special shade of duck-egg blue, roses are in full bloom and every place looks its idyllic best.

Bear in mind that the country's slow pace of life will not suit everyone. Nor will the climate. The winter skies of northern Europe can often be gray and dreary. Buying a house isn't like buying a new pair of drapes: It's a major financial commitment. By renting a property initially, you will be able to ensure that the Emerald Isle is the ideal home for you in January as well as in flaming June.

LONG-TERM RENTALS

Ireland offers a mix of both furnished and unfurnished rental properties, so it won't be necessary to buy furniture if you don't want to. Although renting here isn't complicated, be warned that over the long term, it can work out to be fairly expensive—certainly so if you are thinking of living in Dublin.

The country's rate of home ownership is around 83 percent, one of the world's highest, so there's never a glut of rental properties available. Unlike in Germany, where about 40 percent of families own homes, few Irish people rent for life. In some areas rents have almost tripled in recent years. Last year saw an across-the-board rise of 18 percent in Dublin and 14 percent in the provinces. The booming housing market has led to a clamor for affordable accommodation, particularly from young Dubliners on modest incomes. However, supply can't always meet demand, and so the rents keep on rising.

According to the latest property survey issued by the Institute of Professional Auctioneers and Valuers (IPAV), the national average monthly rent for a house is $563, for a one-bedroom apartment $339, and for a two-bedroom apartment $473.

In the Dublin area, the average monthly rent for a house is $1,009, for a one-bedroom unit $738, and for a two-bedroom apartment $930. Although these

These old buildings beside the river in Clonakilty have been converted into attractive apartments.

© Steenie Harvey

sound like fairly reasonable rents, there is a lot of low-quality housing in the city, and this brings the average down. The averages for Cork are $596, $414 and $548, respectively, while in Limerick the figures are $548, $358 and $470.

THE DUBLIN RENTAL MARKET

Although Dublin is a lot more expensive than provincial towns and rural areas, it has plenty of attractions as a place to live, particularly if you're young and looking for a high-octane lifestyle. And while even dot.com millionaires may find it difficult to afford real estate in the capital, it does makes an excellent base for house-hunting forays along the east coast and into rural counties such as Kilkenny.

Depending on size, quality and distance from the city center, most properties that overseas tenants would consider renting fetch between $800 and $1,500 per month. Furnished one-bedroom studio apartments start at around $575 per month, though these kind of units more typically fetch $650 to $750 in expanding outer suburbs such as Lucan and Blanchardstown. You can expect to pay nearer to $850 to $900 per month for similar properties in leafy Ballsbridge, along the Liffey Quays or in fashionable Temple Bar, the city's refurbished medieval quarter. Students, tutors and others wanting to live almost on the doorstep of Trinity College pay $800 for one-bedroom furnished apartments on Tara Street.

Renting allows ample time to visit different counties and find the right property at— hopefully—a reasonable price.

More spacious apartments and houses in good Dublin areas typically range from $850 to $1,800 monthly. For example, a two-bedroom furnished apartment in a small low-rise block in Clontarf rents for $885 monthly; a similar-sized apartment in a refurbished former distillery rents for $1,120, the same price as a two-bedroom unit on Tara Street.

Apartments in really classy neighborhoods or with sea views can command even higher rents. For instance, a two-bedroom unit with sea frontage at Monkstown rents for $1,535 per month. Townhouses in good neighborhoods like Ballsbridge and Sandymount rent for approximately $1,700, though the corporate sector willingly pays up to $4,000 monthly for quality furnished properties. Maybe I should adjust that figure; the latest listings from the Sherry Fitzgerald agency include a furnished four-bedroom home with a garden in Monkstown for a whopping $5,900 per month.

In traditional residential districts like Rathgar, Terenure and Blackrock, three- and four-bedroom family homes usually rent for between $1,620 and $2,500, with similar homes in Lucan and the newer suburbs fetching around $1,000. Dublin's larger agents also usually have homes in rural county Dublin as well as in Wicklow, Meath and Kildare, satellite counties within commuting distance of the capital.

Within Dublin, both private landlords and realtors advertise in the classi-fied sections of newspapers like the *Irish Independent, Irish Times* and *Evening Herald*. Although most handle property sales, some realtors have their own rentals departments and a host of agencies deal with rentals.

- Sherry Fitzgerald Residential Lettings, 12 Merrion Row, Dublin 2. Tel +353 1 6399290. Fax +353 1 6399295. E-mail: lettings@sherryfitz.ie
- Hooke & Macdonald, 52 Merrion Square, Dublin 2. Tel +353 1 6610100. Fax +353 1 6766340. Website: www.hookemacdonald.ie
- Lisney, 24 St. Stephen's Green, Dublin 2. Tel +353 1 6382700. Email: dublin@lisney.com

THE PROVINCIAL RENTAL MARKET

In provincial towns and cities, the cost of most monthly rentals is between $475 and $950. As in Dublin, much depends on the size of the property, whether it's furnished and where it's located. Galway townhouses and apartments are at the higher end of the provincial rental market because of various factors such as demographic growth rates, good employment prospects and Galway's status as a university city.

Around smaller towns and cities such as Waterford, Sligo, Clonmel and Tralee, you can find nice townhouses and country bungalows for between $470 and $600 per month. Remote—and I do mean remote—rural cottages sometimes surface for as little as $400 per month, though these will undoubtedly take a bit more tracking down. Apartments are also on the increase, particularly in provincial cities. Two-bedroom furnished apart-ments in Waterford typically rent for between $500 to $560 per month.

Ardagh, county Longford, scooped the title of Ireland's tidiest village in 1998.

© Steenie Harvey

Again, the best way to find rental properties is to scan the classified sections of local newspapers or contact agents in an area that appeals to you. Although the vast majority of provincial realtors don't have specific rentals departments, most generally have a handful of rental properties on their books.

You'll find more rental possibilities covered in the Prime Living Locations chapters that follow, but if your heart is set on Kerry, try James North (33 Denny St., Tralee, Kerry; tel +353 (0)66 7122699). At the time of writing the agency's portfolio included Cloher Li, a furnished three-bedroom townhouse in Tralee for $530 per month plus $767 security deposit. They also listed a two-bedroom apartment for $408 monthly plus $530 security deposit.

Or consider Kinsale, the star of county Cork's historic harbor towns. For an evocative address, how can you beat Viking's Wharf, World's End, Kinsale? A furnished three-bedroom cut-stone townhouse, it rents for $944 per month plus $1,888 security deposit. For $472 per month plus $944 security deposit, you could settle into a one-bedroom furnished apartment in a converted boathouse at Creek Lodge, one mile from Kinsale town. Overlooking Kinsale's inner harbor and marina, Compass Hill Cottage is furnished, has three bedrooms, and rents for $767 monthly plus $767 security deposit. These and other Kinsale properties are available through Sheehy Bros, 10 Short Quay, Kinsale, county Cork; tel +353 (0)21 4772338.

Rental Red Tape

Most long-term rentals require you to sign a year's lease. Going by my own experience, it shouldn't be difficult to get settled fairly quickly. Before buying our own cottage near Lough Key in county Roscommon, we rented a house in Sligo for six months, a place we knew well from previous holidays. On Day One, over on a house-finding trip from England, I walked into an estate agent's office in Sligo town. That same January afternoon he drove me out to see a property, a furnished country house four miles from the town center. I was introduced to the house's owner, who spent most of her time in Boston.

On Day Two I accompanied my prospective landlady to her solicitor's office where we signed a lease. I handed over two months' rent, half of which took the form of a deposit, returnable providing we didn't damage the house or its contents. The following week we were here in Ireland, living the country life, and our daughter was discovering the weird new world of an Irish convent school!

Providing they pay the rent, tenants are well protected under Irish law. The landlord is obliged to provide a rent book, or written lease, that includes the duration of the tenancy, the amount of rent, when payment is to be made and by what means—cash, standing order, check, etc. The terms of the lease should also include arrangements regarding utility bills, the amount and purpose of the deposit, and whether pets are allowed.

Signing a lease legally obligates you to pay the rent for the agreed-upon period, regardless of whether you move out before the lease expires. An aggrieved landlord is within his rights to track you down and demand any missing payments if you decide to leave early. Of course, it's quite likely that you'll be able to come to an amicable arrangement should you find a suitable property to buy before the rental lease expires.

Short-Term and Vacation Rentals

If you're thinking of renting for a couple of months rather than a year, you may have to settle for a holiday let, or vacation rental. However, I have seen properties advertised for lease periods of four and six months. The best thing to do is to contact some of the larger agencies with your requirements. Or try the Internet. One useful website for tracking down rental properties is www.irishpropertynews.ie. For example, a four-bedroom house in Galway city was recently available for a four-month period for $1,130 monthly.

Although many properties listed in tourist brochures may seem pricey, rates fall dramatically during the low season. It may even be possible to negotiate an advantageous two- or three-month rental deal with the property's owner. You'll never know until you ask.

A good place to start is with the tourist board's self-catering accommodation guide, priced at approximately $6 and available at all Bord Fáilte offices. This weighty tome lists hundreds of holiday rental properties and includes owners' contact numbers. As all properties marketed through Bord Fáilte must meet certain standards, you can be sure that these homes will be warm and well decorated with all the necessary conveniences. It may seem an obvious thing to mention, but just in case any of you are wondering, all vacation properties are furnished.

In the tranquil green fields of the midlands county of Westmeath, you could rent Lake View, a traditional restored house overlooking Lough Lene. The historic remains of Fore Abbey and its scattering of holy wells and Celtic age churches are nearby, as is an 18-hole golf course. Sleeping five, and with "everything supplied," it rents for $200 per week from October to March; $260 per week during April, May, June and September; $307 during July and August. Contact Margaret and Eugene Carr, Cummerstown, Collinstown, county Westmeath; tel +353 (0)44 66385.

Offering grand walks, excellent seafood restaurants and lungfuls of oxygen-laden air, the pretty harbor village of Ballyvaughan in county Clare sits at the edge of the Burren where rare wildflowers bloom amongst the rocks. Here two-bedroom cottages sleeping two rent for $142 per week during January and February, $585 during July and August. Contact George Quinn, Village and Country Homes, Frances Street, Kilrush, county Clare; tel +353 (0)65 9051977. Email: sales@ballyvaughan-cottages.com.

In the heart of Connemara's Gaeltacht, Hotel Carraroe has a small holiday cottage development with prices at $206 per week from October to April. I stayed here one Easter myself. Don't miss the exhilarating walks along the coral strand and the traditional music in the village pub, *An Cistin* (The Kitchen). Contact Ostan Carraroe, Carraroe, Connemara, county Galway; tel +353 (0)91 595116.

There are a wide range of agencies, though peak season prices tend to be higher than if you made a private arrangement. The Rent-an-Irish-Cottage company has small cottage complexes in Cork, Kerry and many other scenic locations. Most cottages are thatched, and all have open peat fires. Prices go from $160 to $1,356 weekly, depending on cottage size and time of year. At Durrus in Ireland's scenic southwest, a cottage sleeping four rents for $250 weekly in September and October.

July and August are the peak months for vacations in rural Ireland. For cottages in the most popular counties, Cork and Kerry, the rule for advance bookings is to do it as far ahead as you can. Donegal is also chock full during these months. Many Irish families (and many more from across the border in Northern Ireland) plump for holidays in the Republic's wildest and most northernmost county. At this time of year, you'll invariably need to book for a week minimum. It's generally Saturday to Saturday, though there are exceptions. At other times of year, you can usually opt for long weekends or three- or four-day midweek stays.

Trident Holiday Homes has a wide selection of properties throughout Ireland. Also try Irish Cottage Holiday Homes, which acts as a central booking point for numerous small, privately owned cottage complexes.

- Rent-an-Irish-Cottage, 85 O'Connell St., Limerick; tel +353 (0)61 411109. E-mail: info@rentacottage.ie.
- Trident Holiday Homes, 15 Irishtown Road, Irishtown, Dublin 4; tel +353 (0)1 6683534. Website: www.thh.ie.
- Irish Cottage Holiday Homes, 4 Whitefriars, Aungier St., Dublin 2; tel +353 (0)1 4751932. Website: www.ichh.ie.

Dublin? Although you don't usually have to book months in advance to stay in a vacation apartment in Ireland's capital city, I'd advise North Americans to allow at least six to eight weeks to find something nice and centrally located. If you want to stay in the capital, vacation rentals through Trident Holiday Homes (address above) start at $381 weekly for one-bedroom apartments, $444, $635 and $762 for two-, three- and four-bedroom homes, respectively. They're all in nice areas such as Donnybrook and Ballsbridge.

Another option is Jacobs Apartments, in the heart of Dublin city center's financial district. The apartments sleep either two or four and are only a short walking distance from the main shopping areas, Connolly Station and the central bus station. Weekly prices for the two-person apartments are $413 winter, $530 summer. For the four-person apartments, $530 and $650. You can also rent for the weekend (two nights). This costs $200 to $236 for smaller units, $260 to $295 for the larger ones, and $354 to $442 on public holiday weekends. Contact Jacobs Apartments, Booking Office, 21-28 Talbot Place, Dublin 1; tel +353 (0)1 8555660. Website: www.isaacs.ie.

How to Book a Vacation Rental

Each owner and rental company has their own way of doing things, but in a lot of cases the procedure is to pay around 30 percent of the rental price when you place a booking. The balance may be due four to six weeks before the start of the rental date, or on arrival. Electricity, heating and bed linen are often included in the rental price, though in some homes you may have to feed coins into a meter for electricity. You may also have to pay extra ($12 to $24) to rent bed linen and towels. Some property owners also request damage deposits of $80 to $115.

If an agency or privately owned establishment is geared up to take credit cards, you can normally pay the deposit by this method. Visa and Master-Card are the most widely used cards in Ireland. I'm reluctant to send my own credit card details by email, so once I've been offered accommodation, I usually phone in the information.

The other main method of making payment is to go to your hometown bank and obtain a foreign currency draft for the required amount against a recognized bank (that is, a check in euros drawn against the Bank of Ireland in Dublin.) You then send this draft to your chosen agency or individual to be cashed. For peace of mind, send it by registered or certified mail.

Personal checks in dollars are not really acceptable. Although Irish banks take them—I sometimes pay U.S. dollar checks into my own bank—they take a devil of a long time to clear. Even in this supposedly electronic age, I've been told to allow up to 20 days for payment to clear.

Buying Property

A MARKET OVERVIEW
Although there are some lovely properties here, house prices in most

corners of Ireland will likely seem very pricey to many North Americans, not just in Dublin and its satellite counties, but even in those heartland counties that most foreign buyers have never even heard of.

The part of the country where I live, county Roscommon, serves as a good example of how things are. Despite its gentle lakeland scenery, it has never been in vogue either with foreign buyers or Irish city-dwellers in search of summer vacation homes. County Roscommon is over 120 miles from Dublin, offers no spectacular mountains, and (even in the Celtic Tiger economy), jobs are few and far between. Yet a neighbor's bungalow just sold for $122,000. There was nothing special about this house. It was plain, boxy and nondescript. I'm mentioning it to stress that finding bargains is almost impossible nowadays. I certainly don't want to put you off buying a home; all I'm saying is be realistic.

For something habitable in an "unfashionable" inland county—Tipperary, Longford, Leitrim, Roscommon—the starting price is generally $53,000 to $60,000 for old-style cottages and houses. Donegal is worth a look too. In inland areas of this county you can still find cottages in reasonable condition for $65,000, though don't expect to be awakened by seagulls. Another good hunting ground is the border county of Cavan. And put South Sligo and the eastern halves of counties Mayo and Clare on your list too. Any location within these counties is within easy reach of the dramatic western seaboard, though you'll pay an additional premium of around $24,000 for properties with an ocean view.

Admittedly, you'll still see properties in a number of counties priced at around $35,000. However, in most instances all you'll get for this type of money is a shell, a ramshackle cottage that's fit only for a beast of the field to use as a shelter. Nor will your pile of rubble be in a scenic location or have ocean views, not at that price level. In the prettiest parts of Cork, Kerry and Galway, you can pay $70,000 and more for a tumbledown dwelling. Along the West Cork coast, near Castletownsend, $177,000 buys a stone farmhouse with four outbuildings. The selling agent is describing it as "a restorer's dream," but my own description would be "semi-derelict." It's a horrendous price for a renovation project.

Location also dictates the price of modern properties. The average price of a three-bedroom bungalow is $136,000 in county Longford, but $260,000 in county Galway. Crazy prices? They get even crazier in the seaside villages and towns of county Dublin, where families are paying an average of $415,000 for a newly built semi-detached house with three bedrooms. However, not everywhere is quite so unaffordable. For seaside properties at an almost-affordable price, county Mayo can still deliver some good options. Here, newly built holiday homes in the small coastal town of Louisburgh were recently selling for $118,000.

The cost of buying a home has become the biggest downside to the country's recent economic success. Wealthy Irish city-dwellers are still in the market for second homes in scenic areas, and fierce competition continues to drive prices skywards, especially for refurbished homes around the most sought-after villages. Twelve years ago, you had your pick if you wanted to buy a sound little cottage on an acre for under $25,000. Unfortunately, those days are long gone.

The property value wave shows no signs of ebbing and residential values in most counties are still on the upward trend. The latest IPAV real estate survey translates the cost of buying a new home nationally at $145,140. Average prices in selected cities are $214,760 in Dublin, $140,420 in Cork, $139,000 in Galway, and $126,000 in Limerick.

The national average for second-hand homes is $129,000. Broken down on the same basis, the average price for Dublin comes in at $230,000, for county Cork $133,000, for county Galway $130,000, and for county Limerick $122,000. The most expensive part of the country is county Meath, which recorded the highest average of $236,000.

Although statistics provide a useful yardstick, they don't give the full picture. Both national and county averages will include everything from castles to tumbledown cottages. While you can easily pay $250,000 for a smallish second-hand bungalow in the commuter counties of Meath and Kildare, look elsewhere and almost identical properties can still be had for $82,000. Value-for-money continues to exist in counties Roscommon and Leitrim, where rural depopulation has left the price of many old-fashioned properties in the doldrums. Root about here and you'll find country cottages carrying $35,000 price tags, though they're unlikely to be in mint condition.

Basically it all comes down to location, location and location. A village property will always be more expensive than a remote cottage embedded in the middle of nowhere. Plots of land beside the Atlantic and backdropped by mountains are likely to cost at least three times as much as sites of similar size deep in the landlocked midlands. And although Dublin is undoubtedly driving the country's property engine, many provincial towns are experiencing what our realtors describe as "buoyancy." The Killarney Lakes in Kerry, the Galway coastline, the harbor towns of county Cork and the wild green glens of Wicklow are all localities where vendors can and do demand a high premium for properties.

THATCHED COTTAGES

Turf smoke curling above a roof of golden thatch? For many overseas buyers, the ideal Irish home is a simple whitewashed cottage standing on its own emerald green acre. Really old-fashioned cottages have what's known as a half-door: The top half can be opened to let in the light and sunshine while the bottom part keeps out the geese and chickens clucking in the yard. Of course, another requirement is a spectacular view: a rugged landscape of shimmering ocean and brooding mountains. And of course, this cottage has to be in immaculate condition.

Be warned. Thatched cottages in the fairy lands of Connemara now sell for telephone number price tags—it seems ironic that these traditional dwellings were once the exclusive preserve of the poor. Every romantically inclined foreigner is chasing the same dream, and any cottage coming onto the market is soon snapped up. For a cottage in picture-perfect condition in popular Connemara villages such as Clifden or Oughterard, the currency of nostalgia won't get you very far. Buyers are willing to pay well over $200,000.

Things get even more expensive if you want to be within an hour or so of Dublin. At the time of writing, a beautiful thatched cottage was on the market at Tomnalossett, a scattering of houses near Enniscorthy in county Wexford. Two bedrooms, whitewashed walls, neat little garden—and a price tag of $230,000. Serious money. I saw another pretty cottage at Bray in county Wicklow with three bedrooms. Price: $345,000. The least expensive thatched cottage in good condition that I saw on the market this year was at Feakle in county Clare; it was priced at $130,000.

If your heart is set on this type of home but funds are tight, the best county in which to search is Donegal. Thatched cottages in so-so condition still occasionally surface for as little as $70,000, but, as in Connemara, you must be prepared to move fast. However, do note that the typical Irish cottage is not a magic cottage whose living space will somehow miraculously expand the moment you've bought it! Rooms are often tiny and there won't be much storage space.

COUNTRY MANSIONS

Other properties that attract foreign attention are the houses of the Anglo-Irish Ascendancy. Many well-heeled buyers cherish the dream of stepping over the threshold of history into a handsome Georgian rectory buried deep in hunting country, the kind of house where you receive your guests in an elegant high-ceilinged drawing room, play croquet on the lawn, and keep horses in a lush green paddock.

What will such a property cost? Well, Whitfield Court, near Kilmeaden in county Waterford, is priced "in excess" of $4,000,000. Yes, four million. Built in 1841, this Greco-Italian style pile with 11 bedrooms and its own gatelodge sits on 200 acres of parkland and woodlands. Its gardens served as a quirky footnote to Ireland's civil war, fought between Free Staters and Republicans. Apparently Whitfield Court's gardener dispatched a letter to the absent owner. He stated, "There were no casualties and both sides greatly admired your Ladyship's antirrhinums," a flower more commonly known as the snapdragon.

Period properties don't come cheap, even in the unfashionable midlands. Though you can find far less expensive properties than Whitfield Court, affluent buyers are still prepared to spend a lot of money for their own slice of historic elegance. A "Georgian gentleman's residence" in Birr, county Offaly, is on the market for more than $530,000. It has three reception rooms, four bedrooms, and a paved enclosed courtyard with lofted stores and a loosebox for a horse.

If you're interested in period country houses and have at least $400,000 to spend, a number of agents specialize in these types of properties. All the following produce glossy brochures covering properties countrywide.

- Ganly Walters, 37 Baggot St. Lower, Dublin 2; tel +353 (0)1 662 3255
- Hamilton Osborne King, 32 Molesworth St., Dublin 2; tel +353 (0)1 663 4343 / 676 0251
- Jackson Stops, 51 Dawson St., Dublin 2; tel +353 (0)1 677 1177

VILLAGE HOUSES AND COTTAGES

More cost-conscious buyers may prefer something simpler. A favorite area with many foreign buyers is West Cork, where sheltered coves string the coastline and village houses are gaily washed in rainbow shades of teal blue, salmon pink and buttery yellow. If you can handle the trauma, buy a property needing plenty of work. You'll almost certainly see an immediate profit if you restore a place and then resell. Admittedly, you may need vision to see the true potential of many run-down properties, but part the cobwebs and you can still find farmhouses needing modernization in the hinterland of this wonderfully scenic area for $60,000. (Similar farmhouse properties for renovation along the coast are very expensive, though.)

As most buyers want a home that's ready to move into, you can make substantial gains by buying a house in sad repair and then fixing it up. Ireland's restoration projects are literally endless. Maybe your idea of bliss is to renovate a quaint old farmhouse down in the strawberry fields of county Wexford or an old schoolhouse in lakeland Leitrim. And, for the really adventurous, there's even the opportunity to capture a tumbledown castle and bring it back to its former glory days.

Bargains occasionally surface in Wexford, down in the corner of Ireland's southeast. When I was here for the October Opera Festival, I saw a charming five-bedroom home in the seaside village of Kilmore priced at $151,000, which seemed a reasonable price for the area. There were quite a few country cottages at around the $59,000 mark too.

Many foreigners who settle here are individualistic types with a taste for rugged simplicity rather than bright lights and the high life. There are no real on-purpose communities where little knots of Americans, Germans or Brits have created a home-away-from-home expatriate lifestyle such as you find in places like Mexico's Lake Chapala, Portugal's Algarve and the Costa del Sol in Spain. Buy a house in Ireland and you really are buying into the local community.

Further information about property prices can be found in the Prime Living Locations chapters, but here are a few examples of what your money would have bought recently:

Under $50,000

$21,000: Natural stone cottage on half acre near Gurteen, county Sligo. Almost derelict.

$32,500: Former schoolhouse at Gusseraine, county Wexford, dating back to 1834. Price reflects the need for renovation—lots of it.

$33,000: "Extensive repairs are required" on a traditional cottage on three acres near Blacklion, county Cavan.

$44,000: Two-bedroom cottage on half acre at Piltown, county Kilkenny. Cut sandstone frontage, but in need of a face lift.

$49,000: Two-bedroom townhouse to modernize in Carrick-on-Suir, county Tipperary.

$50,000–70,000

$53,000: Quaint country cottage for renovation in quiet rural setting near Collinstown, county Westmeath.

$53,000: Three-room Old World cottage on one acre for renovation near Aclare, county Sligo. A stream runs through the plot.

$65,000: Three-room cottage (580 square feet) in reasonable condition with garage and outbuildings in the midlands' green heart, three miles from the county Longford village of Newtownforbes.

$65,000: Two-bedroom village house, recently refurbished, at Kinlough, county Leitrim.

$69,000: Old-style cottage, newly refurbished, with three bedrooms and stone outbuildings near Frenchpark, county Roscommon.

$70,000–90,000

$76,000: Three-bedroom cottage in good condition on one acre of land near Lattin, county Tipperary.

$77,000: Near Tralee, in the northern half of Kerry, bijou roadside cottage, two-bedrooms, refurbished.

$80,000: Three-bedroom traditional cottage with views of Lough Feeagh. Only four miles from Newport, a small seaside town in county Mayo.

$81,000: Modern three-bedroom bungalow near Castlepollard, a small town in the midlands county of Westmeath.

$88,000: Sunshine-yellow cottage in good condition, two bedrooms, on half acre site at Tubber, county Clare.

$88,000: Traditional farmhouse on two acres near Claremorris, county Mayo. Currently occupied and in reasonably good condition.

$90,000–125,000

$97,500: Refurbished three-story townhouse in Wexford town.

$106,000: Three-bedroom house on one acre, in rural area near Ballyhale, county Kilkenny.

$113,000: Pretty whitewashed cottage at Killatarley, three bedrooms, timbered ceilings, recently restored. Near Lough Conn, a well-known fishing lake in county Mayo.

$124,000: Four-bedroom bungalow in Killorglin, a town in the north of county Kerry.

$125,000-plus

$212,000: Fully restored thatched cottage with three bedrooms on half acre near Ballymacodra, county Cork, 10 minutes from Youghal and 40 minutes from Cork City. Timber-paneled ceilings, ocean views, access to beach.

$236,000: Three-bedroom bungalow at Rossnowlagh, site of one of Donegal's best beaches. Spectacular views of Donegal Bay.

$295,000: Five-bedroom house in the attractive Cork harbor town of Kinsale, noted for its gourmet restaurants.

$708,000: Former lighthouse converted into an eight-bedroom home. On Clare Island, county Mayo, the former stronghold of Grace O'Malley, a 16th-century pirate queen.

BUYING A SITE

If it's the case that you've found the perfect location but no properties on the market suit your requirements, you may want to purchase a plot of land and have a house built to your own specifications. An important point to note is that all buyers, whatever their nationality, must obtain planning permission from the local authority before starting building. Once you start scouring the listings of sites for sale, you'll notice that the more expensive sites are in highly desirable scenic areas and carry the magic words "with full planning permission approved."

Just because a site is for sale doesn't necessarily mean you'll be given the green light to build on it. Ireland now has rigorous planning laws and flouting of the regulations can lead to heavy fines. Lax standards in the past resulted in some charmless areas of "ribbon development" in which a number of coastal areas got brutalized by a seemingly endless string of houses of very dubious architectural merit. Traveling the coast road approaches to Galway city can be a shock to those who remember the days when local people lived in simple cottages instead of huge Spanish-style haciendas complete with incongruous Georgian porticos.

Although it's possible to make a planning application yourself, the devil is always in the details and a fair amount of specialist knowledge is required. Most people leave it in the hands of an architect or builder. Your estate agent will introduce you to firms they have dealt with before. One of the first things they'll do is check that building proposals do not conflict with the local authority's Development Plan, which lays down guidelines pertaining to the area. After submitting plans, they then either seek Outline Planning Permission, which essentially establishes approval as to the general nature of the project—OPP for a three-bedroom residence, for example. Alternatively they can apply straight away for the most common type of permission: Full Planning Permission, which entitles the applicant to start building their new home. They (or you) will also need to have a notice of the proposals published in the local newspaper as well as on a board beside the site. This is to give any interested parties advance warning of your plans and to allow them the chance to object.

Once Full Planning Permission has been obtained, it generally applies for a term of five years. If the house hasn't been completed within this time span, it's necessary to make a renewed application for planning permission.

How much it will cost to have a house built obviously depends on the type of residence you have in mind. Current estimates for building costs are $50 to $55 per square foot. A two-bedroom bungalow-style home averages around $60,000. The cost of the land you aim to build on is another matter entirely. Land zoned for development carries a far higher price than farmland, for which you will not usually be given planning permission to build upon. Just because you read an article in the *Farmer's Journal* saying that county Waterford farmland is fetching $8,850 an acre doesn't mean that *all* land in Waterford averages that amount.

When it comes to land zoned for development, the reality is very different. If you want Atlantic views, serviced sites of less than a quarter of an acre are selling for $88,500 a piece in the south coast counties of Waterford and West Cork. In county Galway, half-acre plots around the villages of Oranmore and Clarenbridge are fetching $59,000 to $71,000, though prices fall to $53,000 in the eastern half of the county around Gort.

Looking elsewhere, half-acre sites where Full Planning Permission has already been obtained can be had for $30,000 in rural county Offaly. However, you'll pay at least double that amount for a prime site of similar size overlooking island-studded Lough Derg in county Clare. Around Dublin and the east coast, vendors can practically name their price for sites in the right location. A site with planning permission for a three-bedroom house in county Kildare sold for $209,000. Just to reiterate: That price was for the site alone; to actually build the house would be extra.

In county Wexford, half-acre sites in inland rural areas are fetching $21,000 to $36,000, but similar sites with sea views sell for as much as $118,000. One of the cheapest parts of the country to buy land on which to build is county Cavan. Here half-acre sites sell for between $18,000 and $27,000.

It's also necessary to obtain planning permission if you intend doing major work on an existing building—for example, adding an extension or converting old stables into a residence. Once alterations are complete, you must make sure your builder gives you a Certificate of Compliance to show that planning permission had been granted and work was carried out according to the specific regulations laid down. Keep this certificate with the property deeds because it's an important document that needs to be produced should you eventually wish to resell.

Planning application fees are approximately $50 for newly built houses and $25 for domestic extensions. Plenty of information can be obtained from local authority offices or the Department of the Environment, Custom House, Dublin 1; tel +353 (0)1 679 3377. Helpful booklets are "A Guide to Planning Permission" (PL1), "Making a Planning Application" (PL2), "Building a House: The Planning Issues" (PL4), "Doing Work Around the House: The Planning Issues" (PL5), and "A Guide to Building Regulations" (PL11).

If you want to discuss ideas with an architect, lists of accredited members for a particular locality can be had from the Royal Institute of Architects of Ireland, 8 Merrion Square, Dublin 2; tel +353 (0)1 676 1703.

Non-Nationals Buying Property

As an American, there's nothing to stop you from buying a house or site in Ireland provided that the amount of land amounts to less than two hectares (five acres). If, however, the property comprises more than five acres and falls outside the boundaries of a town or city, you'll need to seek the consent of the Land Commission. This is a government body, part of the Department of Agriculture & Food.

These regulations apply to all non-EU nationals. Although each situation is considered on its individual merits, note that permission is not always forthcoming, particularly if it concerns the sale of a large tract of good quality farmland. On the other hand, if a property includes a substantial acreage of "wilderness" land, you should encounter no problems. Basically it comes down to what the land was previously used for and what you, the prospective new owner, intend to do with it.

Both national and county averages will include everything from castles to tumbledown cottages.

Those who hold dual Irish nationality or can claim citizenship of any other EU country may purchase as much land as they wish in any area whatsoever without seeking government permission. Once you have been resident in Ireland for seven years, you are also exempt from these special regulations. Another point to note is that the proviso does not apply to any house with a large acreage that falls within a town's boundaries.

Further information is available from the Land Commission, Department of Agriculture & Food, Government Buildings, Farnham St., Cavan, county Cavan; tel +353 (0)49 4368200.

Legal Title of Property

Most residential properties in Ireland are registered as "freehold." This means that title to the property can be held forever and is entirely free of rent. Whether you eventually sell a property or bequeath it to your heirs, its legal title always remains as freehold.

You're more likely to come across leasehold titles in relation to city center houses or commercial properties. A leasehold title can be set at anything from 250 to 999 years and usually comes with an annual ground rent payable to the title holder. The years that are left to run on a lease invariably affect the price of a property, but it's occasionally possible to buy out the lease and obtain freehold title. As leasehold titles can be complicated, do seek legal advice before signing any contracts.

How to Buy Property

Irish properties are sold mostly through estate agents (realtors), also called auctioneers. Unfortunately, there is no real multiple-listing system like in the States, and most agents have their own particular little cache of proper-

This family bungalow in county Sligo operates as a Bed & Breakfast business.

© Steenie Harvey

the Dos and Don'ts of Property Buying

DO thoroughly investigate the area where you intend to buy and visit it at different times of year, not just in summer.

DO talk to locals. They will know what houses in the locality are selling for.

DO visit a number of estate agents to compare properties and prices.

DO use professionals and have legal title to a property approved by a solicitor.

DO remember you haven't legally secured a property until both buyer and seller have signed formal contract documents. Oral agreements count for nothing.

DO arrange insurance coverage. Ideally it should be in place on the day you visit the solicitor's office to sign the final contract.

DO ensure money is transferred through correct banking channels with a proper record of the transaction.

DO make sure sufficient funds are available if buying at auction. Successful bidders have to pay 10 percent of the purchase price on the day of sale.

DON'T buy sight (or site) unseen.

DON'T buy while on vacation. Arrange a proper house-hunting trip. An even better idea is to rent a house before you buy.

DON'T write to estate agents asking for details of "quaint little cottages in western Ireland." They will require you to be far more specific regarding locality and price range.

DON'T be unrealistic. You're not going to find a chocolate-box thatched farmstead for $25,000.

DON'T shave on costs. Get that surveyor's report.

DON'T forget to allow for additional fees and charges.

DON'T start building your dream home without first obtaining planning permission.

DON'T even think about attending an auction if you're one of life's impulsive characters.

ties. This means buyers have to do a lot of legwork to get around to the various offices. Most agents belong to professional bodies such as the Irish Auctioneers & Valuers Institute (IAVI) or the Institute of Professional Auctioneers and Valuers (IPAV). Members must adhere to certain standards of practice and are bonded by deposit protection funds. As a buyer, you will not be liable for the estate agent's fee for selling a property. This is met by the vendor and generally amounts to between 2.5 and 3.5 percent of the sale price.

The main method of sale for residential properties is through "private treaty," whereby a suggested price level is placed on the property. This is only a guideline price and a property may eventually change hands for more or less than the price you'll see advertised in a newspaper or an estate agent's window. It's quite acceptable to make an offer, particularly if a house has been on the market for some time. The owners may be prepared to accept a lower sum than the guideline price.

A guideline price is not binding on the vendor, so ensure any agreement is put in writing. Oral deals are not legally enforceable. Have you heard the term "gazumping"? What it means is the acceptance of a higher offer by the seller, despite having verbally agreed to sell their property to someone else.

Gazumping does happen, particularly in today's market in which house values are continually rising.

Second-hand properties are sold according to the principle of *caveat emptor*—buyer beware. Do make sure any contractual agreement you sign is "subject to surveyor's report." Whether you're interested in a $50,000 cottage or a million-dollar mansion, it would be senseless to go ahead and buy without first engaging a surveyor or architect to check for structural defects. A surveyor's report may save you a lot of money as well as heartache in the long run.

Do *you* know if a house's foundations are crumbling away? The vendors (and their estate agent) are under no legal obligation to tell you so. Should a surveyor actually uncover a horror story, you're entitled to withdraw your offer and get your deposit back—that is, if you've insisted that the contract covers this eventuality, of course. Surveyors' fees average $230. A list of members can be obtained from the Society of Chartered Surveyors, 5 Wilton Place, Dublin 2; tel +353 (0)1 676 5500. Email: info@scs.ie.

Before agreeing to buy a property and put down the usual 10 percent deposit, it's wise to consult an Irish solicitor (attorney) of your own to ensure your interests are properly protected. Although it's not essential, most buyers use a solicitor to handle the actual conveyancing of a property—that is, drawing up a formal contract and getting the deeds transferred into their name.

As well as helping with negotiations on the purchase price, the deposit, the date you can take possession and any special contract conditions, your solicitor will check to ensure the title of the property is free and clear. If necessary, he or she can also obtain permission for the sale from the Land Commission.

The entire process normally takes between six and eight weeks. The balance of the purchase price is paid to the seller only after your solicitor is satisfied that you are acquiring good and marketable title to the property. Your estate agent should be able to point you in the direction of a local solicitor. Alternatively get a list of members from the Law Society of Ireland, Blackhall Place, Dublin 7; tel +353 (0)1 672 4800. Website: www.lawsociety.ie.

The standard fee charged by solicitors is $118 plus 1 percent of the purchase price, plus the 20 percent VAT that has to be added to all professional charges. It all sounds horribly baffling and expensive, but translating it into dollar terms, this is how it works in practice: On a $50,000 property, fees would amount to $618 and VAT to $123.60, $741.60 in total.

Auction Sales

Around 6 percent of Irish properties are sold at auction, and it's these sales that tend to hog the headlines. In general, the type of properties that come under the hammer include a varied selection of Dublin houses, large country mansions and estates, farms with a substantial acreage of grazing land,

and business concerns such as busy town center pubs or hotels in well-known tourist locations.

Auction properties are advertised four to six weeks in advance of the sale date, which gives time for potential buyers to evaluate a property and get a surveyor's report. In the past, some vendors sold at auction because their house had languished on the market for years and any sale price was better than none at all. Nowadays things are different. In an ever-soaring market it can be difficult to put a value on certain types of property, and auction-eers are achieving fantastic results for clients who choose to sell by this method, often 20 percent and more above guideline prices. Astute vendors are also aware that people tend to get carried away at auctions, often bidding more than a property is really worth.

The "reserve" placed on a property is the minimum price a seller will accept. Reserve prices can differ from advertised guideline prices as the seller is not obliged to determine the reserve price until the actual day of the auction. An IAVI directive states that the guideline figure should be within 10 percent of what the auctioneer reckons the reserve price will be. As this doesn't always happen, some would-be buyers suffer immense disappointment when the prize property sells for far more than they anticipated. To rub salt in the wound, nobody is going to refund their out-of-pocket expenses for valuation and surveyor's reports.

Should you decide to buy at auction and your bid proves to be the highest acceptable offer, the purchase contract has to be signed there and then. You must also pay a 10 percent deposit immediately. The balance becomes due when all the legalities have been completed, usually six to eight weeks afterwards.

Unlike with private treaty sales, you cannot contract to buy subject to a surveyor's report being satisfactory. This should have been done before the sale date and you bid unconditionally. If, for any reason, you cannot complete the sale, you can wave farewell to your 10 percent deposit.

Other Charges

Along with solicitors' and surveyors' fees, a number of other charges are involved. Registration fees can be of two types; your solicitor will advise which one is appropriate. Land Registry attracts a levy of approximately $300 and includes registration of any mortgage. The cheaper option, Registry of Deeds, costs around $31 if the purchase is outright, $62 if a mortgage is involved.

STAMP DUTY
This is essentially a government purchase tax. To alleviate the housing problem in Ireland, the band-rates at which new buyers were levied for stamp

Stamp Duty Rates

Current Value	1st Time Buyer Occupying	Existing Owner Occupying	Residential Investment Property
Up to $118,000	NIL	NIL	9%
$118,000 to $177,000	NIL	3%	9%
$177,000 to $236,000	3%	4%	9%
$236,000 to $295,000	3.75%	5%	9%
$295,000 to $354,000	4.5%	6%	9%
$354,000 to $590,000	7.5%	7.5%	9%
Above $590,000	9%	9%	9%

duty were lowered in the last budget, though things have become more expensive for Irish buyers in the market for second homes, such as up-market holiday cottages. In another move to take the heat out the market, stamp duty rates for all investment properties were set at 9 percent. The rules were a lot simpler prior to January 2001, but this is how stamp duty works at the moment. Calculations were made on the basis that 1 euro equals $0.87.

Although Stamp Duty is not levied on the actual construction of new homes, it does apply to the purchase price of sites. However, only very substantial or expensive plots of land attract Stamp Duty. Relief from Stamp Duty is available to first-time buyers of any newly built home if the floor area is less than 125 square meters. If the floor area is greater than this, duty becomes payable on 25 percent of the house price or the site value,

Dublin's renowned for its Georgian doors—these are on Merrion Square.

© Steenie Harvey

whichever is greater. Fees, payable through your solicitor, are made on the day when final contracts are exchanged.

APPLICATION FEE
This will concern you only if you've arranged financing or a mortgage to buy a property. Charged by banks and building societies, it's sometimes levied as a percentage of the loan, typically 0.5 percent, or a flat fee of $118 to $177.

VALUATION FEE
Again, this applies only if you're arranging financing. All lenders require prospective mortgagers to pay for a valuation report on how much any property they seek a loan against is worth. Fees are typically $120 plus VAT of 20 percent.

MORTGAGE STAMP DUTY
Borrowers pay an additional government levy of 0.1 percent (up to a maximum of $590) on all mortgages over $23,600.

House Insurance

For peace of mind, get your house insured. You should arrange coverage from the moment you sign the final contract. In general, premiums are lower in rural areas where rebuilding costs are cheaper and the risk of burglaries is far less than in the cities.

It's impossible to give exact quotations, though the examples below will give you a good idea of current insurance premiums. A home with a thatched roof will be seen as being at greater risk for fire damage than a modern bungalow. Similarly a house with a cellar that is sited beside a river could carry a fair risk of flood damage. Thus it will undoubtedly attract higher premiums than a similar house perched on top of a hill.

House Insurance Rates

DUBLIN AREA			PROVINCES		
Sum Insured	Contents Insurance	Yearly Premium	Sum Insured	Contents Insurance	Yearly Premium
$118,000	$35,000	$286	$83,000	$25,000	$154
$177,000	$53,000	$379	$118,000	$35,000	$207
$236,000	$71,000	$505	$177,000	$53,000	$311
$295,000	$88,000	$623	$236,000	$71,000	$414
$354,000	$106,000	$758	$295,000	$88,000	$518
			$354,000	$106,000	$633

Many insurance companies compete for business, and it's possible to get some good discounts. AMEV, for example, allows a 21 percent discount for clients with a burglar alarm who are over 45 years of age. Guardian PMPA offers a 20 percent discount to customers who already have car insurance with the company. As offers differ from year to year, shop around to get quotes. The best way is by using the Golden Pages of the local phone directory. As with car insurance, the umbrella organization for brokerage firms is the Irish Brokers Association. For a list of members, contact them at 87 Merrion Square, Dublin 2; tel +353 (0)1 661 3061.

Property Taxes

Even if you own a mansion, you won't need to worry about property taxes. Although high-value properties did once attract an annual levy, all property taxes have since been abolished. Rates (local authority charges) apply only to commercial properties, not the residential sector. They vary from county to county. For a small business such as a pub, expect to pay annual rates somewhere in the region of $1,000.

Water is there for the taking unless you belong to one of the country's small number of private water schemes. Charges average $120 per year, but even these schemes are expected to become free shortly.

However, unless you fancy the idea of buying a trailer and hauling all your household trash to the local dump, you'll have to pay for refuse collection. Charges are set by local authorities and private contractors and are levied at an annual rate of between $175 and $235.

PRIME LIVING
LOCATIONS

North Channel

ATLANTIC OCEAN

Tory Island

Fanad
Head

Malin Head

Rathlin
Island

Aran
Island

Donegal

Lough
Foyle

Londonderry

Ballymena

Rossan Point

Donegal

Donegal

**NORTHERN
IRELAND
(UK)**

Belfast

Donegal Bay

Lough
Erne

Lough
Neagh

Strangford
Lough

Erris
Head

Belmullet

Sligo Bay

Sligo

Monaghan

*Dundrum
Bay*

Achill
Island

Mayo

Sligo

Leitrim

Cavan

Dundalk

Dundalk Bay

Castlebar

Roscommon

Longford

Louth

Drogheda

**THE NORTHWEST
PASSAGE**

Clare Island

Clew Bay

Inishturk

Lough
Ree

*Irish
Sea*

Inishbofin

Lough
Mask

Tuam

Westmeath

Meath

River Boyne

**THE WESTERN
SEABOARD**

Galway

Athlone

Lough
Corrib

Galway

Offaly

R. Liffey

Dublin

Dublin

Galway Bay

Kildare

Wicklow
Mountains

Aran Islands

Clare

Laois

Wicklow

Wicklow

Hag's Head

Ennis

Lough
Derg

Carlow

St. George's Channel

Loop Head

*River
Shannon*

Tipperary

Limerick

Kilkenny

Wexford

Limerick

Tralee Bay

Tralee

Limerick

Carrick-on-Suir

Wexford

Rosslare Bay

Killarney

Mallow

Waterford

Waterford

**THE SUNNY
SOUTHEAST**

Kerry

THE SOUTHWEST

Cork

Dungarvan

Youghal Bay

Kenmare River

Caha Mountains

River Lee

Cork

Bantry

Old Head
of Kinsale

Cork Harbour

Mizen Head

Cape
Clear

Galley
Head

Celtic Sea

N

W E

S

13 Prime Living Locations

Although the following chapters on Prime Living Locations do not detail all of the Republic's 26 counties, they will give you a good indication of price levels in the places most foreign buyers are drawn to. Of the unmentioned counties, some are downright unaffordable. Others don't offer a great deal in the way of scenic splendor, not unless you have a peculiar yearning for endless vistas of sugar beet fields or flat brown boglands being plowed up by industrial machines. That's not to say you won't find attractive homes in the unmentioned counties. Ardagh in county Longford really is as pretty as a picture; it deserved to scoop the title of Ireland's Tidiest Village in 1998.

The regions and counties I have highlighted offer properties in all price ranges. But although it's an important consideration, cost shouldn't be the only factor when it comes to choosing where to live. So what makes these particular regions special?

Well, in a way, I suppose my choices have been influenced by my own particular interests: folklore, walking and wildlife. While I've included some urban options, I rather think that most people who dream of a home in Ireland probably desire the kind of environment that attracted me— perhaps a village with wild seascapes all around, or one where the view is of green fields, golden gorse and distant mountains. I'm also drawn to any place that murmurs of long ago—pilgrim paths, prehistoric forts, holy wells—and you don't find those kind of places in cities.

167

Although I'm happy with where I've settled, that doesn't stop me from imagining what it would be like to live elsewhere. One of my favorite memories is this: walking down a deserted lane in West Cork on a hot summer's day, through tunnel-like hedgerows of wild blood-red fuchsias, and coming across a perfect circle of standing stones dating back to before the Celts. Beyond this incredibly ancient place I could glimpse the sapphire shimmer of the sea and little whitewashed homes nestled in the folds of the hills. If any place could be described as a perfect location, this one came close.

The Southwest of Ireland

The southwest, which takes in the counties of Cork and Kerry, is one of the most sought-after areas by foreign buyers. It's easy to understand why. This region has some of the most varied and beautiful landscapes in the whole of Ireland: golden beaches and rugged peninsulas, mountains and lakes, colorful villages where houses are painted in a riot of rainbow colors.

> *This region has some of the most varied and beautiful landscapes in the whole of Ireland.*

Drifting down the coastline, there are just so many places that tug at the heart strings: harbor town Kinsale, Clonakilty, Kenmare, Dingle, dozens of friendly little towns and villages I'm sure you'll fall head over heels in love with. In the chapter on southwestern Ireland, I've also included details on one of the lesser-known counties, Tipperary. Although it lacks a seacoast, its gentle pastoral scenery is very appealing, and full of historic interest too. It's here you will find the awe-inspiring Rock of Cashel as well as the Silvermines Mountains and the still waters of Lough Derg.

The Sunny Southeast

In the southeastern chapter, you'll find details about the counties of Wexford, Waterford and Kilkenny. Wexford, a former Viking stronghold, is almost like a home-away-from-home for me. I come down here every year for the October opera festival and to do some bird-watching. While most people tend to associate seaside counties with summer pleasures, the great swathes of golden beaches that extend round the corner into county Waterford are an absolute joy to walk during the late fall and on a clear crisp winter's day.

The southeast hinterland is pretty special too. One of the most enjoyable vacations I've had in Ireland was a walking tour around Waterford's Nire Valley and Comeragh Mountains. Kilkenny, a town with a real medieval feel to it, is another of my favorite locations. I went there to research an article on Irish witchcraft but spent just as much time exploring the surrounding countryside of green river valleys and tumbledown monasteries. County Kilkenny acts like a magnet to craft workers, and you'll find lovely villages here such as Inistioge and Graiguenamanagh.

The Western Seaboard

Strung with offshore islands, the western seaboard counties of Galway, Mayo and Clare have a wildness about them, and it's no exaggeration to say the changing lightscapes of the mountainous Connemara area are an artist's delight. Renowned for its music and folklore, this is another region that has given me immense pleasure over the years: searching for rare spring orchids in Clare's Burren, climbing the holy mountain of Croagh Patrick in Mayo, and going to Galway to eat oysters, experience the fun of the Ballinasloe Horse Fair and take the ferry to the Aran Islands. It's a great place to live if you want to immerse yourself in traditional ways and, with Galway city within easy reach, enjoy 21st-century amenities at the same time.

The Northwest and Lakelands

If I had to sum up the northwest and lakelands in three words, I'd use unspoiled, uncrowded and undiscovered. This is my own home region and, so

county Clare's stonescaped Burren

© Steenie Harvey

far, it has managed to escape the notice of the crowds. I can't understand why. County Sligo, named by the poet W. B. Yeats as "the Land of Heart's Desire," is beautiful, full of wistful landscapes and fascinating legends. Donegal offers more than 200 miles of spectacular coastline and an intriguing Gaeltacht area where the old music, songs and dances are preserved and celebrated.

Delve into the lakeland counties of Roscommon, Cavan and Leitrim and you'll discover quintessential Ireland—country Ireland, if you like. These three counties of quiet lanes, sparkling loughs and small villages are what I think of as "the real Ireland," the kind of place where everybody knows everybody else's granny as well as their third cousin twice removed. And it's full of historical interest. The Tain, one of Ireland's oldest epic legends, begins at Cruachan, the present-day village of Rathcroghan in county Roscommon. According to the annals, this Neolithic site of earthen raths, standing pillars and a circular bull ring enclosure was the location of Queen Maeve's palace.

I think the reason why most people ignore Ireland's lakelands is that there are no mountains or seascapes—in other words, the kind of picture-postcard landscapes you see in tourist brochures.

Yet I would never say the scenery is boring. My own house overlooks a lough, and on a clear day I've got distant views of the Sligo Mountains. And there are plenty of wonderful walks here too—across the low hills to glittery little loughs, out to holy wells and through the bluebell woods. You do really have to live in the area to appreciate it though. All the best places are out of sight, lost in the tangled maze of back roads. It was only last year that I discovered a mossy stone court cairn from Celtic times, buried in woodlands a couple of miles from my home.

Lough Arrow, south Sligo

© Steenie Harvey

Why Dublin's Not Covered

Why no in-depth look at the Dublin property market? Well, to be honest, I think Ireland's capital and its satellite counties (Meath, Kildare and Wicklow) are ridiculously overpriced. House values in the east of Ireland have absolutely rocketed in recent years, and most young Irish buyers are saddling themselves with huge mortgages simply to get on the first rung of the housing ladder. Leaf through the property sections in the *Irish Times* and *Irish Independent* and you'd think the streets of the capital were paved with emeralds. A two-bedroom apartment in the city center? Yours for a mere $452,000.

Most three-bedroom family residences in the outer suburban residential areas easily command $300,000. In the most sought-after Dublin neighborhoods, you can expect to pay a lot more. During 2000, some Dublin houses sold for over $5 million. But although the $5 million home is still a rarity, let me give you a typical example of an "ordinary" family home. In Dublin's Terenure neighborhood, a four-bedroom family home (1,490 square feet) with two reception rooms, kitchen/dining area, bathroom, garage, and 120 feet rear garden is priced at $429,500. It's not even a detached house, only semi-detached, which means it shares a partition wall with a neighbor.

In the Dublin seaside suburb of Dalkey, $367,000 is being sought for an 860-square-foot bungalow. In Malahide, a new development of semi-detached houses is being sold off-plan: the developer's advertisement reads "prices from $350,000." A period residence (2,580 square feet) in Blackrock "requiring some modernisation" carries a price tag of $734,500. Want to buy a Dublin guesthouse? Be warned that they sell for scary sums; one in the Clontarf area of north Dublin made $960,000 at auction. Most pubs sell in excess of $2 million.

Incidentally, I've seen "retirement location" pages on the Internet indicating pretty stone cottages in Dublin's surrounding countryside sell for between $10,000 and $20,000. The authors neglect to say where exactly these cottages are located and which agents are selling them. It's not surprising: The $20,000 east coast cottage is nothing but a figment of the imagination. Please don't come to Ireland expecting to find such bargains because you'll be doomed to disappointment. Anything remotely habitable in the Meath, Kildare and Wicklow countryside fetches at least $145,000. All these counties are within easy commuting distance of the capital, and buyers are paying premium prices.

A Few More Things to Note

The thing is, Ireland is a divided country—and I'm not talking about Northern Ireland and the Republic. The realm of $5 million homes is a very different place from the Ireland that I know. During my research for this book, I traveled all over the country, and I've just been looking at a realtor's listing sheet I picked up. It shows a nice three-bedroom village house that just sold for $45,200—an exceptionally low price, but it's not alone. There are some other attractive little cottages on the list for $56,500 and $67,800.

These properties were on sale through a realtor in a town called Mohill. It's a very small place—two churches, three supermarkets, a dozen or so pubs, and country lanes leading off in all directions. Now, I'm sure most of you have probably never even heard of Mohill. It's way up in Ireland's northwest, in the lakeland county of Leitrim. You may not have heard of Leitrim either as it's one of those counties the travel guidebooks tend to skip over. There's nothing much here to attract tourists, no showpiece sights, no Blarney Castles, none of that medieval banquet nonsense.

> *Delve into the lakeland counties of Roscommon, Cavan and Leitrim and you'll discover quintessential Ireland.*

What you get instead is Ireland as it used to be—no cinema, no night-clubs, no fancy bistros or coffee shops. Mohill's gastronomic center is the Soup Bowl Café, where you can still get a pot of tea for 60 cents. Despite what you'll see in Dublin, a lot of Ireland's small towns are just like this one: close-knit rural communities that are pleasingly sedate and old-fashioned. When I visited, Mohill was having its big event of the year, the Agricultural Show. The town was absolutely jam-packed with tractors and all kinds of beasts of the field. It's not the kind of place that would appeal to a person who can't live without glitz and glamour, but why are you considering Ireland in the first place? If you're looking for peace, relaxation and a way of life that is still neighborly and civilized, I think Mohill and other places like it will suit you to a tee. What I'm saying is, be adventurous! Head away from the capital, its commuter belt and all those places the travel guides point you towards. Even pricier, high-profile counties such as Kerry and Cork aren't necessarily beyond your reach if you look to places like Listowel and Bantry instead of the tourist localities. Take a foray up to Ballina and the unsung shores of north Mayo, where cozy bungalows with Atlantic views sell for enticing prices. Prefer an Ireland scattered with low hills and little loughs? Try Cavan, undoubtedly the most "undiscovered" county of all.

Affordable cottages in lovely rural locations can still be found in most parts of Ireland—if you know where to look.

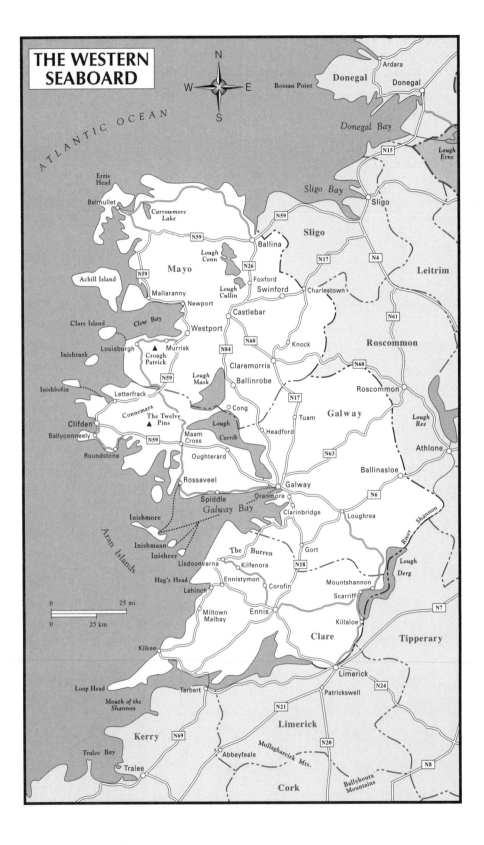

THE WESTERN SEABOARD

N W E S

ATLANTIC OCEAN

Donegal

Ardara

Rossan Point

Donegal

Donegal Bay

N15

Lough Erne

Erris Head

Belmullet

Carrowmore Lake

N59

Sligo Bay

Sligo

Sligo

N59

Ballina

Lough Conn

N26

Sligo

N17

N4

Leitrim

Achill Island

N59

Mayo

Mallaranny

Foxford

Swinford

Charlestown

Lough Cullin

N61

Newport

Castlebar

Roscommon

Clare Island

Clew Bay

Westport

N60

Knock

Louisburgh

Murrisk

Croagh Patrick

N84

Claremorris

N60

Roscommon

Inishturk

Ballinrobe

Roscommon

Lough Mask

N17

Galway

Lough Ree

Inishbofin

Letterfrack

Cong

Tuam

Athlone

Connemara

The Twelve Pins

Lough Corrib

Headford

N63

Clifden

Maam Cross

N59

Ballinasloe

Ballyconneely

Oughterard

N6

Roundstone

Rossaveel

Galway

Loughrea

Spiddle

Oranmore

Clarinbridge

River Shannon

Galway Bay

Inishmore

Gort

Lough Derg

Aran Islands

Inishmaan

Inisheer

The Burren

N18

Lisdoonvarna

Kilfenora

Mountshannon

Hag's Head

Ennistymon

Corofin

Scarriff

Lehinch

N7

Miltown Malbay

Ennis

Killaloe

Kilkee

Clare

Tipperary

Loop Head

Tarbert

Limerick

Patrickswell

N24

Mouth of the Shannon

N21

Limerick

Kerry

N69

Mullaghareirk Mts.

N20

N8

Tralee Bay

Abbeyfeale

Ballyhoura Mountains

Tralee

Cork

0   25 mi

0   25 km

14 The Western Seaboard

Once visited, never forgotten! A land of stone-walled fields and melancholy mountains, Ireland's Wild West offers up all the wilderness you could ever wish for. If you're nostalgic for the "traditional Ireland" of ancient ways and curious festivals, this beautiful region will fit the bill.

County Galway

Few counties can rival Galway for scenic splendor, particularly on cloudless days when the mirror-clear light lends the qualities of feyness and illusion. Forty shades of green? Galway's canvas is painted in a myriad of changing hues: the mountains of the Twelve Bens etched in delicate blues and violets, the uplands a bronzed carpet splashed with golden gorse and the white flecks of sheep. As spring turns to summer, pale waterlilies brocade the loughs, and the countryside around Kylemore Abbey explodes in a pink bonfire blaze of wild rhododendrons. Westward the colorfest is completed by white coral strands and shadowy humped islands that drift like whales in the blue-green swell of the Atlantic.

For many people, the very essence of Irishness seems rooted in this western county. It's a popular location for both foreign buyers and wealthy

Dubliners seeking holiday homes. Both sets of buyers tend to yearn for old-fashioned cottages and farmsteads in the legendary lands of Connemara, the name given to the scenic northern region of the county. For local buyers, proximity to Galway city is a top priority and most prefer modern homes, usually a newly minted bungalow. While it's true that these type of homes hold little appeal for traditionalists, there's no denying they're far warmer and cozier than the vernacular thatched dwellings of times past.

Although house values within the county are considered expensive, there *is* a two-tier market. An hour's drive from the coastline, the small sleepy towns of agricultural eastern Galway are off the tourist trail, and houses are therefore a lot more affordable. Even if Connemara is beyond your price range, you can still have a piece of Galway at prices that won't break the bank. Look to the Fields of Athenry (yes, Athenry exists) and countryside areas around towns such as Ballinasloe, Headford, Loughrea and Tuam.

GALWAY CITY

The West's self-styled "cultural capital" is a medieval seaport city of twisty, atmospheric lanes and scores of traditional music pubs. Galway's origins date back to the 13th century, when a settlement grew up around a castle built by Richard de Burgo. As a trading port, the city developed strong links with other European maritime cities, and it's widely believed that Columbus came here before his epic voyage to the Americas.

a Galway busker

© Steenie Harvey

A stone's throw from the bus and railway stations, the hub of today's city is Eyre Square. Here you'll find all of the big banks and building societies, the grand old edifice of the Great Southern Hotel and also a monument to the Galway Hooker—not an infamous lady of the night, but one of the local sailing boats! Interesting pubs and little specialty shops are found on aptly named Shop

Street, which links Eyre Square to Spanish Arch and the Corrib River, where old wharfside warehouses have been transformed into attractive apartments. Delve into the adjoining lanes and you'll come across tempting little courtyard restaurants and bistros, many specializing in seafood.

University students add year-round vibrancy to the place, but it's in summer that things get really hectic. Galway's arts, music and theater scene has gained legendary status, and legions of tourists from all over the globe arrive to experience festival fever—everything from horseracing to oyster extravaganzas. The 12-day arts festival in July is always tremendous fun, so don't miss it. Its highlight a colorful street pageant, previous themes have centered on Noah's Ark and the Fairy Horde.

House prices in Galway and its suburbs reflect the fact that there has been a population explosion: up from 25,000 inhabitants in the 1960s to around 60,000 today. Over the past 10 years, Galway has held the title of Ireland's fastest-growing city, largely due to an influx of jobs in both tourism and information technology. Major U.S. companies such as Intel, Compaq and Boston Scientific all have bases here. General engineering (26%), information technology (25%) and health-care products (17%) are the dominant sectors. With growth expected to increase further, the city is constantly drawing people into its employment orbit. Once-sleepy communities like Oranmore, Spiddal and the oyster village of Clarinbridge have become an inextricable part of the western commuter belt.

> *Galway's canvas is painted in a myriad of changing hues.*

Official statistics put the average price of new homes in the Galway region at $139,000, second-hand homes at $130,000. However, that's the average for the whole county, and estate agents' guideline prices for solid family homes near Galway city center are more likely to be pitched upwards of $150,000. In the city's sought-after residential neighborhoods such as Taylor's Hill, Kingston Road and Threadneedle, the price of Victorian and Edwardian townhouses can easily soar above $500,000. Within the city itself, the only kind of properties you are likely to find for under $100,000 are former "corporation" houses. These were built by the council to rent out to needy families who couldn't afford their own homes. During the late 1980s and early 1990s, a number were sold to tenants, who have since sold again in the private market. Being on estates, these lookalike homes are not particularly attractive. A typical selling price is $93,500.

Due to the high cost of development land around the city, the majority of newly built developments are apartments. Again, prices aren't cheap. Two-bedroom townhouse apartments in Galway's seaside suburb of Salthill start at $192,000, and three-bedroom duplex apartments fetch

$243,000. In the newly fashionable docks area of the city, a two-bedroom apartment with ocean views is being sold for almost $255,000. Monthly rents for most properties are in $565 to $850. For example, a two-bedroom furnished apartment on Headford Road rents for $768 monthly through O'Donnellan & Joyce.

THE SUBURBS AND BEYOND

Move away from the city environs and prices vary from $50,000 for an isolated cottage in *extremely* sad repair to $565,000 or more for a lovingly restored Georgian mansion in a desirable setting. If you fancy building a dream home here, a typical price for a half-acre site is $51,000, but it can be a lot more. For example, sites currently on the market include a half-acre plot at Moycullen, six miles from Galway, priced at $186,000.

Depending on size and location, refurbished cottages and houses mostly fall into the $80,000-to-$225,000 bracket. The typical two- or three-bedroom bungalow usually fetches at least $90,000 in the eastern half of the county and invariably carries a substantial premium if in a prime scenic area of the west. To cite some typical examples, for $96,000 you could buy a two-bedroom cottage in a quiet rural area near Tuam. However, another two-bedroom cottage in Renville village near Oranmore (a lot closer to Galway and with seaside scenery) is priced at $164,000.

More than anything else, what buyers pay for is location: A bungalow with views of the mountains and Clifden Bay, and within a short walk of a sandy beach, is priced at $407,000. Clifden is the main tourist center of Connemara, so this is an area where you have to expect to pay premium prices. It's renowned for its beautiful beaches. A further attraction is the nearby Championship golf course at Ballyconneely.

CONNEMARA

County Galway's mountainous fringe, Connemara, lies west of Lough

the Claddagh Ring

Although Claddagh village is now just another of suburban Galway's housing estates, the fame of this former fishing community lives on in the shape of Claddagh rings. Usually made of gold, these unusual love tokens have a 300-year-old history. Tradition tells of a local boy, Richard Joyce, who was kidnapped by Barbary pirates while traveling to the West Indies. The corsairs sold him to an Algerian master who taught him the secrets of the goldsmithing trade.

When Richard Joyce returned to Galway in the 1690s, he founded his own goldsmith's shop and designed the Claddagh ring. The clasped hands signify friendship, the crown symbolizes loyalty and, depending on which way you wear it, the heart motif stands for love. If the heart points inwards, you are telling the world that your own heart is spoken for. If it points outwards, you are available and seeking a new suitor!

Corrib and has long been a popular location with foreign buyers. More a state of mind than a map reference, its haunting beauty can inspire both joy and melancholy as well as the urge to grab a paintbrush. Many first-time visitors are surprised that Connemara isn't a county in its own right for this seems to be the Ireland of donkeys, turf stacks and little white-washed cottages that imagination promised.

The well-trampled routes are in north Connemara, mostly around Clifden and the villages of Roundstone, Ballyconneely and Letterfrack. Clifden, home of the Connemara Pony Show, is an exceptionally pretty community where houses are colorwashed in an artist's palette of forget-me-not blue, salmon pink and pale primrose yellow. The town's plethora of craft shops, sweater outlets, pubs and restaurants suggests that North Connemara isn't exactly virgin territory. Estate agents' listings soon confirm that there's no such thing as bargain properties here. Substantial old-style houses within the town center can fetch as much as $282,000, although large modern houses can be had for $181,000 to $192,000. The most inexpensive home in good condition I saw in this area was priced at $135,000.

Like I said, don't expect bargains. West of Clifden, at Ballyconneely, a lovely four-bedroom traditional cottage with views over Errismore and the Atlantic is priced at $255,000. Even one-bedroom cottages "in need of renovation" near the villages of Cleggan and Roundstone can command prices of over $105,000. Roundstone is particularly easy to fall in love with. It's a quaint fishing village with a toy-town harbor where you can watch nets and lobster pots being repaired. Although no planning permission for any new residence had yet been given, an acre site containing the ruins of an old cottage near this village recently sold for $136,000.

Another Connemara village that demands buyers to have fairly deep pockets is Oughterard. Its location is magical, on the western shore of Lough Corrib, which is peppered with uninhabited wooded islets and home to flocks of wild swans. This is the heart of thatched cottage country, but, unfortunately, these storybook dwellings command very high prices and tend to get snapped up like hotcakes. In good condition, a three-bedroom thatched cottage near Oughterard would fetch at least $200,000. However, if you're willing to undertake some restoration work, you can still find old (unthatched) cottages in so-so condition for around $55,000. Be warned, though, that for this kind of price they'll be very small: kitchen/living room, one bedroom, and maybe an attic room built into the roof. Within Oughterard town, two-bedroom apartments fetch $127,000.

This is actually quite a good area to track down affordable properties for long-term rental. Properties available through Matt O'Sullivan's Oughterard office include a two-bedroom fully furnished apartment on the town's Main

Street for $543 per month. A four-bedroom house, fully furnished, in the Portcarron area of Oughterard is available for $588 monthly.

The countryside south of Maam Cross remains more of an uncharted wilderness. Here Connemara's coastline breaks up into a filigree fretwork of peninsulas with islands chained fast to the mainland by stone causeways. This is Iar Connacht—wild, isolated and veined with some of the most penitential roads in Ireland. It's a buyer's best bet for obtaining an affordable slice of Connemara with "renovation project" cottages occasionally surfacing for under $55,000. Though they're getting rare, a tiny one-bedoom thatched cottage was on offer earlier this year for $80,000. The cozier comforts of a small modern bungalow cost around $100,000 in these parts, not too high a price considering that most houses in this mazy land of waterscapes have at least one view of the sea.

The Irish word for "west," *Iar*, also means "the end," a place where everything runs out. A Gaeltacht enclave where most inhabitants speak Irish as their first language, Iar Connacht can evoke fear and dread in urban teenagers. During the summer holidays, scores of city schoolkids are packed off here to improve their language skills. Boarding with local families, both eager and reluctant students are thoroughly immersed in their native tongue.

Not every youngster appreciates the south Connemara experience. No cable TV or discos, just Gaelic games, *ceilidh* nights and the jabber of Radio na Gaeltachta. Irish summer schools bar English-speaking for the duration and also frown on what is quaintly termed "keeping company" with the opposite sex. Rebellious offenders are sent home and, as fees are non-refundable, parental reaction can easily be surmised.

THE ARAN ISLANDS IN GALWAY BAY

Irish is also the day-to-day language of Inishmore (Arainn), Inishmaan (Inis Meain) and Inisheer (Inis Oirr), the Aran Island trio cast adrift in Galway Bay. Leaving aside Aran sweaters, the islanders' most outstanding achievement is managing to create minuscule fields from barren rock, a centuries-old endeavor involving seaweed, shelly soil and animal dung. Cleared stones were used to build the hundreds of miles of gateless walls that prevent the islands' precious soil from being blown away by the Atlantic's buffeting gales.

Farmers and fishermen on the Aran Islands have long been waging battle against the elements. Their stark lifestyle inspired numerous Celtic Revival dramas as well as 1932's classic documentary, *Man of Aran*. Its American director, Robert Flaherty, certainly believed in artistic license. He wanted to show the islanders' continuing dependence on the basking shark industry, even though it had expired half a century before. And so the fishermen set out to capture a monster of the deep, braving a storm in a fragile hide-coated canoe, shaped like a new moon and known as a *currach*. During the tourist season, the documentary is shown three times a day in Kilronan, Inishmore's main village.

Due to the high transportation costs of building materials, houses on the Aran Islands aren't cheap. Few properties are available for renovation, and the $100,000 bungalows of Iar Connacht are likely to cost an additional $20,000 out on the islands. When properties do change hands, they are usually marketed through agents in Galway. At the time of writing, Heaslip's properties included a beautifully restored traditional stone cottage in the heart of Kilronan village on the island of Inishmore, the largest of the three islands. Reflecting the fact that these kinds of properties are highly sought after, it is priced at $226,000.

Island living won't suit everyone. Winter's storms can cut you off from the mainland for days at a time, and you'll have to trust that an army helicopter will manage to get you to hospital in Galway if you are ill. Shops are few and the price of day-to-day essentials is eye-watering. And, like your new neighbors, you'll have to stoically suffer the annual influx of anthropologically minded visitors armed with camcorders and highly romantic expectations.

You're not coming here as a starry-eyed tourist, so don't make the mistake of thinking that everything that appears in those lavishly illustrated coffee table books is gospel fact. Sorry, but Aran women no longer dress in scarlet flannel petticoats and their menfolk wear jeans rather than homespun trousers. Their homes are lit by electricity, not lamps filled with oil squeezed from the liver of the poor old basking shark. As for drowned fishermen being identified through sweaters that sport a unique, personalized pattern, the sad truth is that the story is pure balderdash. This particular item of folklore originated with J. M. Synge's play, *Riders to the Sea*, in which a corpse is recognized by four dropped stitches in a woolen sock.

But Aran sweaters are big business, and it would be commercial suicide to let on that high-powered knitting machines now create the vast majority of them. Aran women only started knitting them in the late 1920s, which rather quashes the notion that the distinctive raised patterns are as ancient as Ogham script. Even so, the carefully fostered myth that designs like Tree of Life, Honeycomb and Trinity have been handed down through the generations as a kind of heirloom is harmless enough—and it certainly helps Ireland's export industry!

THE EASTERN PART OF GALWAY

Galway has a lot more to offer than just its coastal fringe and offshore islands. Bargain hunters should definitely check out the eastern parts of the county. Only 45 minutes from Galway city, deep in the countryside's green heart, Ballinasloe is a trim little town of 6,000 souls drowsing away in the flat limestone pasturelands that mark the county border with Roscommon. Traditional-style slate-roofed cottages in reasonable condition can be had for around $57,000; solid Victorian country houses in need of a face lift, for $90,000.

Although you'll not be getting spectacular scenery, what makes Ballinasloe special is the Great October Fair, Ireland's oldest horse fair, dating back to the 1100s. Fair Week is a snorting, stomping spectacle of horseflesh with around 4,000 beasts passing through the town and dealers engaging in the time-honored language of nods, winks, spits and handshakes. As horse-trading is thirsty work, it's not uncommon for the town's pubs to actually run out of beer!

From dawn until dusk, the Fair Green becomes a heaving sea of hunters, heavy Irish drafts, shaggy-coated Connemaras, tiny Shetland ponies and eye-catching black-and-white piebalds. Known in Ireland as "colored horses," piebalds are prized by the traveling people (gypsies) for whom Fair Week is the highlight of the year. In that long-gone era of cavalry troops and horse-drawn carriages, Ballinasloe's Fair Green was Europe's biggest marketplace for horseflesh. It's said that a French officer bought Marengo, Napoleon's magnificent white charger, here in 1801. And although times have moved on, the October Fair provides visible proof that Ireland still boasts more horses per capita than any place in Europe.

REALTOR ADDRESS BOOK

Heaslips, 27 Wood Quay, Galway; tel +353 (0)91 565261. Email: info@heaslips.com.

Smith & Co, Newtownsmith, Galway; tel +353 (0)91 567331.

Keane Mahony Smith, 37 Prospect Hill, Galway; tel +353 (0)91 563744.

O'Donnellan & Joyce, Mary Street, Galway; tel +353 (0)91 564212. Email: odonnjoyce@eircom.net.

Matt O'Sullivan, The Square, Clifden, county Galway; tel +353 (0)95 21066. Also with offices at Main Street, Oughterard, county Galway; tel +353 (0)91 552503.

Paddy Keane & Co, Main Street, Ballinasloe, county Galway; tel +353 (0)905 42339.

GALWAY CONTACTS

Connacht Tribune (Galway's local newspaper), Market Street, Galway; tel +353 (0)91 536222.

Iarnrod Éireann (rail services), Galway Ceannt Station; tel +353 (0)91 561444.

Bus Éireann Travel Center, Galway Ceannt Station; tel +353 (0)91 562000.

Tourist Office, Eyre Square, Galway; tel +353 (0)91 537700.

County Mayo

Mayo's island-strewn coastline switchbacks from Killala Bay down to Killary Harbor, where it meets up with Galway's Connemara region. Connacht's regional airport, at Knock, provides an easy link to Dublin as well as to a number of English cities. You can also take a train to the capital from the Mayo towns of Westport, Claremorris, Ballina and Castlebar, the county town.

Shaped like a great stone tent, the county's most mesmerizing landmark is undoubtedly Croagh Patrick, Ireland's "holy mountain," whose reputation as a sacred site dates back to at least the time of the pagan Celts. St. Patrick is believed to have spent 40 nights in vigil on its summit in 441 A.D., but whether he performed any snake-charming feats is another matter entirely. Each Garland Sunday, the last Sunday of July, around 50,000 people go on pilgrimage to a mountain-top oratory, some still making the climb barefoot.

Here too are the renowned fishing waters of Lough Conn and Lough Mask. Wealthy anglers often base themselves at Ashford Castle, a fairytale fantasy of a hotel where President and Mrs. Reagan stayed on their Irish visit. A walk through Ashford's woodlands brings you to Cong, a time-stood-still village of crystal rivers, low stone bridges and a market cross. If it looks strangely familiar, that's probably because much of the filming of *The Quiet Man*, the John Wayne and Maureen O'Hara movie of the early 1950s, was shot here. One of the most historic of Irish villages, Cong also has a ruined abbey, founded in 1134 by Turlough O'Connor, the High King of the time. With potential for turning into a guesthouse, a six-bedroom residence in north Cong is currently available for $226,000. In the surrounding area, stone-built cottages (three-bedroom) in good condition change hands for $90,000 to $100,000. One-acre sites with full planning permission to build a dwelling start at $28,000.

Completely unrestored — a very traditional cottage in county Mayo

© Steenie Harvey

WESTPORT

Many foreign buyers elect to buy homes in and around seaside Westport. Laid out in Georgian times, it's an attractive town of wide, tree-lined streets, set-piece squares and a canal flanked by tall, narrow townhouses that give one the vague feeling of being in the Low Countries. Then again, that could come from all the Dutch accents. Westport is a summer tourism mecca and a high proportion of visitors comes from Holland.

Tourist towns always tend to be fairly expensive places and Westport's house prices also reflect its status as an employment honeypot. There is no one major employer in the Mayo area, rather a mix of small industries that take in everything from pharmaceuticals to eyecare products, seaweed processors, electrode and paintbrush manufacturers. Within the town's environs, one-acre sites fetch at least $45,000, and it's now almost impossible to find a three-bedroom bungalow for under $170,000.

However, semi-detached cottages within a five-mile radius of Westport still surface for less than $125,000. Move inland towards Castlebar and the price for small bungalows drops to $108,000. There are also plenty of habitable little cottages on agents' books for around $56,000. Within easy reach of Westport, the most sought-after coastal villages are Lecanvey, Murrisk, Newport and Louisburgh, strung out along the ocean like beads on a rosary. In these communities, the starting price for refurbished cottages with half an acre of land is now at least $100,000, but buyers may have to offer $150,000 or more for a particularly good view of Clew Bay and its islands. Even a renovation project cottage can cost $60,000 with the right view, and two-bedroom harborside apartments at Newport sell for $130,000.

But how about owning your own private island in Clew Bay? About 63 acres in area, Inishturkbeg is a wooded island with views of Achill Island, Croagh Patrick and Nephin Beg mountain. It recently came on the market for $1.08 million. Included in the price was a modern house and a restored cottage.

MURRISK

Back on the mainland, Murrisk is the nearest village to Croagh Patrick and the Garland Sunday pilgrim trail. It's intriguing to discover that the village derives its name from the Muir Iasc, a one-eyed sea serpent that was apparently worshipped by the local inhabitants during Druidic times. Makes you wonder if there was some truth in the legend of St. Patrick banishing the snakes, after all!

Folklore is one thing, but a poignant, real-life story is attached to Louisburgh village, a little farther up the coast. It's that of the Doolough tragedy, commemorated every year by a sponsored walk for Third World famine victims. At the height of Ireland's own great famine, when the potatoes rotted in the fields, a number of starving families banded together and trudged across the Doolough Pass from Killary Harbor to Louisburgh. There they sought admission to the old workhouse but entrance was refused. Almost 600 people died on the hope-

Knock

Ireland's spiritual power plant, Knock is one of the world's foremost Marian shrines and a place of continuous prayer. The village draws vast crowds during the May-to-October pilgrimage season. Some pilgrims spend their entire summer vacation here, taking part in torchlit rosary processions and all-night vigils. Sundays are particularly hectic, often with around 10,000 of the faithful patiently waiting to take Communion in the huge Basilica of Our Lady, Queen of Ireland. Holy days are even busier as almost every Catholic parish will organize a coach trip for parishioners.

Knock's fame stems from the evening of August 21, 1879, when 20 villagers claimed to have seen an apparition of three figures near the gable wall of their church. Bathed in a golden glow, the central figure was recognized as the Virgin Mary. Her unearthly companions were judged to be St. Joseph and St. John the Evangelist, holding the Book of Revelation and accompanied by a lamb. Hovering two feet above the ground, the apparition apparently lasted for almost two hours.

less return journey back across the Doolough Mountains, dark and lonely peaks that fully epitomize the brooding savagery of the scenic west.

ACHILL AND NORTH MAYO

Achill, Ireland's largest island, is linked to the mainland by a road bridge. Although winter weather can be quite squally, Achill encompasses all that's best in Irish scenery: dramatic cliffs and mountains, silvery beaches and wild moorlands. Here you can still find some nice homes at reasonable prices. Most island properties are sold through agents on the mainland, though. Newport agent Frank Chambers recently offered a traditional-type Achill cottage (824 square feet) overlooking Saulia Bay for $78,000. For $90,500, you could have bought a modern bungalow (three bedrooms), half a mile from Dugort and its beach, shops and pub. Dugort is one of the island's main villages.

In north Mayo, the area around Ballina, Killala Bay and the remote Belmullet Peninsula is your best bet for tracking down seaside snips. Small coastal bungalows occasionally pop up for less than $100,000. Not as fashionable as Westport, Ballina is a pleasantly old-

Shaped like a great stone tent, the county's most mesmerizing landmark is undoubtedly Croagh Patrick.

fashioned town on the Moy, one of Ireland's most noted fishing rivers. Just a couple of minutes away from some lovely riverbank walks, terraced townhouses (row houses) sell for $113,000. You can buy cheaper; semi-detached former corporation homes fetch around $51,000 in Ballina, but most foreign buyers don't find these type of estate houses very appealing.

Or consider the county's agricultural heartland, laid out in a patchwork quilt of emerald green fields and brown velvet boglands, all sewn together with gray drystone walls. Around little farming communities such as Swinford, Foxford, Ballinrobe and Claremorris, you can still find fixer-uppers starting at $17,000 and small cottage-type properties in good condition from $67,000. Note, though, that the $17,000 figure relates to a cottage requiring "extensive repairs," and, to be honest, the one I saw for that price was nothing other than a heap of old stones. Cottages requiring "repair" rather than "extensive repair" go for around $30,000.

CLAREMORRIS

On the main Galway-to Sligo-road, Claremorris and its satellite villages are the best place to look for bargain properties. Local agent Martin Finn usually has a wide selection. A three-bedroom newly renovated country cottage, five miles from Claremorris on a corner crossroads, is priced at $71,000.

Why are prices in the Claremorris area substantially cheaper? Well, the first thing that strikes you when strolling around the town is the complete absence of craft stores, gift shops and other tourist outlets—evidence that coach tours never see the place. House values have not been artificially inflated by either foreign buyers or city dwellers in the market for holiday homes, undoubtedly because the landscape doesn't offer up the Ireland of loughs and mountains that exists in most people's dreams. There are no major employers in this area, another factor that always sends house prices upwards.

REALTOR ADDRESS BOOK

Martin Finn, Dalton St., Claremorris, county Mayo; tel +353 (0)94 62216.

Brendan Tuohy, North Mall, Westport, county Mayo; tel +353 (0)98 28000. Email: btuohy@iol.com.

The Doolough in county Mayo—its name means "dark lake"

© Steenie Harvey

Frank Chambers, Main Street, Newport, county Mayo; tel +353 (0)98 41145. Email: frchambers@eircom.net.

Philip McComiskey, Church Road, Ballina, county Mayo; tel +353 (0)96 22433. Email: philipmc@iol.ie.

Collins Estate Agents, Castle Street, Castlebar, county Mayo; tel +353 (0)94 22701.

MAYO CONTACTS

Western People (local newspaper), Francis Street, Ballina, county Mayo; tel +353 (0)96 21188.

Rail Services: Ballina (tel +353 (0)96 71818), Castlebar (tel +353 (0)94 21222), Claremorris (tel +353 (0)94 71011), Westport (tel +353 (0)98 25253).

Bus Éireann Travel Center, Ballina, county Mayo; tel +353 (0)96 71800.

Tourist Information, James' Street, Westport, county Mayo; tel +353 (0)98 25711.

County Clare

From the mighty Cliffs of Moher to the starkly beautiful uplands of the moonscaped Burren and the lush green pastures around Lough Derg, Clare packs lots of goodies into a compact area. For me, it encompasses all that's best about western Ireland. Although prices have risen, prime coastal properties are nowhere near as expensive as in neighboring Galway. Most Irish people would agree that this is a kind of spiritual home for traditional

Neolithic Ireland—the PoulnaBrone Dolmen, county Clare

© Steenie Harvey

music. Enthusiasts will already know about the legendary music pubs of Doolin, Miltown Malbay, Ennistymon and Kilfenora.

ENNIS

Yet there's more to this county than first meets the eye. Strolling the streets of Ennis, Clare's county town and commercial center, take a peek at the window displays of bookshops and newsagents. If you're expecting to see the standard fare of books on local history, the Cliffs of Moher and the wild-flowers of the stony Burren region, you'll probably wonder why self-help guides to using computers and the Internet are given such a high profile instead. The reason? Well, sleepy old Ennis won the prize to become Ireland's first Information Age town.

Ennis has a population of just under 18,000. One of the projects for the new millennium was that 80 percent of households would have computers and be connected to the Internet. For just under $300, a substantial saving on the normal retail price, every family was entitled to collect a computer and a bundle of software packages, and obtain Internet access. The only criterion was that one member of the household could show that he or she can perform five simple computer tasks. Some 83 percent of Ennis households applied, and, so far, 4,600 computers have been delivered. Furthermore, any household still without a telephone could get a free connection.

This ongoing project is being funded by Eircom, the Irish telecom company. Their boffins decided that an ordinary west of Ireland town would make the perfect testing ground for their new technologies. If you like the idea of living in what is set to become one of the most technologically adept communities in the world, prices for new one- and two-bedroom apartments within the town range from $84,000 to $120,000. The most expensive part of town is Bank Square, in the heart of Ennis. Small bungalows and semi-detached houses start at around $97,000, but $140,000 is a more realistic price for the nicer residential neighborhoods. Better value lies out of town in the rural hinterland. In the village of Meelick West, a pretty primrose yellow cottage with two bedrooms was recently available for $84,750.

Naturally, the town is online. If you want to know more about Ennis and the online community, click onto www.ennis.ie.

NORTH CLARE AND BEYOND

Clare's coastline will prove a big draw, but note that the north of the county is more expensive than the south. In north Clare, right on the shores of Galway Bay, Ballyvaughan is a picturesque harbor village with some excellent pubs and restaurants. Don't miss the seafood at Monk's on the quay side. From here you can explore the traffic-free Green Roads of the Burren, old drovers' tracks that lead up into a mysterious world of caves, dolmens, ringforts and the sad remains of famine villages.

the Cliffs of Moher

*a*t one of Ireland's most famous scenic landmarks, you can take an exhilarating eight-kilometer walk along these vertigo-inducing cliffs from the observation point of O'Brien's Tower to Hag's Head. The cliffs tower above crashing Atlantic breakers to a height of almost 200 meters and offer views to take your breath away. Out in Galway Bay, beyond the rocky seastacks and natural arches, are the three misty humps of the Aran Islands. To the south you can glimpse the faraway hills of Kerry; look northwest and you'll see the brooding mountain fastnesses of Connemara. Fringed by a flowery sward of sea pinks, campions and bird's-foot-trefoil, the path to O'Brien's Tower is made of hefty slabs of Liscannor flagstone.

It's easy to escape the crowds as most camera-toting coach tour visitors simply spend a quick 20 minutes walking from the visitor center to O'Brien's Tower and back again. Head instead to the distant Moher Tower and, apart from the occasional backpacker, you can relish the views in complete solitude. The path also forms part of the much longer Burren Way, marked by little arrows on stone markers. As they can sometimes be hard to identify, be careful not to stray too close to the edge. Birds nest all along these cliffs: kittiwakes, guillemots, razorbills, fulmars and various other species of gulls. You may also spot clown-like puffins and the occasional red-legged chough. Look out too for wildflowers such as the white scented flowers of Lady's Tresses, dainty pink Fairy Foxgloves and cushion-like Mossy Saxifrage with its abundant clumps of star-shaped flowers blooming among the sea-sprayed rocks between May and August.

Springtime is especially magical for it's then that the Burren's limestone pavements are transformed into a flowery carpet of rare wildflowers. Species include purple spotted orchids, mountain avens and vivid blue gentians. Although properties here are not inexpensive, you can still find reasonable value on the southeastern edge of the Burren, particularly around the villages of Kilfenora of the high Celtic crosses and lake-surrounded Corofin. For example, $107,000 buys a two-bedroom cottage at Kilfenora. However, modern bungalow residences and holiday homes along the coast are changing hands for at least $140,000—sometimes a lot more. A three-bedroom bungalow on Ballyvaughan's promenade carries a price tag of $198,000. Within the town, a five-bedroom townhouse with good potential for being converted into a bed-and-breakfast is priced at $271,000.

Doolin is another desirable coastal village, perfectly positioned between the Burren and the Cliffs of Moher. As well as traditional music every night, those who live here can enjoy unrivaled views of the Aran Islands. Again, it's a brilliant location for botanists and ramblers who enjoy seeking out the remains of historical churches, castles and prehistoric ruins.

At the lower reaches of North Clare are the seaside resorts of Liscannor and Lahinch. Renowned for its unique flagstones with their fossilized pattern surfaces, Liscannor is the more traditional of the two. You can still see black-hulled *currach* boats in the harbor, and the curative powers of St. Brigid's Well continue to attract local people on February 1. Lahinch is more of a golfer's hangout. Here the Championship links course along the dunes dates back to 1893 and was originally intended for the sole use of officers of the infamous Black Watch regiment.

A new development was recently launched in Liscannor, a mix of apartments and small holiday homes. Prices range from $73,500 to $166,000. Built in a more traditional style, a two-bedroom cottage has just come on the market priced at $140,000. Again, though, prices for larger properties will probably seem staggering, especially those that have sea views. Most Irish buyers want large, modern properties, not traditional cottages, and they'll pay ridiculous sums. For example, a five-bedroom bungalow in Liscannor is on the market for $424,000.

Most folks in this area go into Ennistymon for their main shopping. Its streets are lined with old-fashioned shop fronts and market traditions date back to the Napoleonic wars. Come on a Tuesday for the weekly street market. Come on Friday for the cattle market. Come at any time to take a scenic walk along the riverbank to the Cascades, where you can occasionally see leaping salmon when the waters are in full spate. Half a mile from town, pretty three-bedroom cottages on half an acre fetch $96,000—and you can just about glimpse the sea. Within the town itself, terraced townhouses (you probably know them as row houses) cost around $85,000.

MOVING INLAND TO KILLALOE

For one of Clare's prettiest inland locations, make tracks for Killaloe and the shores of Lough Derg. Sheltered by the Slieve Bearnagh hills to the west and the Arra hills to the east, Killaloe is an attractive little place perched on a neck of land where the Shannon River flows out of the lough on its journey towards Limerick. You can walk into county Tipperary by crossing the 13-arched bridge spanning the river. The immediate locality is littered with historical remains: medieval churches, round towers and those bibles in stone, high Celtic crosses, one of which carries inscriptions both in old Irish *ogham* lettering and Norse runic script. Locals claim this was once Ireland's capital. The most famous of the High Kings, Brian Boru, is said to have had a palace known as Kincora where the present-day town now stands. Best known as a sailing and watersports center, today Killaloe does a good summer tourist trade with European visitors who enjoy messing about in boats.

Although Killaloe townhouses can be had for $113,000, don't expect a waterfront location for that price. Buyers are willing to pay incredible sums to look out on to the lough and glimpse Holy Island. A magical island laden with legends, Holy Island's other name is Inishcealtra. Marked by a high round tower, here too is a collection of ancient chapels, an anchorite's cell and early Christian gravestones dating back to the 7th century. Thought to have been founded by St. Colm, the island was an important monastic site until it fell to Viking raiders. Until the 1830s, the island's holy well was a popular place of pilgrimage, but the Church discouraged visits after revelries got out of hand. Some local girls were carried off by men intent on what you might describe as "inappropriate relationships."

To give you an example of prices in this area, two-bedroom apartments at the marina sell for $175,000. Depending on house size and acreage, good quality detached properties around Killaloe and the nearby communities of Scarriff, Tuamgraney and Mountshannon start at around $130,000. At that lower end of the price scale, the enchantingly named Honeybee Cottage comes with two bedrooms and one acre of land, but with countryside, not lakeside, views. If you want a large house with panoramic views of Lough Derg, $396,000 is the asking price for a five-bedroom bungalow at Scarriff.

REALTOR ADDRESS BOOK

Philip O'Reilly, 22/24 Abbey St., Ennis, county Clare; tel +353 (0)65 6844448. Email: info@philiporeilly.com.

Costelloes, 5 Abbey St., Ennis, county Clare; tel +353 (0)65 6821299. Email: info@costelloe.com.

Paddy Vaughan, 89 O'Connell St., Ennis, county Clare; tel +353 (0)65 6820131.

John Vaughan, Parliament St., Ennistymon, county Clare; tel +353 (0) 65 7071477. Email: sales@johnvaughan.net.

Harry Brann, Killaloe, county Clare; tel +353 (0)61 376380.

Pat Mulcahy, Killaloe, county Clare; tel +353 (0)61 376176.

CLARE CONTACTS

Clare Champion (local newspaper), Barrack St., Ennis, county Clare; tel +353 (0)65 6828105.

Rail services to Dublin via Limerick from Ennis; tel +353 (0)65 6840444.

Bus Éireann, The Railway Station, Ennis, county Clare; tel +353 (0)65 6824177.

Tourist Office, Arthur's Row, Ennis, county Clare; tel +353 (0)65 6828366.

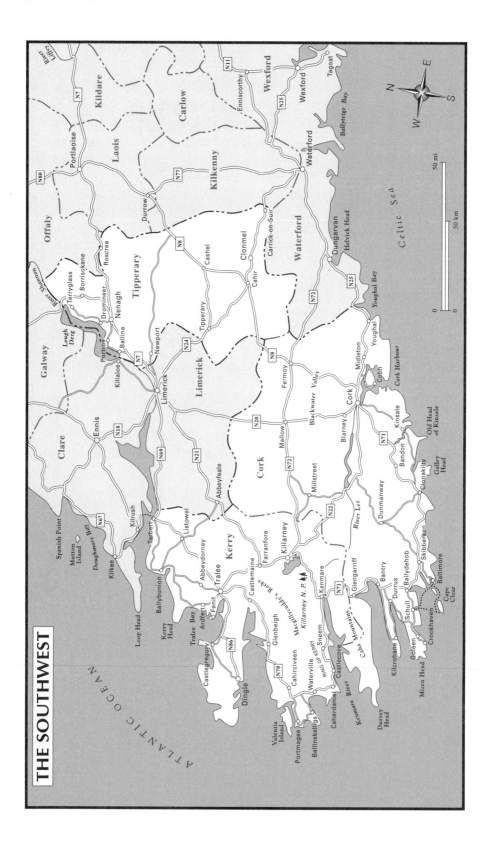

THE SOUTHWEST

15 The Southwest

The paintbox villages of the southwest are a favorite hunting ground for foreign home buyers. Even if you do decide to buy elsewhere, be sure to feast your eyes here on some of Ireland's most colorful and spectacular landscapes.

County Kerry

Despite the annual horde of summer visitors, Kerry delivers sheer poetry. Nothing detracts from the bewitching beauty of its landscapes, where mountains are reflected in looking-glass loughs and flotillas of islands drift out of a muslin mesh of sea mist. You'll never forget the first time you actually see this enchanted kingdom for yourself: the silver-thread waterfalls spilling down from the Slieve Mish, Derrynasaggart and Macgillyguddy's Reeks mountain ranges, the mirror-bright lakes of Killarney, the rocky Atlantic peninsulas with their basking seals and occasional frolicking dolphin.

For many people, the county is synonymous with the famous Ring of Kerry, the 112-mile circuit around the Iveragh Peninsula, which claims the bulk of the county's scenic goodies. With the National Park right on its doorstep, Killarney is where most visitors stay; the town itself (pop. 13,000) is almost entirely given over to the tourism trade. Although Killarney makes an excellent holiday base, it lacks the sense of intimacy you'll find

in many of the other towns and villages strung around the Iveragh Peninsula. Traveling in a clockwise direction, the litany of lovely coastal towns
and villages includes Kenmare, Sneem, Caherdaniel, Waterville, Ballinskel-
ligs, Portmagee, Valentia Island and Cahirciveen.

THE RING OF KERRY AREA

My own favorite Ring of Kerry location is the Derrynane-Caherdaniel-
Castlecove area. You don't have to choose between mountain and coastal
vistas. Here you've got the full glory of both, and the hauntingly desolate
monastic island of Skellig Michael is only a boat ride away. For ramblers,
this is one of the waystations on the 135-mile Kerry Way. The surrounding
area is an archaeologist's playground of forts, souterrains and standing
stones. Those fascinated by the natural world will come across unusual
flora such as the Kerry lily, kidney saxifrage, bee orchid and blue-eyed
grass. It's not uncommon to meet up with the local wildlife either. Foxes,
stoats, hares, seals and otters abound in this area.

As with all such heavenly places, house prices tend to be quite high if
you're looking for a refurbished property of any size. Is your dream a cut-
stone home in beautiful condition, three bedrooms, sitting on 2.5 acres
with both sea frontage and mountain views? Two miles from Caherdaniel,
Heron Water House fits the bill—and at $294,000 the price reflects the
desirability of this area. Steep, certainly, but the value is in the view, south
over Kenmare Bay towards the peaks of the Beara Peninsula.

But that's not to say this part of Kerry is totally unaffordable. If an ocean
view is not a priority, an old-style end of terrace cottage with three small
bedrooms and views of the Caha Mountains is currently on the market for
$66,000. In fair condition, this cottage is six miles from the colorful town of
Kenmare. Within Kenmare town itself, recently built three-bedroom homes
sell for around $153,000. On Blackwater Pier an old-style two-bedroom
house in need of some repair (but habitable) is on the market for $90,500.
Four miles from Kenmare, in a scenic rural area, a perfect gem of a traditional farmhouse (four bedrooms) has an asking price of $181,000.

In general, the view factor dictates the price of all Kerry properties. Say
you're looking for a four-bedroom bungalow you could turn into a little
B&B business. One suitably sized home, near Farranfore, is priced at
$113,000. This village is 20 miles from Killarney and well away from the
picture-postcard scenery. About $158,000 buys a similar bungalow within
walking distance of Waterville village, on the Ring of Kerry's northern
stretch between Lough Caragh and Dingle Bay. Views of the mountains and
the Skellig Rock in the distance, yes. Seashore lapping right up to the door,
no. For a residence with ocean frontage, you might have to pay in the
region of $250,000.

With those kinds of prices, you may wonder how local people on low

Killarney's Lakes

estling within the 27,000 acres of Killarney's National Park, girdled by mountains, are the three magical lakes that conjure up one of Ireland's most quintessential images. The largest is Lough Léin, the Lake of Learning, which gained its name through the scholars who were rowed over to Inisfallen Island, a renowned center of education in medieval times. Boatmen still take visitors to this tumbledown monastic settlement, originally founded by St. Finian the Leper in the 7th century. As well as being the place where the *Annals of Inisfallen* were written, it's said Brian Boru, High King of Ireland, studied here during his youth.

Muckross Lake is the middle lake.

Stopping points include the ruins of a 15th-century abbey laid to waste by Cromwell's soldiers in 1652, the Victorian magnificence of Muckross House and gardens, and the Torc waterfall that cascades off the mountains. Following the track around the north shore of the lake brings you to the Old Weir Bridge and the Meeting of the Waters, where a small river tumbles down from the Upper Lake. The entire area is excellent walking and cycling country; rent a bike from O'Neills, Plunkett Street, Killarney (tel +353 (0)64 31970). If you're traveling by car, a grandstand panorama over the Upper Lake towards the Purple Mountain can be had from Ladies View, where Queen Victoria and her ladies-in-waiting came to picnic.

incomes can afford south Kerry properties. Well, town suburbs provide some answers, and it's still possible to buy semi-detached row houses in Cahirciveen, Tralee and Killarney for $67,000. These aren't the kind of properties that most foreign or holiday-home buyers want, so the market is purely local and not subject to the same ever-upward pressures. Indeed, some urban properties can be reasonably affordable and attractive too.

If you've got time and enthusiasm, dilapidated cottages in the mountain foothills of the Iveragh Peninsula still sell for under $50,000. Realtors describe these sad-eyed hovels as "fixer-uppers," but many are complete wrecks and would seem to be completely beyond redemption.

But don't write off Kerry yet. You *can* buy good quality cottages here for between $60,000 and $75,000. For an affordable slice of the county at a bargain price, the best hunting grounds are in the north of the county, around Listowel and Tralee. With a population of around 20,000, Tralee is Kerry's main town and home to the whimsical Rose of Tralee festival. "Roses" of Irish descent from all over the globe come to take part in what is more a celebration of Irishness than a straightforward beauty contest.

NORTH KERRY

Much of North Kerry consists of hilly green fields rather than dramatic mountain scenery, and if this is your first view of the county, you'll wonder what all the fuss has been about. There isn't much to distinguish it from the rural parts of county Limerick, linked to North Kerry by the county border and with much similarity in house prices. The landscape alone explains why you can buy substantial village houses and refurbished cottages in good structural condition for $70,000, three-bedroom country bungalows for $118,000, or stone farmhouses, completely refurbished and redecorated, for $107,000. You're likely to come across such properties in the rural hinterland of villages such as Abbeyfeale, Ardfert and Abbeydorney.

The North Kerry coastline between Tarbert and Fenit is nowhere near as breathtaking as the Iveragh Peninsula, but many Irish families vacation in this area and there are a number of golf courses here. The most popular resort is Ballybunion where a centuries-old family vendetta resulted in an estimated 3,000 eager participants battling it out on the beach in 1834! Interesting buys around this little seaside town include a two-bedroom refurbished cottage for $96,000 and a modern four-bedroom bungalow for $198,000.

North Kerry isn't entirely bereft of gorgeous seascapes and mountain fastnesses. You'll find plenty to enthrall you on the wild Dingle Peninsula. Some 30 miles long and with a backbone of mountains, it reaches into the ocean to the west of Tralee and is one of western Europe's richest sites for monastic beehive huts and other archaeological curiosities. The Dingle Peninsula sees far fewer package tourists than the Iveragh Peninsula, largely because its ribbon-thin roads just weren't designed for coach tour traffic.

DINGLE

With around 1,200 inhabitants, 52 pubs and some excellent seafood restaurants (try Doyle's), the main settlement is harbor-town Dingle, which has a thriving fishing fleet and does a lucrative trade in taking visitors out to spot

Reminiscent of an upturned stone boat, the Gallarus Oratory in county Kerry is a beautifully preserved relic of an early Christian church.

© Steenie Harvey

Fungie, the famous resident dolphin. The villages scattered west of Dingle town are Irish-speaking, so this is a bilingual town. You'll certainly hear the chatter of Irish in An Café Litearta (the Literary Café), which sells books as well as coffee.

Urban cottage-type homes within Dingle town start at $113,000, two-bedroom apartments at $135,000, and small townhouses from $147,000. Elsewhere on the Dingle Peninsula, you can buy traditional two-story rural houses for $169,000, but modern bungalows are quite expensive, perhaps because just about everything here comes with a view of both mountains and ocean. Want the kind of silver-screen views seen in the movie *Ryan's Daughter*? It was filmed at Inch Beach, a spectacular spot where four-bedroom bungalows change hands for almost $300,000. Two miles from Dingle town, beside Beenbawn beach, a three-bedroom bungalow with views towards Dingle harbor is priced at $260,000.

REALTOR ADDRESS BOOK

Daniel Hannon, 6 Main St., Listowel, county Kerry; tel +353 (0)68 21577.

Pierse & Fitzgibbon, Property Ireland, 25 Market St., Listowel, county Kerry; tel +353 (0)68 21244.

Sean Daly, 34 Henry St., Kenmare, county Kerry; tel +353 (0)64 41213. Email: info@seandaly.com.

Sean Coyne, 2 Main St., Killarney, county Kerry; tel +353 (0)64 31274. Email: coynekil@iol.ie.

Wm Giles, 23 Denny St., Tralee, county Kerry, tel +353 (0)66 7121073.

James North, 33 Denny St., Tralee, county Kerry, tel +353 (0)66 7122699.

John Moore, Green St., Dingle, county Kerry; tel +353 (0)66 9151588.

KERRY CONTACTS

The Kerryman (local newspaper), Clash Industrial Estate, Tralee, county Kerry; tel +353 (0)66 7121666.

Rail services to Dublin from Tralee (tel +353 (0)66 7123522) and Killarney (tel +353 (0)64 31067).

Bus Éireann services to many destinations from Tralee (tel +353 (0)66 7123535) and Killarney (tel +353 (0)64 34777).

Tourist Information, Beech Road, Killarney, county Kerry; tel +353 (0)64 31633.

County Cork

Sandwiched between Waterford and Kerry, cosmopolitan Cork is Ireland's largest county. Rich in folklore, music and wildly seductive landscapes, it's a place that many foreign buyers feel is perfect for raising a young family, starting a new business venture or simply enjoying their retirement. Like neighboring south Kerry, the scenery is simply dramatic—imagine a hinterland of mountains, loughs and wooded river valleys, all fringed by a craggy coastline of cliffs, coves and pristine beaches. That's Cork.

The Gulf Stream climate ensures that winters are mild, and cottage gardens rarely see snowfalls. Primroses start blooming in the hedgerows in February and shops stock the new season's vegetables sooner than anywhere else. An added bonus is the county's wide range of sporting activities, which include everything from golf to yachting, hill walking, fishing and fox hunting. Outside of Dublin, the southwest coastal region is the country's main tourism mecca, so there are plenty of opportunities for anyone considering a business venture.

House values within the county vary enormously. Whatever your budget, it shouldn't be too hard to find something suitable. As a rough guide, the dearest locations are villages within easy striking distance of Cork city, high-profile harbor towns such as Kinsale, and pretty color-washed villages such as Eyries on the Beara Peninsula, where all the village houses are painted in rainbow colors: mint green, sky blue, primrose yellow, pale lavender. You would be surprised at how many buyers fall in love with a coat of paint. In Eyries, the quintessential beauty spot village, any little cottage that does come on the market sells for at least $113,000.

The biggest problem with county Cork is its sheer size. It can be hard to decide on the best place to begin a house-hunting quest. In general, realtors in Cork city are more likely to deal with properties in the eastern

color-washed Clonakilty, county Cork

© Steenie Harvey

half of the county, between the border with county Waterford and Kinsale, which has its own local agents. If you're more inclined towards West Cork, try Clonakilty, Skibbereen or Bantry for the widest choice of properties and agents.

CORK CITY

Although you probably haven't come to pound the city streets, it's hard to resist spending a day or two in Cork city, wandering the engaging lanes around the Lee River. With a population of around 180,000, this is the Republic's second-largest city and has its own university as well as a thriving arts and culture scene. Early birds find the best bargains at the flea market on Coal Quay or head to the covered English Market, which at one time was barred to Irish traders. Produce ranges from locally made cheeses to drisheen, a sausage made from sheep's blood.

Properties within the city are quite expensive. It's almost impossible to find a three-bedroom semi-detached home for less than $125,000. Apartments (558 to 728 square feet) in a new development on the Old Youghal Road start at $119,000.

CORK'S HARBOR TOWNS

Journeying east to west along the coast road, the first of Cork's old harbor towns is Youghal. Pronounced "yawl," its town walls date from the 13th century and Sir Walter Raleigh was the mayor here in 1588. Next comes Cobh, pronounced "cove," whose huge natural harbor was the embarkation point for around 2.5 million of last century's emigrants. The Heritage Center chronicles some of their sad stories and also remembers the days when the transatlantic liners, the *Titanic* among them, put into port here. Under British rule Cobh's name was Queenstown and its 19th-century terraces have something of the look of an English seaside town. Three-bedroom terrace (row) houses here fetch around $107,000.

On to fashionable Kinsale, which has its own seafaring history. Pubs carry names such as the Spaniard and the Spinnaker. If you walk along the clifftops to Old Head, you can gaze out to where the *Lusitania* went down in 1915 with the loss of 1,500 lives. A center for yachting, sea angling and golf, the town's alleyways are steep and cobbled, houses are painted in a rainbow of pastel colors, and 11 of its 35 restaurants are of the gourmet variety.

With only 2,500 year-round residents, Kinsale really comes to life as a summer port resort, and almost half of its properties are sold for investment purposes. Modern three-bedroom bungalows in the surrounding area start at around $152,000, but town properties with a view are much more expensive. Within the town center, two-bedroom apartments sell for $147,000, but two-bedroom duplex apartments overlooking the harbor can fetch as much $446,000. Crazy prices ... and they just seem to be getting crazier all the time. One of the latest Kinsale homes to come onto the market is priced at $655,000; it's no mansion, just a four-bedroom bungalow residence with nice river views. Even restoration properties—if you can find one—go for silly sums. Most cottages were snapped up long ago, but I did see an old schoolhouse for conversion at $102,000.

If you want to live in the Kinsale area for a while, it would make a lot more sense to rent a property. Expect to pay around $565 per month for a one-bedroom apartment and from $735 for a two-bedroom. Duplex apartments with harbor views are substantially more expensive, around $1,350 monthly. At the time of writing, a renovated cottage (three bedrooms) beside Garrylucas beach was available for rental through Sheehy Brothers. With an attractive front garden and a pathway to the beach, the rent for this cottage is $735 per month if taken on a yearly let, $850 monthly if rented solely for the summer months.

West of Kinsale is colorwashed Clonakilty, a pretty heritage town with a magnificent array of traditional hand-painted shopfronts. Its citizens are very proud of the local delicacy, Clonakilty Black Pudding. If you feel queasy about tucking into pig's blood sausage, a good place for a pub seafood lunch is An Sugan. Much of Neil Jordan's film *Michael Collins* was filmed hereabouts, and it was in Clonakilty that the Free State general went to school.

As always, when it comes to the price of properties, much depends on the view. Simple two-bedroom coastal cottages can still be had for $102,000 to $115,000, but they don't linger on the market for very long. At the time of writing, Kerr's had a pretty cottage at Castlefreke, 15 minutes from Clonakilty. With wonderful panoramas of the West Cork coastline, this was priced at $113,000.

backstreets of higgledy-piggledy Kinsale, county Cork

SKIBBEREEN

Protestants founded bustling Skibbereen, but its name became a byword for Catholic suffering and the severe hardships endured by the peasantry during the Famine years. Even though today it's a prosperous farmers' town, memories never fade and visitors are encouraged to follow the Skibbereen Trail around sites associated with An Gorta Mor, the Great Hunger.

Country cottages for restoration in the Skibbereen area start at around $45,000, but at this price we're talking about cottages that need lots and lots of tender, loving care. ("Ruins" are also available for $17,000 to $28,000.) However, I did see one old farmhouse not in too grievous a condition for $40,000. You could probably estimate spending the same again on restoration costs, but there's a tidy profit to be made. Similar farmhouses that have already had a makeover fetch at least $100,000 in this vicinity, usually quite a lot more.

For a cottage that's immediately habitable, $65,000 is a more realistic starting figure in the Skibbereen area. There are some attractive old properties hereabouts. At the time of writing, $113,000 was the price of a traditional blacksmith's forge. With cut-stone frontage, it has already been converted into a three-bedroom home. Or how about an old mill to restore into vacation apartments? At the time of writing, Hamilton Osborne King's Cork office had a 17th-century mill near Skibbereen that was still in working order until 15 years ago. Delivered by ships that moored alongside the mill, grain was hoisted up into the five-story building by hand. Some 18,000 square feet in size and priced at $283,000, the mill sits on the water's edge, across the bay from Castletownsend.

Skibbereen's nearby coastal villages are a big draw for foreign buyers. Although most village populations in West Cork number fewer than 500 year-round residents, they're always swollen with summer visitors and so have a good selection of traditional music pubs and restaurants.

The Big Fella

many scenes in Neil Jordan's movie *Michael Collins* were shot in the West Cork area. Played in the film by Liam Neeson, Michael Collins was born in 1890 near Clonakilty. Often referred to as "the Big Fella," he was a major figure in Ireland's War of Independence (1919–1921). Using "flying columns" and assassination squads, he organized a ruthless campaign of guerrilla warfare against the British, which eventually resulted in bringing the old enemy to the negotiating table.

Sent to London by Eamon de Valera to negotiate a truce, Collins put his signature to the treaty that partitioned the island of Ireland. In doing so he signed his own death warrant. Southern Ireland split into pro- and anti-treaty factions and former comrades-in-arms were soon spilling their own blood in a bitter civil war. On August 22, 1922, the anti-treaty forces caught up with Collins at Beal-na-Bleath, near the West Cork village of Macroom. His car was ambushed, and rather than fleeing, Collins engaged in a shoot-out that resulted in his death.

BALTIMORE AND NEARBY VILLAGES

South of Skibbereen, Baltimore is a lively port and sailing center with a ruined castle that goes by the magical name of Dún na Sead, the Fort of the Jewels. Its former inhabitants, the O'Driscoll clan, enjoyed a million-dollar view over Roaringwater Bay and Carberry's Hundred Islands. Ferries make the journey over to Sherkin Island and Cape Clear Island, a noted site for bird-watching, lying on one of the migratory passage routes. One of the strangest events in Baltimore's history occurred in 1631 when 200 of the inhabitants were snatched by Barbary pirates and shipped off to Algiers as slaves. Haven't got a clue what homes sold for in those days, but you can easily pay $270,000 for a three-bedroom house here today.

Other sought-after villages on Roaringwater Bay include Ballydehob and Schull. Lovely villages, without doubt, but if you want a good quality hide-away with harbor views, expect to pay for it. A three-bedroom farmhouse near Ballydehob certainly has the picturesque panoramas—and also a $333,000 price tag to match. However, the Victoria Murphy agency did have an exquisite schoolhouse, already converted into a home, for $164,000. Some of West Cork's best beaches are to be found along this stretch of the Mizen Peninsula. The queen of them all is Barleycove, on the road between the villages of Crookhaven and Goleen, where you often see artists trying to capture the beauty of the place on canvas.

With Dunmanus Bay on one side and Bantry Bay on the other, remote Sheep's Head Peninsula takes a 12-mile plunge southwestwards from Durrus village. It's another splendid spot to get out the easel and paint-brushes. Priced at $130,000, a fully restored two-story farmhouse with pink-washed walls and four bedrooms was recently available through Key Properties.

If you decide to check out properties away from the coast, avoid county Cork's best-known village, Blarney. Too twee for words, it's a real tourist trap and traffic is simply horrendous. Coach tour after coach tour delivers hordes of would-be stone kissers, all convinced the Blarney Stone has the power to turn them into silver-tongued charmers. Personally, I wouldn't spend $4 to bend over backwards from a great and giddy height to slaver over some lump of rock! On the other hand, if you've got a money-spinning idea, it may be just the place; it's a village where tourists are very easily parted from their cash. Blarney Woolen Mills alone manages to sell 900,000 sweaters to convoys of the credulous every year. Although three-bedroom semi-detached houses and four-bedroom bungalows in the village fetch $130,000 and $215,000, respectively, you can find modest two-bedroom cottages within the rural locality for under $100,000.

Midleton is a 17th-century market town and home to the Jameson whiskey distillery. Townhouses here can be found for $85,000. Or look to the Blackwater Valley, dotted with castles and ancient sites. Main towns and villages along the valley include Fermoy, Mallow and Millstreet, which hosts one of Ireland's largest horse shows. On the Bandon River, the countryside surrounding Dunmanway and Bandon delivers up plenty of habitable properties from $50,000 to $100,000 and is especially good for hunting down bargain cottages for refurbishment. Recently built three-bedroom row houses in Bandon town sell for $84,000.

REALTOR ADDRESS BOOK

John Kerr, 17/18 Ashe St., Clonakilty, county Cork; tel +353 (0)23 34944. Email: info@kerr.ie.

Matt O'Sullivan, Emmet Square, Clonakilty, county Cork; tel +353 (0)23 33367.

Sheehy Bros, 10 Short Quay, Kinsale, county Cork; tel +353 (0)21 4772338. Email: sheebros@iol.ie.

Key Properties, Bantry, county Cork; tel +353 (0)27 50111. Email: tom@keyproperties.net.

Hamilton Osborne King, 11 South Mall, Cork City, county Cork; tel +353 (0)21 4271371. Email: infoc@hok.ie.

Keane Mahoney Smith, 44 South Mall, Cork City, county Cork; tel +353 (0)21 270311. Email: admin@k-m-s.com.

Victoria Murphy & Daughter, 14 Pearse Square, Cobh, county Cork; tel +353 (0)21 4811014. Email: victoriamurphy@indigo.ie.

CORK CONTACTS

The Corkman (local newspaper), 39 Main St., Mallow, county Cork; tel

beside the seaside—Barleycove, West Cork

+353 (0)22 42394. Also *The Examiner and Evening News*, Academy St., Cork; tel +353 (0)21 4272722.

Rail services direct to Dublin, indirect routes to Waterford and Killarney; tel +353 (0)21 4504888.

Bus Éireann services most Irish cities and large towns from Cork; tel +353 (0)21 4508188.

Tourist Information Office, Aras Fáilte, Grand Parade, Cork; tel +353 (0)21 4273251.

County Tipperary

"It's a long way to Tipperary," goes the old World War I marching song. Certainly it's far enough away to have escaped becoming part of the Limerick, Cork or Waterford city commuter belts. Although this is Ireland's largest inland county, its charms are understated by most tourist guides and so still has the air of a well-guarded secret. If peace and tranquillity top your shopping list, take a Trip to Tipp and check out its sleepy market towns and even sleepier villages. However, house prices are by no means inexpensive. The county is becoming increasingly popular with affluent Dublin buyers looking to buy weekend homes and take up the traditional rural pursuits of hunting and fishing.

Walled on its southern horizon by the smudgy blue bastions of the Galtee and Comeragh mountain ranges, in the west by the Silvermines Mountains and Lough Derg, Tipperary is essentially farming country. Its central Golden Vale produces prime herds of beef and dairy cattle, and local agents often find it hard to keep up with the demand for good quality pasture. As this is also excellent hunting country, any period-type property with a couple of paddocks and outbuildings for stabling generally finds plenty of eager buyers.

CASHEL

Properties are particularly pricy around Cashel, a heritage town that's home to one of Ireland's most splendid historical sights. Once the seat of the Kings of Munster, the Rock of Cashel rises above the Tipperary countryside like the mirage of some Celtic Acropolis, crowned with an array of ecclesiastical stonework dating back to medieval times: a round tower, intricately carved high crosses, a ruined cathedral and a castle tower house. It was from this lofty eyrie that St. Patrick reputedly plucked a shamrock to illustrate the doctrine of the Holy Trinity.

But as Cashel is the one Tipperary town to which tourists flock in great numbers, it may prove a good location for anyone seeking a guesthouse opportunity. At the upper end of the market, Hill House, a Georgian house with eight bedrooms, an acre of walled garden, and superb views of the

Rock of Cashel and the town's 13th-century cathedral has just come onto the market with a price tag of $565,000. Obviously, you'd need a lot of guests to make it pay for itself.

I know it sounds ludicrous, but by Dublin values, a Georgian residence priced below $1 million is seen as a steal. Hill House comes with oodles of elegance too. You can easily imagine a harpsichord tinkling away in the drawing room, a frock-coated master of the house writing in his journal in the study, and ladies in frothy muslin dresses playing croquet on the lawn.

Any Georgian "gentleman's house" or rambling old rectory in good condition does not come cheap, but away from the grand country house market, smaller properties throughout Tipperary are more affordable. Numerous rural cottages come into the $45,000-to-$60,000 range, and modern two-bedroom bungalows begin at around $80,000. However, those sort of price levels indicate that a property will be very much off the beaten track. You'll pay rather more to gaze over Lough Derg or be within striking distance of the county's prettiest towns—Clonmel, Roscrea, Cahir, Cashel and Carrick-on-Suir. Just because of its name, you may feel it's worth having a look at Tipperary town, but, to be honest, it's rather drab and disappointing. The only real reason to come here is for the twice-weekly cattle mart or if a horse race is scheduled.

SOUTHERN TIPPERARY
On the county's southeastern border, surrounded by cider apple orchards, Carrick-on-Suir (pop. 5,500) sees far fewer visitors than Cashel. A riverside market town, its history goes back to the Middle Ages when it was an important center for the wool trade. Here you can buy pretty three-bedroom cottages and bungalows within three miles of the town for around $135,000. Within the town itself, a two-bedroom townhouse for refurbishment was recently available for $47,500. Newly built townhouses start at around $93,000.

South Tipperary's main town for work, shopping, restaurants and realtors is Clonmel. With around 20,000 inhabitants this is as close as the county gets to big city lights. Just 10 miles west of Carrick-on-Suir, it's another riverbank town of atmospheric backstreets and quayside mills surrounded by good hill-walking territory. Overlooked by Slievenamon Mountain, a quaint two-bedroom cottage with a number of outbuildings and an acre of land sells for $70,000 to $75,000, but spankingly modern three- and four-bedroom villa-type bungalows fetch $110,000 and up. The Keane Mahoney Smith agency here also handle rentals. One- and two-bedroom furnished apartments go from $375 to $475 monthly, three- and four-bedroom furnished houses from $430 to $590 monthly.

There's still a quaint, old-fashioned air to Clonmel, and it gives a good inkling of what a Georgian coaching town must have been like. Down from the turrets of the West Gate, Hearns hotel was once the home and head-quarters of Charles Bianconi, who came over from Lombardy, Italy, to found Ireland's first coach service in 1815. The Bian was a horse-drawn two-wheeler that carried both the mail and up to six passengers, who sat back-to-back facing the roadside.

NORTHERN TIPPERARY

North Tipperary's chief town is Nenagh. Although not a particularly pictur-esque town, its realtors generally have a good supply of inexpensive cot-tages in the rural hinterland, where narrow forested roads climb up from Newport into the Silvermines Mountains. As their name suggests, this was once a center for silver mining though the term "mountains" is something of an exaggeration. The highest point, Keeper Hill, towers to a rather under-whelming 2,217 feet (676 meters). The range links up with an intriguing-sounding plateau called the Devil's Bit, and most local kids can reel off the story about how this gap in the hills came by its strange name. Long ago, the Devil himself flew over Tipperary and just for the hell of it, decided to bite a chunk out of the mountains. Finding that it wasn't the most palatable of snacks, he spat it out, and that's how the Rock of Cashel was formed. Or so the legend goes.

In this part of north Tipperary, ready-to-move-into cottages on a typical one-acre patch of land start at around $60,000. Some really tempting homes are available if you're willing to pay fractionally more. At the time of writ-ing, $68,000 would have bought a pretty, whitewashed "village street" cot-tage with two bedrooms and a garden at Cappawhite. However, most family bungalows (four bedrooms) fall into the $152,000-to-$210,000 price range.

the Age of Wonders

*G*reat ones for lists and catalogs, the long-bearded sages of the Middle Ages weren't content with just seven wonders of the world. Two miles east of Roscrea town is a place that used to be known as the 31st Wonder of the World: a sacred Celtic isle called Monaincha or Insula Viventium, the Island of the Living. Reputed to hold the secret of everlasting life, its only hint of past glories is a little ruined church. Sadly, the site has long been dispossessed of its island status by drainage schemes.

In previous centuries only the wealthy could afford the services of a doctor and the Irish peasantry were more concerned with having a pain-free life rather than traveling to remote islands in a quest for immortality. The High Crosses of Ahenny and one of the Crosses at Kilkieran are crowned with remov-able capstones, sometimes known as mitre stones or bishop's hats. Tipperary lore sug-gests that headache sufferers sought to relieve their pain by placing these capstones upon their own pates. It seems a curious notion. There you are with a throbbing migraine and you want to balance a *boulder* on your head? Should you run out of aspirin, you may be better off seeking relief from the waters of St. Kieran's Well, beside Kilkieran churchyard. It too reputedly cures headaches.

West of Nenagh and the Silvermines Mountains is the Tipperary shore of Lough Derg, part of the famous Shannon River navigation scheme. Always busy in summertime with boating visitors, the shore is strung with little marinas and attractive lakeside villages such as Terryglass, Dromineer, Garrykennedy, Portroe and Ballina, the latter linked to Killaloe in county Clare by an arched stone bridge. The two counties and their lakeshore villages are in friendly competition to win the tourism battle, so there's no shortage of good restaurants, curio shops, traditional music pubs and summer festivals. House prices are similar to the Clare side of the shore: upwards of $200,000 for luxury bungalows with doorstep panoramas of the lough. For example, $282,000 will land you a nice four-bedroom bungalow at Terryglass, suitable for converting into a small bed-and-breakfast establishment.

REALTOR ADDRESS BOOK

John Lee & Son, Main St., Newport, county Tipperary; tel +353 (0)61 378121.

William Talbot, 52 Keynon St., Nenagh, county Tipperary; tel +353 (0)67 31496.

Shee & Hawe, 62 Main St., Carrick-on-Suir, county Tipperary; tel +353 (0)51 640041. Email: sheeandhawe@propertypartners.ie.

Barry Walsh Estates, 91 Main St., Carrick-on-Suir, county Tipperary; tel +353 (0)51 640528.

Keane Mahoney Smith, 20 Parnell St., Clonmel, county Tipperary; tel +353 (0)52 21601. Email: admin@kms-clonmel.com.

Tom Pollard & Co, Emmet St., Clonmel, county Tipperary; tel +353 (0)52 22755. Email: tpollard@iol.ie.

TIPPERARY CONTACTS

Rail services from Clonmel to Cork, Limerick and Rosslare with connections to Dublin from Limerick Junction; tel +353 (0)52 21982. Trains also call at Nenagh and Carrick-on-Suir (but not Cashel); for routings call Thurles Station at +353 (0)504 21733.

Bus services between most Tipperary towns and Dublin, Cork and Limerick. Hub of Bus Éireann's operations is Carrick-on-Suir; call +353 (0)51 879000.

Nenagh Guardian (local newspaper), 13 Summerhill, Nenagh, county Tipperary; tel +353 (0)67 31214.

Tourist Information, Sarsfield St., Clonmel, county Tipperary; tel +353 (0)52 22960.

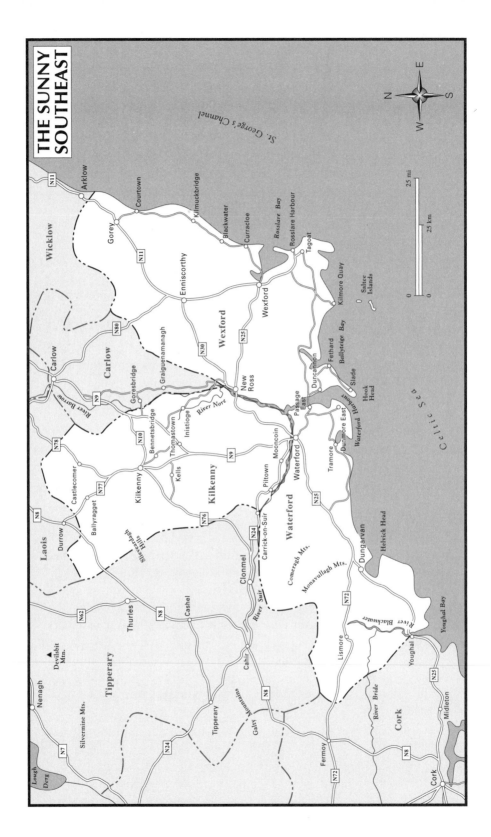

16 The Sunny Southeast

When I think of the southeast, I see gorgeous green meadows, ancient abbey ruins, pretty villages and horses galloping along sandy beaches. Despite the savage Viking and Norman past, this is Ireland at its most gentle. Even the weather here usually decides to be kind!

County Kilkenny

Don't ignore Kilkenny just because it doesn't possess a coastal fringe. Its verdant green landscape is pastoral perfection, dotted here and there with picturebook villages, shady woodland copses, ramblers' tracks and winding rivers banked by lacy white clouds of cow parsley. Lost in the fields are some hauntingly beautiful monastic settlements, and you'll also stumble across a wealth of high crosses, round towers and castles dating from Norman times. An added bonus is Kilkenny town, the country's best-preserved example of a medieval city.

Sometimes called the Marble City, Kilkenny town is the place to head first. Although wandering around its castle, abbeys and maze of crooked lanes can make you feel as if you're trapped in a time warp, the modern world is always there when you need it. Kilkenny has good train and bus service to Dublin. If you're driving, it's 70 miles from the capital by road, far enough to deter the commuter crowds. With around 20,000 inhabitants, this is a large town by Irish standards and thus laden with all the essentials: excellent shops, health services, restaurants, the Watergate theater and three annual arts festivals. And, if you suddenly develop an arid throat, you'll find 68 pubs and St. Francis' Abbey, now the headquarters of the Smithwicks Brewery.

Rather than demolish their ancient buildings, Kilkennians simply give them a new lease on life. The tourist office is located in the Shee Alms House on Rose Inn Street, built as a paupers hospital in 1582 and used as such until 1830. Dating back to 1284, the home of the infamous Witch of Kilkenny on St. Kieran's Street is now a popular pub-restaurant. On Parliament Street, Kilkenny's Archaeological Society and the genealogical county records have found a home in the Rothe House, built by a wealthy merchant for his young bride in 1594. One of the town's more recent architectural ventures was the construction of the Castle's new coachhouses and stables in 1760. Set in a flower-filled courtyard, these buildings are now used by local craftspeople and the Kilkenny Design Center.

Although Kilkenny's old black marble pavements were lifted in 1929, much else remains to distract you from your house-hunting plans: pleasant riverside walks below the Castle, St. Canice's Cathedral, the Black Abbey and the Tholsel, where medieval villains were publicly burnt at the stake. No one really knows how long people have been walking through the dark passageway of the Butterslip, but records show that in 1616 market traders were using it. Nowadays people buy their dairy produce in supermarkets, but older residents can still recite a traditional rhyme about the Butterslip:

> *If you ever go to Kilkenny,*
> *Look for the hole in the wall.*
> *Where you get twenty-four eggs for a penny*
> *And butter for nothing at all.*

Unfortunately, houses within Kilkenny town don't sell for "nothing at all" prices. It's an affluent community with people employed in the service industries, brewing and food production. Avonmore Foods employs hundreds of workers at its Kilkenny plant on the road to Ballyragget. House prices vary considerably and, as always, much depends on location and the type of home. One of the town's most sought-after residential addresses is Sion Road, which tracks the broad, bosky vale of the Nore River. Here an elegant nine-bedroom residence, currently run as a bed-and-breakfast establishment, is on the market for $1,017,000.

At the other end of the price scale, refurbished Victorian row houses in the heart of the city sell for $124,000 to $141,000. Modern semi-detached family houses with three bedrooms start at $102,000 in the suburbs but are nearer $135,500 in the most attractive residential neighborhoods. Cottages (two bedrooms) in good repair on the city's rural outskirts can fetch $124,000, but the deeper you move into the countryside, the more the price falls. In need of modernization rather than extensive repairs, a two-bedroom cottage near Ballyragget is priced at $52,000.

South Kilkenny's countryside brims with enticements, particularly if you concentrate on the small towns and villages beside the banks of the Barrow, Nore, Munster and Suir rivers, all excellent fly-fishing rivers. If your new neighbors aren't involved in farming, chances are they do something arty with clay, crystal, wool, gemstones, wood or leather. This part of the country has a very high concentration of craftworkers. There's always room for new blood and new ideas, and just because you've never done anything remotely crafty in your life doesn't mean it's too late to start. The Crafts Council of Ireland runs courses in jewelry making, pottery, blacksmithing and design skills from its training center in the Castle Yard in Kilkenny town. Whether you're a veteran craftworker looking for a new market or are interested in taking a course, you can contact them there or telephone +353 (0)56 61804. Email: ccoi@craftscouncil-of-ireland.ie.

Along with ancient Thomastown, Kilkenny's main craft clusters are the villages of Goresbridge, Graiguenamanagh, Stoneyford and Bennetsbridge. Thomastown takes its name from Thomas Fitzanthony, a Welsh-Norman

It costs a lot to buy an Irish pub these days. This Kilkenny pub changed hands for over $450,000.

© Steenie Harvey

the Witch of Kilkenny

Born in Kilkenny in 1280, Alice Kyteler was the daughter of a wealthy Norman banker who established a money-lending venture in the town. The business eventually passed into Alice's hands through inheritance, but the ecclesiastical authorities of the day were staunchly opposed to women engaging in trade and she made many enemies. As in many other witchcraft cases, money may have been the reason behind her eventual downfall. Seemingly a woman of healthy appetites, Alice worked her way through four husbands, all of whom mysteriously expired for no apparent reason. Some townsfolk believed that she had poisoned the lot of them; others whispered that it was the work of the Devil.

At her trial in 1324, the Bishop of Ossory accused her of heresy and of trafficking with his Satanic Majesty. Witnesses swore that they had seen Alice and her maidservant slaughtering cockerels and sweeping dust from the town's streets to the house of William Outlawe, Alice's son. In the murky world of medieval magick, this was a form of transference whereby dust represented gold and Kilkenny's wealth would all fall to William. In other words, witchcraft.

The court found the defendants guilty. Alice and her servant Petronella were sentenced to be burnt at the stake, William to be hanged. However, Alice managed to engineer an escape and fled to England while William bought his pardon by funding the reroofing of the choirstalls in St. Canice's Cathedral. Only the poor servant girl paid the ultimate penalty. Petronella was burnt at the Tholsel, outside Kilkenny's City Hall, along with many of her mistress' possessions. The house on St. Kieran's Street where Alice and Petronella lived now goes by the name of Kyteler's Inn.

knight who founded this place of time-toppled medieval walls and castles in 1197. Less than two miles down the road, Jerpoint Abbey silhouettes the skyline. Today its towers and cloisters are in ruins, but this was once one of the finest Cistercian abbeys in Ireland. As an example of typical prices in the surrounding area, $99,000 is being sought for a three-bedroom bungalow close to Jerpoint Abbey, a grand location with all the history you ever wanted within walking distance.

The medieval monks couldn't get enough of county Kilkenny's real estate. Five miles west of Stoneyford, they took over Kells Priory, a former Norman castle with seven gray towers and massively thick curtain walls that perches above the King's River, a tributary of the Nore. Now abandoned to time and the elements, Kells is made even more atmospheric by the fact that the government seems to have forgotten its existence. There's no ticket office, no guided tours, no designated visiting hours, just you, the sheep, and maybe a ghost or two.

Nor did the holy men neglect to colonize the banks of the Barrow River. With the 13th-century Cistercian splendor of Duiske Abbey on the doorstep, Graiguenamanagh's name actually means "the grange of the monks." Here, on 3.5 emerald acres, a modern seven-bedroom farmhouse with a sauna, a range of outoffices and a paddock is available for $565,000.

Not all farmhouses are as expensive, and obviously a lot depends on location, state of repair and the amount of land being sold with the property. About $96,000 buys a two-story farmhouse on one acre of land at Piltown, in the south of the county near the Kilkieran high crosses and the Suir River. Note, though, that it also requires some refurbishment and repair. In Inistioge, a pretty whitewashed farmhouse with the same amount of land indicates the value that these types of properties can command once restoration has taken place. The vendors are seeking $170,000.

Pronounced "inishteeg," this adorable little village is backdropped by dark, goblin woods on the banks of the Nore River below Thomastown. An 18th-century 10-arched bridge spans the river, and around the grassy square, lined with a shady canopy of lime trees, most pubs and shops have kept their original facades. It's not all that surprising to discover that Inistioge has been featured in a number of recent movies. One was the romantic weepy *Circle of Friends*, adapted from a novel of the same name by Irish writer Maeve Binchy.

Another Inistioge property currently on the market is Fourpenny Rock, a Regency-style sporting lodge with four bedrooms. In a sylvan setting overlooking the Nore Valley, it's priced at $282,500. Any Georgian house is likely to prove a good investment in the long run. Built in simple classic style, these types of residences will never go out of fashion. After all, nobody is building them any more!

What if you want an ordinary little village house? Look around Piltown, where small cottages for refurbishment start at $40,000 and detached two-story village houses in reasonable condition at $56,000. As this locality is so close to the county border, note that Carrick-on-Suir (county Tipperary) agents tend to handle properties here. Attractive Kilkenny villages near the county Waterford border include Dunkitt and Kilmacow; delightful village houses here sell for $79,000 to $89,000.

Slip through a crack in time and explore medieval Kilkenny.

© Steenie Harvey

REALTOR ADDRESS BOOK

J. David Hughes, 20 Parliament St., Kilkenny, tel +353 (0)56 63437; and Main St., Graiguenamanagh, tel +353 (0)503 24437.

Fitzgeralds, 24 Patrick St., Kilkenny; tel +353 (0)56 70888.

M. F. Grace, Callan, county Kilkenny; tel +353 (0)56 25163.

Walter Walsh, Mill St., Thomastown, county Kilkenny; tel +353 (0)56 24485.

Ganly Walters Boyd, 5 William St., Kilkenny, tel +353 (0)56 64833; and Lowe St., Thomastown, tel +353 (0)56 24600.

KILKENNY CONTACTS

Rail service to Dublin and Waterford; tel +353 (0)56 22024.

Bus Éireann service to Dublin, Cork and Waterford; tel +353 (0)56 64933. From the Parade, Kavanagh's runs buses to Cashel in Tipperary via Kells and Fethard, also to Carlow, Thurles and Portlaoise; tel +353 (0)56 31106.

Tourist Information, Shee Alms House, Rose Inn St., Kilkenny; tel +353 (0)56 51500.

County Wexford

Filling Ireland's southeast corner, maritime Wexford has a strong agricultural base and has been inhabited since prehistoric times. Although converted to Christianity by St. Ibar in the 5th century, its name comes from the Norse word *Waesfjord*, meaning "sandy harbor" or "harbor of mud flats." The Viking invaders who settled here were followed in 1169 by the Nor-

Deer farming is becoming a popular agri-business.

© Steenie Harvey

mans, for whom Wexford was their first Irish port of call. Then as now, the county's main settlement was Wexford town. Unfortunately, relatively few traces of the distant past remain. For that you can thank Cromwell, who attacked the town in 1649, putting an estimated three quarters of its 2,000 citizens and all of its Franciscan friars to the sword.

Today, around 16,000 people live in the Wexford town area with smaller numbers concentrated in Gorey, Enniscorthy, New Ross and Rosslare Harbour, the main ferry port to South Wales in Britain. Over a quarter of the population is aged between 25 and 44, and employment is found in a diversity of both multinational and indigenous enterprises, everything from food production and data processing and light engineering to the manufacture of pharmaceutical products and car components. In addition, Wexford has benefited from the government's decentralization program. A number of State departments have relocated here; they include the Environmental Protection Agency and Teagasc, the State's agricultural research center.

> *Golden sandy beaches are county Wexford's star attraction, and many have been awarded the European blue flag for excellence.*

Despite the economic boom, young local couples haven't been priced out of the market and, unlike in Dublin, it is possible for them to get onto the housing ladder. Two-bedroom apartments in Wexford town can still be had for under $90,000 and small terraced row houses for $74,000 to $85,000. However, larger showpiece apartments in top locations around the harbor and quays can cost over $100,000. One of the latest developments is the Goodtide Harbor Apartments. Properties range in size from 488 to 987 square feet and cost between $104,000 and $186,500.

Although Wexford town is no longer a commercial port—the Slaney estuary is too silted up with centuries of river mud—it still has the feel of a seafarers' hangout. One of its most famous sons was John Barry, who emigrated to America and founded the United States Navy. Its ribbon-thin streets can get very boisterous during the summer Viking Festival, though for classier entertainment you should come for October's Opera Festival.

Golden sandy beaches are county Wexford's star attraction, and many have been awarded the European blue flag for excellence. Near Gorey, in the north of the county, you'll find beautiful strands beside the villages of Ballymoney and Courtown; the endless golden chain then continues through Morriscastle, Kilmuckbridge, Blackwater and Curracloe, which was featured in the recent Tom Hanks movie, *Saving Private Ryan*. Along with miles of forest walks and sand dunes, there are excellent marina facilities here, and residents are right beside one of Europe's most renowned nature reserves, the North Sloblands. During the winter months, the Slobs provide a feeding ground for around 10,000 migratory Greenland white-fronted

a Night at the Opera

even non-operagoers have probably heard of Bizet's *Carmen* and Strauss' *Die Fledermaus*. But have you ever had the chance to enjoy *Fosca, I Cavalieri di Ekebu* or *Sarlatan*, the tragi-comic tale of a quack doctor who falls in love with a beautiful hypochondriac? At the Wexford festival, an 18-day October extravaganza of opera and more, you could have seen all of the above-mentioned operas in recent years.

Along with its Nordic setting, the hammers, fire, and alcoholic Lutheran pastor of *I Cavalieri di Ekebu* had given this particular opera something of a cult status in Sweden. But the Wexford performance of *Sarlatan* was the first on stage since its last production 60 years before, at Brno in Czechoslovakia. The career of its Czech composer, Pavel Haas, was cut brutally short when he went to his death in the gas chambers of Auschwitz in 1944.

Since Wexford's Opera Festival began in 1951, the focus has been on bringing to light obscure operas that for one reason or another have been unjustly neglected or forgotten. The festival attracts an international crowd of opera lovers, and you can also sample street theater, poetry readings, choral recitals, lectures, stand-up comedy and music that ranges from foot-tapping Irish traditional to the haunting strains of gypsy violins. Wexford town itself takes on a carnival atmosphere with storekeepers competing for best festive window display, and *artistes* and audiences alike throng the cafés and bars along Main Street and the Quays. No other small-town Irish festival offers such a perfect excuse for revelers to get out their evening dresses and dinner jackets!

Tickets for the three showpiece operas aren't cheap. Last year's prices were pitched at just under $60 for each performance. Daytime and late night events are more affordable, costing between $9 and $15. For booking and information about this year's festival, contact Wexford Festival Opera Box Office, Theater Royal, High St., Wexford town, county Wexford; tel +353 (0)53 22144.

geese, more than half the world's entire population. South of Wexford town lies Rosslare Strand and Carne. Round the corner to the south coast proper and you'll come across Kilmore Quay, Fethard, Hook Head and Duncannon.

As no location within the county is more than a two-hour drive from Dublin, Wexford is a favorite location for second-home buyers. Consequently prices are fairly buoyant and, depending on whether it has sea views or not, the typical three- or four-bedroom family bungalow-type property falls somewhere between $115,000 and $230,000. For example, $146,000 would currently buy a mint-condition three-bedroom bungalow close to Tintern Abbey and within easy reach of the beaches of Duncannon and Fethard-on-Sea.

Think $170,000 for a bungalow at Curracloe. At Rosslare Harbor, a five-bedroom bungalow, currently run as a bed-and-breakfast residence, is on sale for $220,500. That's not to say cheaper properties can't still be found. Ten minutes' drive from Wexford town, near Murrinstown village and Johnstown Castle, a three-bedroom refurbished cottage on a 0.75-acre site is available for $79,000. And although this is an inland location, if you look due south you can see the ocean and the distant smudge of the Saltee Islands, whose surrounding treacherous waters gave rise to the nickname "the graveyard of a thousand ships." If you prefer to buy a plot of land within telescope sight of the coast and build a home, half-acre sites with planning permission start at $29,000.

If your heart is set on a thatched property, the area around the fishing village of Kilmore Quay is your best bet. Lining the main street, almost all the local houses are pictures of whitewashed, thatched perfection. Like every visitor who turns up for July's seafood festival, you too will probably want to own one. All well and good if you have deep pockets—are you prepared to part with $249,000? That's the price that Wexford agency Kehoe's quotes for two small adjacent thatched cottages here that could be converted into a larger family home. Outside the village prices drop—for example, to $102,000 for a small non-thatched modern bungalow.

I also like the Duncannon area, though again, properties are quite expensive. Three-bedroom bungalow properties sell for $156,000. South of Duncannon, some lovely walks criss-cross the largely deserted Hook Peninsula, pointing into the ocean like a witch's bony finger. The lighthouse on the headland dates back to the 12th century, and the peninsula itself is dotted with crumbling castles, forts and abbeys.

This area has another and very curious historical claim to fame. Ever heard the phrase "by hook or by crook"? Cromwell coined it during his campaign to capture Waterford city, which lies a few miles west across the county border. What he was referring to were two possible landing points: Hook in Wexford and Crooke in county Waterford. The city would fall to his army by Hook or by Crooke.

Although the Wexford coastline seems to hold all the aces, don't ignore the hinterland, where there's a good choice of attractive cottages and small houses in move-into-tomorrow condition for $75,000 to $100,000. Locals have a tendency to give fanciful names to their cottages. At Bridgetown, 10 miles from Wexford town, Foxes Hollow is a two-story cottage with four bedrooms priced at $96,000. At Tagoat village, not too far from a number of sandy beaches, the same price is sought for the Thrushes Nest, a pretty whitewashed single-story cottage with beamed ceilings. As there are plenty of trees in the half-acre garden, perhaps the name isn't too fanciful; the thrush is quite a common bird in Ireland and it has a beautifully sweet song.

At the other end of the price scale, $622,000 buys a seven-bedroom property (4,325 square feet) at Ferrycarrig, three miles from Wexford town on the Enniscorthy road. It could be run as a guesthouse and a gym/games room is already in place. The village attracts plenty of visitors for this is the site of the Irish National Heritage Park, a kind of outdoor historical theme park with re-creations of everything from Neolithic burial tombs to a replica Viking shipyard complete with replica Viking longship.

Carry on northwards along the road through the heart of strawberry-growing countryside and you'll come to Enniscorthy, a little town on the banks of the Slaney River. Twenty minutes' drive from the beaches and back-dropped by the Blackstairs Mountains, this busy little town has plenty of waterfront inns, brightly painted shopfronts, a 13th-century castle and an annual summer strawberry festival. "It's the biggest small town in the world," claims one enthusiastic local realtor, "a town that's rocketing from nowhere."

Starting price for a two-bedroom terraced (row) house within the town is $73,500, newly built modern houses start at $99,000. A good-sized apartment (527 square feet) costs around $67,000, though if you're not fussy about a view, you can buy a one-bedroom apartment within the town for $45,000. In the immediate surrounding countryside, $90,000 would be a typical price for a renovated cottage, though you can pay a lot more. A 250-year-old stone cottage, impeccably restored and with views of the Blackstairs Mountains, is priced at $175,000.

One of the nicest villages is Ferns, with yet another collection of castle and abbey ruins. This was once the base of the Kings of Leinster, whose number included the notorious Dermot MacMurrough, who invited the Normans over to Ireland and thus brought about centuries of English rule. Three-bedroom modern bungalows here fetch $135,000.

Realtor Address Book
Corish's, Custom House Quay, Wexford town, county Wexford; tel +353 (0)53 22288.

Kehoe & Associates, Commercial Quay, Wexford town, county Wexford; tel +353 (0)53 44393.

Michael O'Leary, The Bullring, Wexford town, county Wexford; tel +353

With skills and know-how, there are plenty of self-employment opportunities.

(0)53 24611. Also with an office at Slaney Place, Enniscorthy, county Wexford; tel +353 (0)54 35061/37322.

Simon Kavanagh, Templeshannon, Enniscorthy, county Wexford; tel +353 (0)54 35335.

Warren Estates, Main St., Gorey, county Wexford; tel +353 (0)55 21211. Email: property@warrenestates.com.

Haythornewaite Auctioneers, Selskar, county Wexford; tel +353 (0)53 46046. Email: wexprop@iol.ie.

WEXFORD CONTACTS

The Guardian (local newspaper), Thomas St., Gorey, county Wexford; tel +353 (0)55 21423.

Rail service to Dublin, Rosslare Harbour, Enniscorthy and Wicklow; tel +353 (0)53 22522.

Bus Éireann service to Dublin, Rosslare Harbour, Gorey, Limerick and Killarney in Kerry; tel +353 (0)53 22522. Private buses to Enniscorthy and county Carlow with Kavanagh's; tel +353 (0)53 43081.

Tourist Office, Crescent Quay, Wexford town, county Wexford; tel +353 (0)53 23111.

County Waterford

Waterford is the Crystal County, renowned throughout the world as the home of the exquisitely crafted crystal that shares its name. With around 44,000 people, Waterford city is the county's main population center and also the southeast's biggest commercial port, always busy with freighters and container ships. Although much of Waterford's outskirts are a featureless sprawl of industrial development, it's proud of its reputation as a working city. Thanks to its strategic location on the Suir river estuary, this is a true trading settlement and has been for over a millennium. While you probably wouldn't want to live within the city confines, do pay a visit, for at its heart lies a fascinating kernel of historical heritage. Surrounded by the remnants of medieval walls, its streets and lanes track back through the centuries to the time of the Victorians, the Georgians and even the Anglo-Normans, who wrested the settlement of Vadrafjord from the Vikings in 1170 during a three-day siege.

The city's most famous Norman landmark is Reginald's Tower, a stone replacement for the original wooden watchtower built by Reginald the Dane in 1003, where guard could be kept over the longships in the harbor. The tower has witnessed an incredible amount of history. The all-conquering Norman lord Strongbow and the Irish princess Aoife held their wedding feast here above the rubble and ashes of the fallen Viking city; it has served as a royal guesthouse, a military arsenal, a mint and a jail. And although the

the Crystal Connection

*a*s an object of desire, Waterford crystal is just about unsurpassable. It rings sweet as a bell and gleams with an almost magical silvery brilliance. The great mystery is how something so beautiful can be created from such mundane mineral products as red lead, silica sand and potash. Producing this luxury crystalware demands great skill, and it takes between eight and 10 years for the glassblowers, cutters and engravers to fully learn their art.

Waterford's connection with crystal making dates back over 200 years, to 1783 to be precise, when George and William Penrose founded the Waterford Glass House on the city quayside. The new crystal business quickly flourished and went on to win a number of gold medals at the Great Exhibition in London. Unfortunately for the Penrose family and their workers, the firm went out of business in 1851, mainly through the British government's imposition of a crippling import tax on the raw minerals needed to produce this heavy crystalware.

With Irish independence came the urge to breathe new life back into old crafts. Waterford crystal was reborn in 1947, relaunching its wares on the world market four years later. So successful was the revival that the company had to move to larger premises on Cork Road. Today the factory employs around 1,600 people, and visitors can take a workshop tour and do serious damage to their credit cards in the Crystal Gallery. Even a tiny crystal napkin-holder will cost you at least $25.

motto on the city's coat of arms is *Urbs intacta manet Waterfordia* (Waterford remains unconquered), the besieged townsfolk did eventually surrender to Cromwellian forces in 1650.

To give you an idea of house prices within Waterford city, single-story urban "cottages" with one bedroom fetch from $54,000 to $68,000. A two-bedroom home in semi-detached suburbia close to the Technical Institute costs around $118,000. If you are looking to rent, the Halley Grace agency quotes $510 per month for a three-bedroom home.

With county Cork to the west and county Wexford to the east, Waterford's coastline has sandy coves, clifftop walks and some particularly attractive harbor towns and fishing villages. Coastal property prices tend to be fairly high as the area is a easy commute to both Waterford city and Cork city. If you want to be near Waterford city, the most affordable area is inland, tracking westwards along the Suir river valley. Look around villages like Portlaw to find refurbished terraced village houses for $76,000 and detached cottages in the surrounding countryside for $67,000 to $79,000.

In the southeast of the county, eight miles from Waterford city, Dunmore East is a lovely fishing village and holiday retreat with plenty of thatched cottages and a busy harbor that entices many ocean-going yachts from Europe. The village seems to have the lot: a 12th-century castle, a 19th-century lighthouse, some good inns and restaurants, clifftop and woodland walks, and great beaches. Ladies' Cove is right in the village while a short stroll south brings you to Counsellor's Strand, a beach awarded for cleanliness and safety that flies the much-coveted EU Blue Flag.

Although no thatched cottages were for sale at the time of writing, three-bedroom semi-detached bungalows near Dunmore East's golf club were on sale for $163,000. It's a highly sought-after area, and some 0.33-acre sites with planning permission now fetch $110,000; prospective residents are willing to pay over the odds to bask in the mild Gulf Stream weather. It's so mild here that palm trees grow in gardens, and if you fancy trying your hand at wine-making, it's possible to grow certain varieties of grapes. Not that you have to break your back digging and delving—I always like gardens that resemble wildflower meadows, and there are lots of those around here.

Traveling west, the next place you'll come to is Tramore, but unless you have kids in tow, you'll probably pass straight through. A traditional blue-collar seaside resort, its safe golden beach is perfect for the bucket-and-spade brigade to build elaborate castles and bury snoozing dads in the sand. The huge Trabolgan "holiday village" is here, and when it rains the crowds descend on Splashworld, an indoor leisure center with swimming pools, water slides and chutes. Fine for a family day out, but do you really want to live in a town of penny arcades and burger joints? If so, two-bedroom vacation bungalows around the town can be had for $73,500.

Leave Tramore behind, drive across Great Newtown Head, and you're back in the world of deserted coves and sleepy-hollow fishing villages. Anywhere around Annestown, Bonmahon, Stradbally, Clonea or Ballinacourty makes an idyllic retreat, but the location factor means you have to pay at least $150,000 for a three-bedroom bungalow with sea views. For those looking to build a property, a typical one-acre site with outline planning permission for a residence is likely to cost upwards of $50,000. Yet move a short distance inland and you can still find old-style cottages in decent repair for $70,000.

Next stop along the coast is Dungarvan, the administrative center for county Waterford. It's a good base for making property forays into east Cork, the West Waterford hinterland, and around the Comeragh Mountains that straddle the county's northern border with Tipperary. Brand-new three-bedroom townhouses sell for $141,000; apartments overlooking Dungarvan Harbor start at $78,000 (one-bedroom) and go up to $152,500 (three-bedroom). Smaller apartments here rent for around $510 monthly.

Thankfully, not all rural properties are so pricy. Habitable homes in the Nire Valley area still surface for less than $120,000. One $118,000 gem I liked the look of was a two-bedroom traditional stone cottage that had already been renovated. Sitting on 0.75 acre, it has gorgeous mountain views and a gurgling stream at the bottom of the garden. Near the county Tipperary border, the Nire Valley qualifies as a secret place, perfect for anybody wanting to live off the beaten track. I took a walking holiday in this unspoiled area last fall, staying in Ballymacarbry village and hiking the lavender ridgetops of the Comeraghs, gentle mountains that rise only to

2,625 feet (800 meters). Steeped in legend, dark jewel-like loughs lie deep in corries in the mountains' rocky flanks and local lore whispers of fairy cattle emerging from the waters on moonlit nights. Although part of county Waterford, the Nire Valley's nearest town is Clonmel in Tipperary. Check out agents there for local properties.

REALTOR ADDRESS BOOK

O'Shea & O'Toole, 11 Gladstone St., Waterford city, county Waterford; tel +353 (0)51 876757. Email: info@osheaotoole.com.

Lawrence & McDonald, 15 Parnell St., Waterford city, county Waterford; tel +353 (0)51 853199. Email: lawrencemacdonald@tinet.ie.

Phil Cusack, Main St., Kilmacthomas, county Waterford; tel +353 (0)51 294364.

Eamonn Spratt, Grattan House, O'Connell St., Dungarvan, county Waterford; tel +353 (0)58 42211.

Halley Grace, 8 Arundel Square, Waterford; tel +353 (0)51 875187. Email: halgrace@indigo.ie.

WATERFORD CONTACTS

Waterford News (local newspaper), 25 Michael St., Waterford City, county Waterford; tel +353 (0)51 874951.

Rail service to Dublin, Kilkenny, Limerick and Rosslare; tel +353 (0)51 873403.

Bus Éireann service to Dublin, Cork, Limerick, Galway, Kilkenny and Rosslare; tel +353 (0)51 879000.

Tourist Information Office, The Quay, Waterford city, county Waterford; tel +353 (0)51 875823.

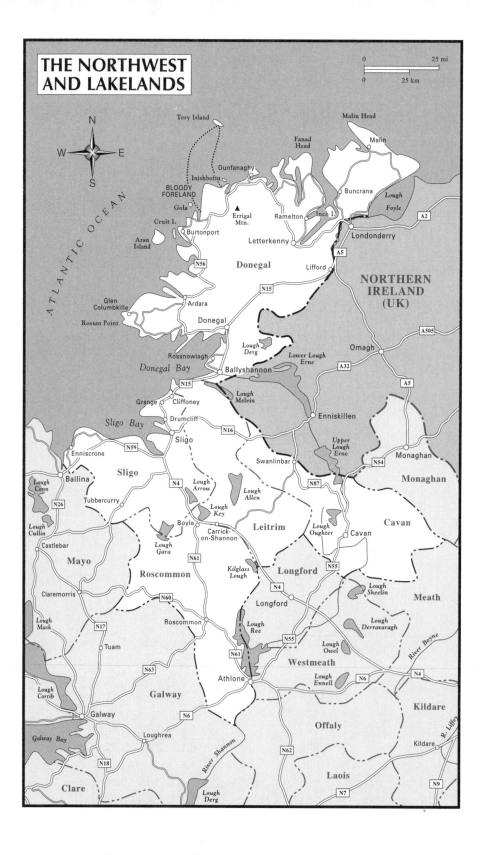

17 The Northwest and Lakelands

Far from the well-worn tourist trails, the underrated counties of Ireland's Northwest and Lakelands are an ideal choice for getting away from the usual stresses of modern life. Perhaps more so than anywhere else, it's here that bargain hunters will find some of the country's most affordable properties.

County Sligo

A land of literature and legend, Sligo is synonymous with the poet William Butler Yeats, who spent many childhood summers here. Dubbed "Yeats Country," its most distinctive landmark is Benbulben, a flat-topped table mountain famed in Irish mythology as the site where the hero Diarmuid met a sticky end on the tusks of a magic boar.

Many places throughout the county resonate with eerie magic: the Lake Isle of Innisfree, shimmering Lough Arrow and Lough Gill, the bluebell glades of Slish Wood, and the dolmens and stone circles of Carrowmore, a mysterious necropolis whose secrets date back to Bronze Age times. Here too is Knocknarea, traditionally held to be a hollow hill and one of the

225

strongholds of the *Sidhe* (the fairies). Crowned by a cairn, Knocknarea is also reputed to be the final resting place of Maeve, a tempestuous goddess-queen who waged battle against Ulster's warriors for possession of the Brown Bull of Cooley.

Sligo Town

With 19,000 citizens, the county's only sizable settlement is Sligo town. On the quality of life scale, it has all the right ingredients: a good general hospital and services, train links to Dublin and a vibrant array of cultural activities. It also has a wonderfully unvamped center retaining much of the character of times past. Visit a time-warp pub like Hargadon's on O'Connell Street and you'll feel as if you've been transported back to the last century, especially during winter when a pot-bellied stove blazes in the main bar.

A land of literature and legend, Sligo is synonymous with the poet William Butler Yeats.

On the banks of the Garavogue River, Sligo's shopping streets are always busy, drawing in people from Leitrim, Roscommon and south Donegal, whose own little towns aren't quite so well stocked. Cinemas, restaurants and the Hawk's Well theater give the town a year-round bustle; regular summertime events include the Arts Festival and the Yeats' Summer School, attended by scholars from all over the world.

Within Sligo town's environs, three-bedroom homes start at around $96,000. Four-bedroom houses within a five-mile radius can go from $124,000 to $280,000 or more—a lot depends on area. It's a good place to find rental properties. The town's estate agents enjoy a lively rentals market, thanks to sizable numbers of hospital staff and students from the Regional Technical College seeking accommodation. Depending on size and location, good quality country properties can be had for between $650 and $850 a month. Apartments within town generally rent for between $450 and $620 a month.

Cottages and small country houses in fairly good condition can occasionally be picked up for as little as $45,000 in remoter corners of the county. For this price, though, you'll have to search in the south of the county, well away from the ocean. As everywhere else, the price of homes usually depends on proximity to town or coastline. In rural backwaters, there are still quite a few traditional-style cottages in various states of repair selling for under $34,000. However, move the exact same cottage to the coast and there's every likelihood its price will have doubled.

Attractive north Sligo villages for living the country lifestyle include Carney, Cliffoney and Grange. At Drumcliffe, W. B. Yeats is buried in the Protestant churchyard; his great-grandfather was once rector here. Under the shadow of Benbulben, the gravestone bears an epitaph Yeats penned himself: "Cast a cold eye on life, on death. Horseman, pass by!" A traditional country house here is currently on the market for $147,000, which seems an exceptional price considering it has seven bedrooms.

SOUTH SLIGO

The south of the county has more of an unexplored feel. At Ballymote, $39,500 buys a modest two-bedroom cottage on a half-acre plot, but the garden is in need of some loving care and attention. In these parts it's rare to come across the kind of gardens filled with hollyhocks, sweet peas and old-fashioned damask roses the word "cottage" always conjures! A far prettier cottage with a conservatory and flowering shrubs in the same area is priced at $107,000.

Other good places in south Sligo to find fairly inexpensive bucolic bolt-holes is in the countryside around Tubbercurry and Gurteen villages. Schiller's recently had a small cottage built from natural stone and blue bangor slate, priced at $20,500. As you can probably guess, though, a cottage at that price requires extensive renovation—and no electricity was on site. (Though a powerline is nearby and thus easily connected.)

Small cottages in good structural condition start at around $40,000, but not all will necessarily come with the trappings that most of us expect nowadays. A cottage is currently available for that price near Ballymote village. Sound structure, electricity and water already connected, but no bathroom or septic tank for getting rid of waste. I remember inspecting a similar cottage in county Sligo when I was looking for my own Irish home

Rosses Point, county Sligo

© Steenie Harvey

the fairy folk

Sligo's folk heritage chronicles countless strange stories about apparitions of the land. In his *Fairy and Folk Tales of the Irish Peasantry*, W. B. Yeats concluded that when the pagan gods of the Celts were no longer worshipped, they diminished in the popular imagination until eventually they turned into "the good people," or fairies. During the 19th century, it was also reputed that fairies were fallen angels or, alternatively, the heathen dead. Barred from heaven, they weren't wicked enough to deserve a place in hell and so had to live out a shadowy existence in secret places: caves, hollow hills, burial mounds and the ancient earthen forts known as raths.

Superstition warned that it was important to treat these ancestral spirits with respect. Fairies held the power to bring wealth to a farm or to give fishermen a good catch. When neglected or badly treated, they could turn spiteful. Thanks to *pishogues* (fairy spells), hens stopped laying eggs, milk turned sour and livestock fell sick. And any-one who cut down a fairy thorn tree or built a new dwelling across a fairy path could expect to suffer an unpleasant accident. But naturally every spell had its counterspell; the four-leafed shamrock, a symbol of good luck, was thought to guard against other-worldly bewitchments.

The best-known character in folklore is the leprechaun, or fairy shoemaker. Legend claims that if you catch one he'll lead you to a crock of gold. However, if you take your eyes off him for just one second, he'll disappear. A more menacing figure is the banshee (*bean sidhe*) for it's said that the sound of her eldritch wail outside a house signifies a death in the family. In some tales the banshee appears as a beautiful young woman wearing fine clothes; in others she is described as a wizened old crone draped in a shroud. Sighting the *bean nidhe*, the fairy washerwoman, is also a premonition of disaster. In heroic myths, warriors doomed to fall in battle often see her beside water. She is wailing and washing out bloodstained clothing—theirs.

to buy. I asked the agent why he was showing it to me; how was I expected to manage without a lavatory? "Do what folks have always done," he said. "Use the field." Incredible though it seems, there are still some elderly people living in old-fashioned hermit's cottages who see nothing odd about not having a bathroom. One has to presume that they bathe in a tin tub in front of the fire.

The two main seaside villages in the north of the county are Rosses Point (site of an 18-hole links course that holds regular tournament events) and Strandhill, popular with surfers. At low tide you can walk across from Cummeen Strand to Coney Island and look out to sea from the Wishing Chair in which St. Patrick reputedly sat. This, I hasten to add, is not the Coney Island in New York! Properties in these two villages are very expensive: newly built family homes start at $226,000 and spacious bungalows fetch just under $250,000.

Further south, Enniscrone is trimmed by a five-mile stretch of golden sands and is another stop for golfers on the western links trail. Believers in the powers of thalassotherapy come to immerse themselves in the village's curious seaweed baths, here since Edwardian times. If you're looking for something large enough to run as a B&B business, four-bedroom bungalows sell for around the $175,000 mark.

REALTOR ADDRESS BOOK

Schiller & Schiller, Ardtarmon Castle, Ballinfull, county Sligo; tel +353 (0)71 63284. Email: schiller@iol.ie.

Des Butler, Quay St., Sligo; tel +353 (0)71 45923.

Sligo Estates, Quay St., Sligo; tel +353 (0)71 43425. E-mail: sligoestates@eircom.net.

Matt Mulholland, Markievicz Road, Sligo; tel +353 (0)71 42845.

McCarrick & Sons, Tubbercurry, county Sligo; tel +353 (0)71 85050.

SLIGO CONTACTS

Sligo Champion (local newspaper), Wine St., Sligo; tel +353 (0)71 69222.

Rail service to Dublin, stopping at Longford, Mullingar and a number of other stations en route from Macdiarmada Station, Sligo; tel +353 (0)71 69888.

Bus Éireann service to Dublin, Galway, Ballina and Derry in Northern Ireland, Macdiarmada Station, Sligo; tel +353 (0)71 60066.

Tourist Office, Temple St., Sligo; tel +353 (0)71 61201.

County Donegal

The distance from Dublin to Donegal's heartland is barely 150 miles, but it really can feel like traveling to the opposite ends of the earth. Best known for its tweeds, Donegal's name means "Fort of the Foreigner" (Dún na nGall), a reference to the 9th-century Viking invaders who established forts here. Geographically part of Ulster Province, this is the Republic's northernmost county, a place of blue, windswept mountains, heathery moorlands and small communities where the welcome is warm and generous. The Irish language remains in daily use along its western fringe, particularly around Gweedore (Gaoth Dobhair), and it's still fairly common to hear handweavers' looms clattering away in many a cottage.

Ramblers soon discover that Donegal is a walkers' paradise with over 400 miles of jigsaw-puzzle coastline. Toy-town fishing ports give way to long pristine beaches punctuated by cliffs, caves and rocky promontories that absolutely teem with birdlife. Scenic splendors include the Bloody Foreland, Horn Head and the giddy heights of Slieve League whose sea cliffs (1,972 feet) are the highest in Europe. At the center of the county is quartz-tipped Mount Errigal and Glenveagh National Park, 25,000 acres of blanket bogs and forested mountains with roaming herds of red deer.

The map shows that Donegal shares a border with Northern Ireland. How close you are to what is euphemistically termed "the other tradition" is evidenced by the July 12 celebrations in Rossnowlagh, a seaside village just north of Ballyshannon town. Rossnowlagh is home to the Republic's only Orange Order Parade, during which Protestant men wearing bowler hats and orange sashes march through the village to pay tribute to King Billy, or William of Orange, who defeated the Catholic King James II at the Battle of the Boyne in 1690.

For many years "the Troubles" kept timid travelers away from these parts and also ensured house prices remained at bargain-basement levels. Just recently, I was amazed to see an asking price of just $40,000 for a cottage at Ballybofey. Although this particular cottage was very tiny—only one bedroom—you can still come across some very reasonably priced homes here. At the time of writing, Letterkenny agent Paul Franklin had some really enticing buys on his books: a period-style stone built cottage overlooking a river estuary for $73,500 and a three-bedroom cottage at Raphoe for $78,000.

THE EASTERN SIDE OF DONEGAL

According to another local realtor, the east of the county still offers Ireland's best value properties. However, too many villages along Donegal's eastern edge have a gloomy, run-down feel. Fishing, clothing manufacture and tweed production are the county's major industries, and they're all sited away from the border. The Celtic Tiger is still to pay a visit to communities like Pettigo, where only 30 percent of the working-age population is employed.

THE WESTERN SIDE OF DONEGAL

In the more scenic west, and especially on the coast, properties sell faster

Traditional farmhouses for renovation can sometimes still be found.

© Steenie Harvey

and for a lot more money. You may have to go up to around $100,000 for a small modern bungalow. That's the kind of price they're fetching in the small town of Dungloe. However, all of Donegal's western coast is vacation home territory, and you'll be in competition for prize properties with city buyers from Dublin, Belfast and other places. The good news is that most second-home buyers are seeking modern properties in sight of the sea, and they tend to ignore the habitable little cottages in the folds of the hills that can still be unearthed for less than $65,000. And if your dream is to own a tavern, recent sightings of pubs for sale included one on the Inishowen Peninsula for $249,000.

Donegal's remoteness is another factor that has helped keep the cap on the property market. Trains don't come this far north and most local bus services can only be described as infrequent. But while the county's sense of separateness has an undoubted charm, prospective new residents ought to weigh all the pros and cons of buying a property here, particularly if planning to live in Ireland year-round. Yes, summers can be glorious but the gray gloom of winter is another proposition entirely. You're in for a dose of Ulster weather: Mist rolls in, rain drizzles down, and you may come to feel that your little home feels rather like a prison. Donegal isn't the ideal location for anyone suffering from SAD, seasonal affective disorder.

APPEALING TOWNS IN DONEGAL

Even so, Donegal is undoubtedly popular with Dutch and German buyers, who seem to like the idea of living in a place where sheep outnumber people. The best places to begin a house hunt are in the county's main towns: Letterkenny, Buncrana, Moville Ballyshannon, Donegal town and the seaside resort of Bundoran. All have a good choice of realtors with properties spread over the county.

In the southern half of Donegal, one interesting buy was Wood Lodge, a Georgian residence on the shores of Donegal Bay, a mile from Mountcharles village and five miles from Donegal town. Recently run as a guesthouse, it was priced at $430,000; the grounds also contained a small lodge, divided into three self-catering apartments. Coming down the price scale, a former smallholding at St. John's Point has been converted into a small vacation home development. Two- and three-bedroom apartments are priced at $62,000 and $68,000, respectively.

Also in south Donegal, Ballyshannon is a lively town of steep, characterful streets that hosts a big folk festival over the August Bank Holiday. Newly built semi-detached houses here currently sell for $77,000. Although they may not fit your image of "romantic Ireland," the majority of Irish buyers prefer to buy new if they can.

One of the main drawbacks in buying centuries-old properties is that they often require you to spend quite a lot on maintenance. Priced at

$99,500 and a short walk from the nearby seaside resort town of Bundoran, a modern three-bedroom bungalow beside the salmon-rich Drowes River typifies the ideal home for many Irish families.

Donegal covers a huge area (this is the second-largest county after Cork), and it can take hours to get from the commercial fishing port of Killybegs to the county's northernmost tip, Malin Head. Its footloose flocks of sheep, Irish-language signposts and extremely narrow roads laced with scary hairpin bends make for extremely slow driving times, so don't go thinking you'll be able to inspect more than a handful of homes in a day or two.

> *This is a place of blue, windswept mountains, heathery moorlands and small communities where the welcome is warm and generous.*

Once you hit the house-hunting trail, one western Donegal village you might want to check out for properties is Glencolumbcille, an Irish-speaking community of whitewashed cottages on the sheltered side of the Slieve League peninsula.

Credited with converting Scotland to Christianity, St. Columbcille (aka St. Columba) lived here during the 6th century, and the hilly neighborhood is studded with holy sites and prehistoric curiosities. On the saint's Pattern Day, June 9, villagers take part in an evening pilgrimage around the sacred places. Summers can be quite lively with tourists coming to check out the village's traditional music pubs and wandering around the open-air folk museum for a glimpse into the rural past. Refurbished cottages around here and Glenties village can be had for $75,000 to $80,000; a farmhouse to restore was priced at $90,000.

SCENIC DONEGAL

Following the coastal road northwestwards, you'll come to the Bloody Foreland. It takes its name from the setting sun, which paints the peninsula a fiery crimson. This is a wonderful drive, full of twists and turns, and glimpses of the islands of Inishbofin, Inishdooey, Arranmore and Tory. A little further on, at Sheephaven Bay, Dunfanaghy village is one of the most captivating stops on the magical seven-mile Atlantic Drive that links Rosguill Peninsula to the giddy heights of Horn Head. To help attract visitors to this remote corner, local people have transformed Dunfanaghy's former workhouse into a heritage center that chronicles the hardships of the Famine years of 1845 to 1847.

Those who enjoy outdoor pleasures will find an 18-hole links course here along with wonderful walks around Killahoey Beach, Ards Forest Park and out to crumbling Doe Castle, built in the 16th century by Scottish mercenaries. It's a much sought-after location where newly built three-bedroom vacation cottages sell for around $100,000.

Across the bay, Downings is another engaging little hamlet where fishing

St. Patrick's Purgatory

fancy the idea of a three-day break on an island marooned in the middle of a remote lake for just $22.50? Accommodation, food and the boat ride too? Of course you do, so let's set sail with Mr. Snow the ferryman to Station Island and a retreat wryly described by past visitors as "Ireland's holy health farm." Six miles north of Pettigo, the island with its cluster of grim buildings known as St. Patrick's Purgatory is the location for the toughest pilgrimage in Christendom: Lough Derg.

Donegal's Lough Derg is not to be confused with the lake of the same name in Clare. This isn't a place where you find cozy pubs, pleasure crafts and watersports. What you get instead is a chance to quite literally renounce the world, the flesh and the devil. The three-day course in pain and suffering is almost shockingly medieval and would undoubtedly test the ascetic resolve of a Trappist monk. On arriving on the island, the first thing that happens is that you are deprived of your footwear—socks and shoes aren't given back until you leave the island. Your bare and bloody feet spend the next three days stumbling over the jagged remains of beehive cells where monks of the early Celtic church lived out their days in lonely isolation.

Chanting long patterns of prayer, pilgrims also take part in a vigil, which effectively means being deprived of sleep for 36 hours. Nor can they take any comfort in the pleasures of the table; there's only one meal a day served at St. Patrick's Purgatory and it consists of dry toast and black tea. First chronicled back in the 1100s, the Lough Derg pilgrimage used to be even tougher than it is today. Pilgrims once spent the vigil inside a cave instead of the basilica. Having suffered Lough Derg's agonies myself, I can promise you that the pilgrimage is an experience you'll never forget.

No advance booking is necessary for these pilgrimages, which take place between June 1 and August 15. (The last one of the year starts on August 13.) For less hardy pilgrims, one-day retreats costing $13.50 also take place throughout the year and do need to be booked in advance. For more information contact The Prior, St. Patrick's Purgatory, Lough Derg, Pettigo, county Donegal; tel +353 (0)72 61518.

---

boats land catches of salmon, lobster and crab. In this part of the county properties are fairly expensive. Dormer bungalows with three to six bedrooms are priced between $135,000 and $186,000. "Dormer" is a word you'll come across fairly often in relation to cottages and houses. If you're puzzled by the term, what it generally refers to is an original single-story dwelling that now has a loft conversion, whereby extra rooms have been built into the roof space.

The next spit of land is the Fanad Peninsula, separated from the Inishowen Peninsula by Lough Swilly. The lough has many myths associated with it. One is that its name comes from *Suileach*, a 400-eyed water monster that was slain by the local hero, St. Colmcille. To cross from one peninsula to the other first entails a southerly journey back through Ramelton (sometimes spelled Rathmelton) to Letterkenny. More a village than a town, Ramelton dates back to the 17th century and was the setting for *The Hanging Gale*, a major 1995 TV drama that commemorated the onset of the Great Famine. Townhouses here can still be had for $68,000.

The Inishowen Peninsula (Inis Eoghain, Owen's Island) takes its name from Owen, son of Niall of the Nine Hostages, who is credited in some folk tales with capturing St. Patrick and taking him from Wales to Ireland. Once part of the great northern kingdom of the Ui Neill clan, it's one of the wildest and most beautiful spots in the whole country with evocative prehistoric sites such as the circular stone fort at Grianan Aileach. For properties in this area, look to agents in Moville and Carndonagh.

Small thatched cottages in good condition occasionally surface for around $85,000, while three-bedroom bungalows with sea views fetch around $158,000. Within Moville town, three-bedroom Victorian row houses are around $68,000 and, for anybody seeking a development project, the town's Mercy Convent recently came on the market priced at $452,000.

ARDARA
Another of my own favorite Donegal villages is Ardara, a stone's throw from the wild Atlantic shores of southwest Donegal. If you have a yen for huge deserted beaches and mysterious sea caves right on the doorstep, then this is one of the most perfect locations in the whole of the northwest. Ardara itself is protected from the sea breezes by steep, heather-clad hills, its cluster of pink, white and teal-blue dwellings nestling in their valley like some secret forgotten settlement. Long renowned as a center for tweeds and knitwear, it's a place where spinning wheels are not regarded as museum pieces.

Each June the village hosts an old-fashioned weaver's fair with displays of spinning, carding and loom weaving. The hub of village social life is Nancy's, a historic inn whose labyrinthine passageways lead to tiny rooms where traditional musicians gather around open fires. Here it costs $140,000 upwards for houses with enough rooms to offer B&B, though I did see a three-bedroom bungalow on the Killybegs road priced at $90,000.

REALTOR ADDRESS BOOK
Rainey Estate Agents, Market Square, Letterkenny, county Donegal; tel +353 (0)74 22211.

Anderson Auctioneers, Main St., Donegal town, county Donegal; tel +353 (0)73 22888.

Sean Meehan, Main St., Bundoran, county Donegal; tel +353 (0)72 41351.

McElhinney & Son, Main St., Bundoran, Co Donegal; tel +353 (0)72 41261.

McCauley Properties, Market Square, Malin Road, Moville, county Donegal; tel +353 (0)77 82110. Email: sales@mccauleyproperties.com.

Paul Franklin, 25/26 Academy Court, Oliver Plunkett Road, Letterkenny, county Donegal; tel +353 (0)74 88000. Email: franklin@indigo.ie.

DONEGAL CONTACTS
Donegal Democrat (local newspaper), Donegal Road, Ballyshannon, county Donegal; tel +353 (0)72 51201.

Bus Éireann offices at Ballyshannon (tel +353 (0)72 51101), Donegal town (tel +353 (0)73 21101), and Letterkenny (tel +353 (0)74 21309). Buses to Dublin, Cork and Galway and points in between, to Northern Ireland, a number of local routes including Killybegs and Bundoran.

Tourist Information Office, Derry Road, Letterkenny, county Donegal; tel +353 (0)74 21160.

The Lakelands: Counties Cavan, Leitrim and Roscommon

Sparsely populated and with very little in the way of tourist sights, the low-key Lakelands are worth considering if you yearn for an Ireland where you can get even further away from it all. Apart from anglers and boating enthusiasts, these counties see few foreign visitors, probably because the scenery is serene rather than spectacular. Along with dozens of little loughs, the border county of Cavan has an undulating landscape of drumlin hills, shaped for all the world like upturned egg boxes. Leitrim is another border county of forested glens and rushy wetlands where smart white cruisers lazily drift along the Shannon River and its tributaries into Lough Ree and the more pastoral landscape of Roscommon. Lough Ree is a place where it may pay to carry a camera. Old folk tales whisper of the Lough Ree Monster, a hump-backed creature that seems to be a cousin of the equally shy and elusive monster, Scotland's Loch Ness.

St. Barry, patron of Tarmonbarry parish in county Roscommon, reputedly crossed the river Shannon in a stone boat.

© Steenie Harvey

THE APPEAL OF ROSCOMMON

This really is small-town Ireland, steeped in old-fashioned ways and provincial pastimes. One of the biggest centers of population in the lakeland region is Roscommon town, at the last census count, home to just 3,600 people. Most other "towns" number around 2,000 residents, so you soon get to

Lady Betty

R oscommon town's Old Gaol housed plenty of accursed characters in its heyday, the most infamous being Elizabeth Sugrue. Widely known as Lady Betty, she practiced an unusual profession for her time: that of a hangwoman. One deliciously creepy rumor says that if you stand outside the jail walls when the moon is full, it's possible to hear the futile cries of former inmates who had an appointment with the Lady.

Betty gained the position in 1780 and you could say it was through being in the right place at the right time. Convicted of the murder of her own son at Roscommon Sessions, she had been sentenced to death along with 25 other assorted ruffians. The prisoners thought they had won a reprieve when the hangman didn't turn up at the appointed hour, but they hadn't bargained on Betty. Hoping to save her own neck, she volunteered to dispatch her fellow sinners.

The ploy worked. On condition that she continue to ply the hangman's duties without reward, black-hearted Betty got her own death sentence withdrawn. A zealous soul, she devised a more effective gallows system and took over the task of public floggings. If tales are to be believed, she also indulged in torture, drank whiskey from a skull, and became a dab hand at drawing charcoal portraits of her victims.

know local names and faces. Go into a remote country pub and conversations will revolve around the weather, local politics and the price sheep are fetching at Tulsk and Drumshanbo markets. You often see locals playing the 25-card-game, an unfathomable combination of whist and brag, where winners compete for "fierce prizes" that sometimes take the form of livestock. Don't get involved unless you want to go home with a heifer!

Individuals who buy properties here tend to have renounced the consumer-driven world and exchanged the rat race for drowsy tranquillity and a very simple lifestyle. Unless you are perfectly happy with few good restaurants, theaters or fashion stores, it may be too laid-back for most American tastes. However, this is a part of the country where many properties have remained at fairly affordable levels. In 1988, I bought a little mint-condition cottage (two bedrooms, kitchen, sitting room and bathroom) on an acre of land overlooking Lough Key in county Roscommon for just $13,000. Although you will have to pay at least $50,000 for a similar cottage in this area today, it's still fairly good value compared to other parts of Ireland.

THE LOUGH KEY AREA

Laced with bluebell woods and studded with islands, the Lough Key area is increasingly popular with Dubliners seeking holiday hideaways, so prices aren't the cheapest in the Lakelands. However, it is fairly accessible. Even if you're without transport, it's easy enough to reach this part of the world. Trains run south to Dublin and north to Sligo from the nearby town of Boyle, which has a reasonable selection of stores for day-to-day shopping and its own summer arts festival.

At the time of writing, Sligo agent Schiller was marketing a three-bedroom rural bungalow/cottage near the county Roscommon village of Frenchpark, about 12 miles from my own home. Priced at $51,000, the house looked very similar to the one I bought. It was lived in until recent years, so it doesn't need major repairs, just modernization and decoration. Egan's also has a number of nice little cottages from $57,000. I know it will be gone by the time you read this, but just to illustrate that you can still find some good bargains here, the agency's current "star buy" is a beautiful thatched cottage near the town of Ballaghadereen. Thatched cottages are quite a rare sight in county Roscommon. This one has three bedrooms and is priced at $142,000. Other properties you could move into immediately include a pretty whitewashed farmhouse with three bedrooms, some out-buildings and an acre of land priced at $89,000. A farmhouse with a larger plot (15 acres) used for growing organic vegetables is for sale for $203,000.

LAKELANDS' COTTAGES

Although you certainly won't find any around Lough Key, the Lakelands region is the likeliest area to track down country cottages for $15,000. But don't get excited; these days you're likely to find one only in the middle of nowhere—and it will undoubtedly require a lifetime's work to refurbish it to anything resembling modern requirements. At the time of writing, you could have bought ramshackle cottages for this price near the border village of Swanlinbar in county Cavan and at Loughlynn in the unscenic western half of county Roscommon. But (and it's a big but) you get what you pay for. A sum of $15,000 is unlikely to buy even a scrap of basic home comfort.

The capital value of Irish properties is increasing every year. This county Roscommon property near Lough Key could also bring in rental income.

© Steenie Harvey

What exactly do you get for $15,000? Alas, not a lot. Probably a corrugated iron roof covering a tiny sitting room, a kitchen with an old-fashioned cooking range and one bedroom. Perhaps best described as "something to suit a desperate man," cottages such as these were built in the days when farm laborers weren't concerned with bathroom facilities and were happy to use an outhouse toilet or the fields. Near Killeshandra in county Cavan, $24,000 buys a cottage with five rooms; $53,000, a large two-story country farmhouse with four bedrooms. Both, however, are in poor condition.

However, most areas of the Lakelands can be good bargain-hunting territory if you're looking for a house you can call home. For example, in the Arigna Hills in north county Roscommon $34,000 buys a traditional-style cottage near the Miner's Way walking trail down into Keadue village. Every August the village hosts a harp festival in honor of Turlough O'Carolan, a blind 18th-century harpist who was the last of the great Irish bards. His grave lies a mile from Keadue, at Kilronan, where pilgrims still visit St. Lazair's holy well. The sacred spring reputedly holds the cure for backache, and you can walk through shadowy woods beside Lough Meelagh where an ancient court cairn evokes the mysteries of the Celtic past.

THE APPEAL OF LEITRIM

The Lakeland region's main pocket of affluence is Carrick-on-Shannon. The county town of Leitrim, its marina is one of the biggest on the Shannon and provides a base for cruiser companies. The area has become even more popular with the recent opening of the Ballyconnell Canal, which links the Shannon with the Erne River in county Fermanagh. Unlike a decade ago, vacationers can now continue their boating odyssey upriver through Leitrim's countryside into Northern Ireland. Naturally enough, many break their journey to stock up on supplies and discover Carrick's waterfront pubs, so the town is always full of good-natured bustle.

French and German visitors adore their boating holidays, and quite a few return to buy homes in the area. Riverside properties always find eager buyers from both home and abroad, so vendors take full advantage and the premium can be as high as 25 percent for a Shannonside residence. Another factor that has pushed up house values around Carrick has been the opening of a wood-pulp plant employing around 500 people downriver at Drumsna. New three-bedroom townhouses in Carrick start at $130,000. The average price of a two-bedroom modern bungalow in the immediate area is $85,000. Country cottages in good condition around Carrick's satellite villages also fetch more than in remoter corners of the Lakelands. For example, a two-bedroom Old World cottage at Eslin Bridge is priced at $68,000.

A little north of here, at Mohill, you could buy a sound little cottage on an acre site within walking distance of the town for $57,000. There are some grand walks in this area, and I've seen pine martens, foxes and badgers in the woods bordering the road to Lough Rynn. Four miles from Mohill, the Lough Rynn estate's most notorious owner was William Clements, the third Earl of Leitrim who treated his 19th-century tenant farmers little better than slaves and allegedly exercised the *droit de seigneur* on local brides-to-be.

Other interesting properties currently available through Mohill agents Lloyds include a former station house, now converted into a home and priced at $90,500. A period-style country house (four bedrooms), a short distance from the canalside town of Ballinamore, is priced at $136,000.

Something different? Although Ireland is more associated with stone cottages, in county Cavan you could buy a Scandinavian-style house. On the outskirts of Belturbet, a market town on the Erne River, a new development of timber homes built on stilts is being marketed as a holiday home project. Enclosed by parkland, properties come with two, three or four bedrooms and prices are $153,000, $170,000 and $198,000, respectively. Sizes range from 850 to 1,250 square feet, and all the homes sit on their own half-acre plot. Owners also have fishing and boating rights.

REALTOR ADDRESS BOOK

Eugene O'Dwyer, Main St., Virginia, county Cavan; tel +353 (0)49 8547622. Email: ejodwyer@eircom.net.

Robert Clarke, Holborn Hill, Belturbet, county Cavan; tel +353 (0)49 9522294.

O'Reilly, Taylor & Tweedy, Main St., Cavan town, county Cavan; tel +353 (0)49 4331599.

James Cleary, Main St., Castlerea, county Roscommon; tel +353 (0)907 20540.

Vincent Egan, Elphin St., Boyle, county Roscommon; tel +353 (0)79 62464.

Wm Farrell, Main St., Carrick-on-Shannon, county Leitrim; tel +353 (0)78 20976.

Mervyn Lloyd, Main St., Mohill, county Leitrim; tel +353 (0)78 31066. Email: mlloyd@propertypartners.ie.

LAKELAND CONTACTS

Leitrim Observer (local newspaper), St. George's Terrace, Carrick-on-Shannon, county Leitrim; tel +353 (0)78 20025. Also *Roscommon Herald*, Patrick St., Boyle, county Roscommon; tel +353 (0)79 62004.

Train service to Dublin from Boyle, tel +353 (0)79 62027; Castlerea, tel +353 (0)907 20031; and Roscommon town, tel +353 (0)903 26201 in county Roscommon; from Carrick-on-Shannon, tel +353 (0)78 20036 in county Leitrim.

For bus service phone Bus Éireann's Sligo office at +353 (0)71 60066 or Busaras at Store St., Dublin, +353 (0)1 836 6111.

Lakeland's Tourist Information offices are seasonal. For information on Roscommon and Leitrim, contact Bord Fáilte's Sligo office on Temple St. at +353 (0)71 61201. For Cavan contact the Dublin office on Baggot St. Bridge at 1850 230 330.

Part V

Earning a Living

18 Working in Ireland

*N*one of us can live on fresh air alone. Unless you have a regular income, think carefully about how you are going to support yourself. In some aspects, Ireland has become a land of opportunity but finding paid employment may depend on the skills you can offer. Although there is still no open-door jobs policy for non-European Union nationals such as North Americans, a number of possibilities have opened up over the past couple of years. Labor shortages in information technology companies and also nursing and construction have eased restrictions in these sectors.

Another possibility is self-employment. Moving to a new country is a major life change in itself, but maybe now is the time to think about becoming your own boss too. And even if you can afford to bid farewell to the nine-to-five grind, not everyone wants to give up work completely. So why not spend a few hours each week volunteering for a worthy organization?

Ireland's Economy

First, a word about the business climate. Many foreign investors still think Ireland's economy is solely agricultural, a place whose only exports are pigs, butter and potatoes. While it's true that the country is nowhere near as industrialized as the rest of Europe, immense changes have occurred in recent years. Agriculture is no longer the mainstay of the economy, though it does of course remain a key contributor. Within this sector, the emphasis isn't just on livestock farming but also on large-scale production of wheat and barley. The food-processing industry is equally important; big companies like Kerry Group and Avonmore Waterford have stock market quotes.

But did you know that Ireland is the world's second-largest exporter of computer software, after the United States? The information technology business is going gangbusters and benefiting both indigenous companies and big multinationals. Employing around 24,000 people, the software export sector garners an estimated 6.6 billion worth of annual business in euros.

The boom has come about mainly through offering attractive tax-advantageous packages for foreign companies to relocate to Ireland, but successive governments have also operated a tireless policy of promoting the country's advanced technology services. The Industrial Development Agency (IDA) and Enterprise Ireland do much sterling work behind the scenes.

The Republic's big advantage in attracting inward investment is through charging multinationals a very low level of corporation tax. Although this is set to rise from 10 to 12.5 percent in January 2003, it's still an enticing deal for companies looking for a gateway into the wider European marketplace.

Continuing growth doesn't just depend on the IT sector. Ireland is also a base for many foreign companies involved in telecommunication, chemicals, pharmaceuticals and textiles. Exploration companies have found a number of oil and gas deposits off the southern coastline. And in the service sector, banking and insurance companies keep churning out huge profits and Dublin itself is the home of the International Financial Services Center (IFSC). International banking companies in the IFSC operate there on an offshore basis, which means foreign investors can roll up profits tax-free. However, just in case you're wondering, Irish people cannot take advantage of offshore accounts in their own country. Residents wanting to hold offshore investments have to look to places like the Channel Islands or Isle of Man.

The Labor Force

Although on a definite downward trend, unemployment still blemishes parts of the country. While only 3.6 percent of the available labor force is currently jobless (138,700 people in total), the percentage figure disguises the fact that unemployment is often extremely high in rural counties and also on inner-city housing estates. Not everyone has the skills to participate in Ireland's technological boom.

Another thing that you may not have realized: Much of Ireland's labor force is unionized and very happy to be so. Any liberal leanings you may have will be severely tested when you find yourself stuck at the airport, unable to leave the country because aircraft maintenance crews have downed tools. And you're unlikely to be humming *The Red Flag* if your mail has been gathering dust in a sorting office for three weeks and more. These things can and do happen. Although not up to the same level of bloody-mindedness as their French comrades, Irish unions can be fairly "bolshie."

Despite all the shouting about the Celtic Tiger, there has been growing unrest amongst an aggrieved public sector workforce, many of whom feel they aren't getting a fair share of the economic cake. Pay disputes have led to strikes and threatened strikes among the ambulance service, sewage and water workers, train drivers, airport baggage handlers and trash collectors. This year's major dispute was a teachers' strike. At the time of writing, their 30 percent pay claim is still unresolved, and pupils in many senior schools have taken to the streets to protest the disruption of their education.

WORKERS WANTED

Rapid growth in the Irish economy in recent years has resulted in labor shortages in some sectors such as information and computing technologies, building professionals and nursing. To facilitate recruitment of suitably qualified people from non-EU countries, a working visa and Work Authorisation Scheme has been set up. This makes it possible for prospective employees with job offers from employers in Ireland to obtain immigration and employment clearance in advance from Irish embassies and consulates. The new scheme does not replace the old work permit procedure, it is simply a faster alternative. The working visa is initially valid for two years.

At present, the designated categories are information and computing tech-

Skilled construction workers are in demand.

© Steenie Harvey

nologies professionals and technicians, architects, construction engineers, quantity surveyors, buildng surveyors, town planners and registered nurses.

With Ireland producing around 40 percent of Europe's packaged software and 60 percent of business applications software, the IT sector has particular need of graduates with technology degrees. Somewhat worryingly, a recent report revealed that there is a 30 percent dropout rate from Ireland's university courses in computer sciences. At present, there is a huge demand for C++ and Java VS developers, systems administrators and IT consultants. The rewards start at around $18,500, rising to $61,000 and above for more senior positions.

> *Did you know that Ireland is the world's second-largest exporter of computer software, after the United States?*

Information on current skills shortages and job vacancies can be found on the Internet websites of FAS, the State Training and Employment Authority (www.fasjobs-ireland.com), and also Forfas, a state body that promotes industrial and technological developments (www.askireland.com).

It's also worthwhile checking out newspaper websites that carry information on job vacancies. Try the *Irish Examiner* (www.examiner.ie), *Irish Independent* (www.loadza.com), *Irish Times* (www.ireland.com), *Sunday Business Post* (www.sbpost.ie) and *Sunday Tribune* (www.tribune.ie).

Work Permits

Unless you can claim Irish or other EU citizenship, or qualify for a working visa under the Work Authorisation Scheme, you'll need a work permit to obtain paid employment in Ireland. You can't apply for one yourself; work permits are issued only to *employers*, not employees.

Employers have to contact the Minister for Enterprise, Trade and Employment before any prospective employee arrives in the country. A work permit gets issued only if the Ministry is satisfied that an employer has taken all reasonable steps to recruit a suitably qualified person from Ireland or the European Union.

Yes, Americans do work here, but most are employed by large U.S. multinationals in positions requiring high levels of know-how. If you're a computer whiz kid, involved in scientific research, or a manager who has already climbed a good way up the corporate ladder, you're undoubtedly a highly valued member of the workforce. No doubt your skills will be needed for the success of your company's Irish operations, and multinational employers no longer have to obtain work permits for those here on terms up to four years. However, even if you already work for a U.S. multinational with an Irish outlet, work permits are *not* issued for more run-of-the-mill jobs outside the technology sector. Numerous overseas companies set up in Ireland to avail themselves of generous grants, incentives and tax breaks. What Ireland gets from the deal is new jobs for the local workforce. In most instances, if an employer requires manual, clerical and secretarial staff, the company must make these positions available to Irish or other EU nationals.

For more information contact Work Permits Section, Department of Enterprise, Trade & Employment, Room 105, Davitt House, Adelaide Road, Dublin 2; tel +353 (0)1 6313079; fax +353 (0)1 6313268.

Self-Employment

Self-employment is a different kettle of fish entirely. New country, new career? If you have an entrepreneurial flair and like the idea of working for yourself, you can do so. Maybe you've been toying with the notion of going into the antiques trade, starting a boat-building business or owning a restaurant, coffee shop or pottery studio. Or maybe you're the crafty type who could design greeting cards decorated with pressed wildflowers or carve mythical figurines from pieces of bog oak. And here's an idea: How about providing a relocation service for other Americans wanting to move to Ireland?

Ireland goes organic

© Steenie Harvey

Anybody out there with a green thumb? Well, please come and open a good plant and tree nursery in my locality. Get permission from the Land Commission to buy a large plot of the Irish countryside and you may even want to consider growing mushrooms on a commercial scale—a Jordanian immigrant in my own area is doing just that. Making a living from the land doesn't have to mean crops and cattle. Agri-business ventures take in everything from quails' egg production to making goat cheese to running pet kennels. I know an English couple in Leitrim who make a living growing herbs, and one Swiss lady in Roscommon has set herself up as a traditional harness and saddle-maker.

Pubs and guesthouses are homes with an obvious in-built business potential. If a home with an income sounds like your type of thing, why not consider a small shop? Many retail outlets have owner-accommodation above the actual business premises. You'll be amazed at how many Irish towns are crying out for a health food store, for instance. At present, we shoppers in Boyle and Carrick-on-Shannon have to make a 40-mile roundtrip to Sligo for our Puy lentils and goat milk yogurt.

Leaving aside the question of whether to buy an existing business or start an entirely new venture, as an American citizen you're first going to have to jump through the bureaucratic hoops. For EU citizens there are no restrictions. Any Dutch, German or British national can start enterprises without having to seek what's known as Business Permission. So, if you can claim Irish or other EU citizenship, do so; this slashes through all the red tape at a stroke.

Obtaining Business Permission

In the tortuous prose of governmental directives, Business Permission is "the permission of the Minister of Justice, expressed in writing, to allow a particular person or group of persons to engage and become established in business in the State for a particular period of time." All non-EU citizens need to obtain such permission.

Business Permission is not granted automatically, and a lot will depend on the nature of any proposed venture. In general, you must satisfy the Ministry of Justice that the granting of approval would:

- Result in the transfer to the State of capital in the minimum sum of an equivalent of $332,000. This minimum investment can be waived if:
  a) the minister is satisfied the application is justified for the purpose of pursuing activities as self-employed persons
  or
  b) that you are the spouse or a dependent of an Irish or EU national.
- At the very least, maintain existing employment within an existing business;
- Add to the commercial activity of the State;
- Substitute Irish goods for goods that would otherwise be imported;
- Be a viable trading concern and provide the applicant with sufficient income to provide for him/herself without resorting to non-contributory social welfare, or paid employment for which a work permit is required.

how much to buy a business?

- Newsagency/food store business (no owner accommodation) in Tralee, county Kerry. Price: $23,000 plus annual rent of $7,760.
- Grocery store in Drinagh, county Cork. Currently trading as the local post office and national lottery agency, the property has living accommodation and two refurbished apartments. Price: $221,000.
- Bar with rear beer garden and living accommodation with three upstairs bedrooms in Freemount village, Charleville, county Cork. Close to shops, church, community hall and G.A.A. ground. Price: $254,000.
- Self-contained coffee shop with seating for 40 diners at Bundoran, county Donegal. Price includes a five-bedroom bungalow overlooking Donegal Bay and Bundoran golf course. Price: $260,000.
- Post office, Courtmacsherry, West Cork. Includes semi-detached residential accommodation; a small parcel of land on the waterfront is included in the sale. Price: $277,000.
- Seven-bedroom guesthouse with large ground floor area currently used as a children's creche in Tralee, county Kerry. Price: $332,000.
- Newsagents with overhead living accommodation in Kiltimagh, county Mayo. Also sells lottery tickets, tobacco, confectionary, videos and giftware. Price: $388,000.
- Convenience store/supermarket with five-bedroom residential accommodation in Riverstown, county Sligo. Sells all main food lines, gas, fuel and also operates as a small newsagency. Price: $415,000.
- Long Lake House, Sneem, county Kerry. Luxurious five-bedroom guesthouse on the Ring of Kerry. Property includes a fitness and relaxation center with sauna, steam bath and whirlpool; separate accommodation for another four guests in a cedar chalet. Price: $2,210,000.
- Busy inn in the center of Newbridge, county Kildare. Includes self-contained owner's apartment. Price: $2,763,000.

All applications for Business Permission need to be accompanied by the following documentation:

- A passport or national identity papers;
- A registration certificate if you are already living in the State;
- A statement of character from the police authorities of each country in which you have resided for more than six months during the 10 years preceding an application;
- A business plan, preferably endorsed by a firm of accountants.

Applicants normally receive the Minister's decision within one month. On receiving approval, you're allowed to start your business or commence trading immediately but will need to register (or renew an existing registration) with the Garda in the area in which you intend to live and work.

Permission to reside in the State is given in conjunction with the validity of Business Permission, initially a period of one year. One month before Permission expires, you'll need to reapply to the Justice Ministry to renew your permit and also to submit audited accounts and evidence of compliance with tax laws. If everything is in order, Business Permission will be renewed for an additional five years.

You can obtain detailed information about Business Permission from the

Immigration Division, Department of Justice, 72 St. Stephen's Green, Dublin 2; tel +353 (0)1 678 9711.

More Red Tape

How much time you'll need to spend on paperwork will depend on the type of business. You'll certainly have to keep accounts and comply with applicable legislation. Regardless of your citizenship status, it's vital to ensure that any requisite planning permissions have been obtained, all fire and public safety requirements have been met, and tax certificates are in order.

The size of any business will dictate whether you need to employ staff. For instance, that tree nursery somebody is going to come and thrill me with would probably be fine for a couple to handle on their own. But what about a busy guesthouse? You may wish to bring in an extra pair of hands to help serve breakfasts and clean the rooms. When it comes to employing help, Ireland is no different from most other countries in that a black economy does exist. Needless to say, wages are often paid without tax deductions, but this is illegal and you'll be putting your Business Permission at great risk.

There is now a national minimum wage in Ireland. Should you decide to go ahead with those mushroom tunnels and employ people to pick them, you'll need to pay your workers a minimum of $4.87 an hour to do so. The whole arena of employment legislation is complex, but you must certainly know your employees' rights regarding hours worked, holiday entitlements and dismissal procedures. Get it wrong and you could pay staggering sums of compensation.

If you do employ people, you'll need not only to take care of your own income tax but also to ensure the correct amount of tax is deducted from your employees' wages. It's your responsibility to pay it to the tax man, so get acquainted with the 60-page "Employer's Guide to PAYE," obtainable from the Revenue Commissioners.

Enter the VAT Man

Any business with an annual turnover of more than $22,100 for goods or $44,200 for services needs to register for Value Added Tax, or VAT. Essentially this is a hidden sales tax collected by suppliers of goods and services on behalf of the Revenue Commissioners.

VAT is undoubtedly the self-employed person's biggest headache. For example, running a pub or a restaurant entails a lot more than simply dispensing hospitality. Like it or not, part of the job involves becoming an unpaid tax collector. Valuable time needs to be spent updating records in readiness for the VAT officer's regular inspections. It's not an easy task when there are five general rates of VAT in operation.

Although you will eventually be passing this tax on to customers, wholesalers and distributors also charge you VAT on stocks supplied. When calculating the amount of VAT to be levied, you deduct the amount you have been charged from the amount payable. Should you mistakenly pay out more in VAT than necessary, the good news is that you can claim a refund.

Plenty of advice is available at local VAT offices. Addresses are given in the 68-page "Guide to VAT" available from the Revenue Commissioners (Indirect Taxes), Stamping Building, Dublin Castle, Dublin 2; tel +353 (0)1 6792777.

The Bed-and-Breakfast Business

Along with local vacationers, Ireland receives more than 4 million foreign visitors each year—and they're all looking to sleep somewhere. As many vacationers opt to stay in private family homes rather than hotels, if you can keep house and cook a hearty breakfast this may be the perfect little business venture for you. The potential for making money certainly exists. Especially during high summer, demand for lodgings often exceeds supply. It can be extremely difficult to find a B&B with vacancies in the popular coastal towns and villages of Galway, Kerry and West Cork. On my last trip

So You Want to Buy a Pub?

Pubs have become amazingly expensive; few sell for less than $220,000 these days. Anything below that price undoubtedly has very few customers and so turnover will be extremely modest indeed. And while a quiet pub may suit a first-time buyer, it's unlikely to prove to be a little goldmine. With many Dublin pubs commanding $2.5 million and more, buyers have been looking to the provinces. Consequently prices have rocketed there too. The selling price depends on various factors: turnover, quality of the premises and owner accommodation, location, and potential for increasing custom such as through food sales or functions. One of the largest agents handling the sale of pubs countrywide is Gunnes (Licensed Division), 18-22 Pembroke Road, Ballsbridge, Dublin 4; tel +353 (0)1 668 2588.

Other names in the pub property market include Irish Pub Sales (Church St., Athlone, county Westmeath; tel +353 (0)902 73838), an umbrella organization for pub realtors throughout the country. They'll let you know which of their members serves a given area. The Carlow branch always seems to have some nice propositions for first-time buyers in the southeast corner of the country, so for a pub here contact George Sothern, (Irish Pub Sales, 37 Dublin St., Carlow Town, county Carlow; tel +353 (0)503 31218). Rooneys (99 O'Connell St., Limerick; tel +353 (0)61 413511) has a good selection in counties Limerick, Tipperary and Clare. In the midlands try John Earley (Goff St., Roscommon Town, county Roscommon; tel +353 (0)903 26579).

to county Cork in August, I found every B&B in the harbor villages of Schull and Baltimore completely booked.

A home that pays for itself is a beguiling prospect. Owning a B&B can supplement a pension income and may even help to fund the purchase of a house. However, the key to financial success is choosing the right location. Most vacationers look for lodging within easy walking distance of towns with plenty of restaurants and music pubs. A house that's eight miles down a country road is likely to get paying guests only when the choicer locations nearer town have been taken.

Dublin aside, Ireland's west and southwest regions have the greatest appeal. Areas such as the border counties and midlands don't register as high in the public imagination. Remember the vast majority of non-Irish visitors never venture into unfashionable counties such as Roscommon and Cavan. Suitable properties will be less expensive in these counties, but you won't find many bed-and-breakfasters ringing the doorbell. And note that trade is seasonal: Even B&Bs in prime touring locations achieve full occupancy only 180 days of the year.

Depending on facilities available, most provincial B&Bs charge between $22.50 and $30 per person, per night. Those providing evening meals charge an additional amount, usually between $10 and $15. Homes do not have to conform to any particular architectural style; they range from townhouses to farmsteads and modern bungalows.

If the idea of running a B&B business captures your imagination, avoid hotels and stay in a few private homes yourself. It will give you the best insight into the standard of accommodation and service you'll need to provide.

Although not all B&Bs are registered with Bord Fáilte (the Irish tourist board), getting your name on their accommodation lists will almost certainly deliver more guests. To be on the register, homes must meet certain minimum standards and for starters need at least three guest bedrooms. For exact requirements regarding room size, facilities and so on, contact Bord Fáilte, Baggot St. Bridge, Dublin 2; tel +353 (0)1 602 4000. Advisory visits to prospective guesthouse owners currently cost $56, and a further $56 is levied when a home becomes eligible for listing. This fee is payable annually.

You could buy a B&B that already has an established trade or purchase an ordinary residential home and then refurbish it to tourist board standards. In both cases, the cost of any property will depend on house size, existing facilities, state of repair and, most important of all, location.

Volunteering

Wanted: Volunteers for the Special Olympics World Summer Games, which are being held in towns and cities throughout Ireland in 2003. The largest sporting event ever to be held here, organizers are expecting 7,000 athletes to participate. Some 30,000 support people will be needed.

Around 33 percent of Irish adults regularly commit themselves to some form of volunteer work. Some people volunteer a few times a year when they have spare time; others give a regular commitment of several hours per week. Opportunities vary and hundreds of organizations would love to hear from you. A recent survey showed that more than a third of Irish voluntary groups have fewer volunteers than they require. It's not simply a case of standing on a corner in the rain, shaking a collection tin for a good cause—though people are always needed for flag days and other fund-raising, of course.

For instance, you may be interested in the field of adult education—one-on-one literacy programs that help people to read and write, English-language classes for asylum seekers, or educational programs in museums. You may wish to get involved with a local youth group or a conservation organization, planting trees and repairing stone walls. Age support groups are always looking for volunteers to befriend, assist and entertain older people in hospitals or clubs, as well as visit them in their own homes.

There are many other forms of social services where helpers are needed—working with the homeless, asylum seekers, and the prison service; manning telephone helplines for victims of rape or domestic violence. Maybe you would enjoy working in a charity shop or with animals. Opportunities range from volunteering with your own animal for pet-facilitated therapy to assisting with the care of abandoned animals at kennels or undertaking interpretative work at a zoo.

An excellent starting point for finding out what opportunities are

Why wait? artwork for the asking

currently available is Ireland's Volunteer Resource Centre. This helps match volunteers to organizations in need of helpers, and posts are listed on their website at www.volunteeringireland.com. If you can't access the Web, contact them at Volunteer Resource Centre, Coleraine House, Coleraine Street, Dublin 7; tel 01 872 2622, fax 01 873 5280, email: info @volunteeringireland.com. These are just a few of the many groups and organizations that were listed on the website at the time of writing.

- Saint Patrick's Football Athletic Club in Dublin seeks volunteers for the turnstiles as well as for program selling, stewarding and hospitality. The season runs from August to April, and the commitment is three hours twice monthly, an average of 18 games during the soccer season. Work for nine games and be a guest for nine games. Qualities needed are an ability to communicate and deal with people, reliability and punctuality.
- PEATA, the Irish Organization for Pets and People, needs volunteers to make regular visits to nursing homes and hospitals, sharing with the residents the pleasures of a pet's company. Minimum of one hour per week. Obviously you must have your own pet and have an interest in the welfare of others.
- The Society of Saint Vincent de Paul needs assistants for their charity shops in Kildare, Wicklow and Dublin. A minimum of three hours a week, Monday through Saturday. Skills needed are a willingness to enjoy working within a team and promoting the work of the shop.
- Conservation Volunteers Ireland has projects throughout the country— dry stone walling, woodland management, bulb planting, hedge laying, bench construction, etc. No experience is necessary.
- If you're able to commit two hours per week, the Visitor's Centre at Dublin's Mountjoy Prison is looking for people with listening skills who can provide support to prisoners' relatives and help in the tea-bar and kiddies play area. Obviously you must be a tolerant, non-judgmental type of person.
- Age Action Ireland needs a book reviewer who will read literature regarding services for older people, then write a short review for the monthly bulletin. The organization is Dublin-based, but the work can be done in the volunteer's own home.
- Amnesty International's Dublin office requires a press assistant for eight hours per week who can maintain a database and records of contact and media, adapt/write press releases, deal with inquiries from the media and help organize press launches.
- Dublin Zoo needs an assistant with good communication skills for their Discovery Center for a minimum of three hours weekly. The work involves helping to set up exhibitions and shows, group tours and information walkabouts.

19 Investing in Ireland

lthough Ireland's economy has turned in a stellar performance in recent years, relatively few outsiders associate the Emerald Isle with major profits and prosperity. Yet for the last decade, this has been Europe's fastest-growing economy, recording double-digit growth figures in the late 1990s. The pace has slowed down in recent months, but estimates issued by the Irish Economic and Social Research Institute predict that the average percentage GNP growth over the medium term (2001 to 2005) will be 5.1 percent. Despite the volatility of world stock markets, commentators expect that Irish participation in Europe's single currency will bring about lower interest rates, thus giving a further shot in the arm to the economy.

Since joining the European Union, the structure of the Irish economy has experienced dramatic changes. During the late 1980s and throughout the 1990s, the manufacturing sector came to be dominated by information technology companies, many foreign-owned. Consequently Ireland's fortunes are entwined with what happens in the rest of the world. For example, any slowdown in the U.S. economy has a ripple affect, and there have already been a small number of job losses in the IT sector.

Despite this, things still look rosy in the Irish economic garden. With the advent of the European single currency, Irish exporters are finding it easier to sell products to other EU countries, often at the expense of British competitors who aren't part of the single currency club. At the

255

moment, Ireland's main trading links are with continental Europe and the U.K., which buys around 60 percent of exports in total. Exports to the U.S. and Canada amount to just over 20 percent.

Investment Options

A thriving economy goes hand in hand with rising house values and, as pointed out in the property sections of the book, the Dublin housing market has delivered huge windfalls for property investors who got in on its recent soaraway act. Can these massive rises continue? Isn't the bubble going to burst? Well, the pundits have been asking those questions for the last five years now, but my own view is that buying Dublin property solely for its investment potential is only for the brave or the foolhardy.

However, with deposit interest rates likely to remain low, you may be looking for a more rewarding investment than what is on offer through high-street savings institutions. An obvious alternative is the stock market, which has the potential to offer greater returns. At the end of 1995, Dublin's ISEQ Index closed at 2,216. In January 1997 it stood at 2,860, an increase of almost 29 percent in 12 months. In April 1998 it touched 5,461, and although there have been corrections in recent months, the economy continues surging ahead. At the time of writing, the Index stood at 5,869.

Over the long term, equities have outperformed other types of investments such as property, bonds and savings accounts. However, nothing can ever be taken for granted and you should always remember that shares can go down as well as up.

Ireland's top 10 Companies

RANK BY MARKET CAPITALIZATION	SHARE PRICE (EUROS)	12-MONTH HIGH	12-MONTH LOW	SECTOR
Elan Corp	58.50	67.00	40.00	Pharmaceuticals
AIB Group	12.72	13.55	8.74	Banking
Bank of Ireland	10.90	10.96	6.36	Banking
CRH	19.26	20.45	14.64	Building
Eircom	2.54	3.98	2.29	Telecoms
Ryanair	11.80	12.45	7.40	Transport
Irish Life	12.40	13.40	7.70	Insurance
J. Smurfit	2.15	2.32	1.74	Paper/Packaging
Kerry Group	12.30	15.10	11.75	Food Mft
Galen	14.01	16.33	8.51	Pharmaceuticals

Buying Irish Shares

There are a number of ways to purchase Irish equities. The first, direct investment in a company, is when a stockbroker buys a designated amount of shares on your behalf. As most Irish stockbrokers also deal on the London market, you're not necessarily limited to the small amount of stocks that make up Dublin's ISEQ Index. Indeed, some homegrown companies have bypassed the Irish marketplace completely and gone instead for a sole London listing.

Dealing costs vary widely. Any transaction, no matter how small, costs a minimum of $67 in commission fees if done through the Bank of Ireland, which has its own stockbroking arm. On the other hand, if you choose an execution-only broker, dealing costs will usually be much less expensive. The brokerage company I use is Fexco, which currently charges commission fees of just under $15 on deals of $1,130 or less. Contact them at Fexco House, Ely Place, Dublin 2; tel +353 (0)1 637 3080.

Other stockbrokers who welcome small investors include:

BCP Stockbrokers, 72 Upper Leeson St., Dublin 4; tel +353 (0)1 661 7111/668 4688.

Bloxham Stockbrokers, 2/3 Exchange Place, Dublin 1; tel +353 (0)1 829 1888.

Butler & Briscoe, 3 College Green, Dublin 2; tel +353 (0)1 677 7348.

Goodbody Stockbrokers, 122 Pembroke Road, Ballsbridge Park, Dublin 4; tel +353 (0)1 667 0400.

Despite the risk factor of equities, the government also takes a bite out of your investment. Stamp duty is 1 percent, and so on a $2,000 deal you pay tax equivalent to $20. When selling shares, you'll be subject to Capital Gains Tax (CGT) on any profits made. Current rate of personal CGT is 20 percent, but you're allowed an annual allowance equivalent of just over $1,100 before paying tax. If you've made losses on other shareholdings during the tax year, these can be offset against a CGT bill. More tax is due if a company pays shareholders dividends, either 20 or 42 percent, depending on your income tax bracket.

Spreading the Risk

An alternative to direct equity investment is pooled investments. You may already be clued up on these by holding U.S. mutual funds. In Ireland, mutual funds are called unit trusts and unit-linked funds. The moneys paid in by investors are pooled together in units in the investment company's assets, which can include property, equities and government gilts from both Ireland and overseas. With these types of investments, the tax liability on profits is paid by the investment fund and you won't have to meet a personal CGT bill. In general, banks, building societies and life assurance companies sell pooled investments. Some funds concentrate solely on holding Irish assets while others hold baskets of British, Continental European or worldwide stocks.

Although most life assurance companies have a minimum level of $2,300 to $5,700 for investors looking to stash away a lump sum in unit-linked funds, Bank of Ireland and Allied Irish Bank also have plans whereby you can make monthly investments ($57 minimum). This is a good way to invest for the long term because if the stockmarket heads south, your monthly investment buys more units. Recommended holding term is five years at least, but there's nothing to stop you cashing in units earlier.

Seeking the right product in what can seem a bewildering financial maze does take time. One of the most tax-efficient packages on offer is a PIP, a Personal Investment Plan. Similar to a unit trust in that it holds a broad mix of stocks, you can realize greater profits with a PIP because the fund pays a lower 10 percent rate of tax on profits. To qualify for this special tax rate, at least 55 percent of the fund has to be invested in Irish equities, 10 percent of which must be in stock of developing companies. Again, you can alleviate the horror of finding you've put a lump sum into a plunging stock market by making monthly investments: $113 per month minimum with Bank of Ireland and Allied Irish Banks, $57 per month minimum with the Educational Building Society (EBS). A PIP with the EBS has the added attraction of a 3 percent bonus if held for 10 years.

First, land your salmon!

© Steenie Harvey

Tracker Bonds

Another type of stock market–related investment is a tracker bond. Most (but not all) trackers carry a two-pronged guarantee, the most important being that your original capital is returned after the set term of the investment. Any guarantee on profits depends on the index (or indices) the bond is "tracking" rising; should the chosen stock market commit suicide, at least you get your money back. However, capital isn't always guaranteed, so make sure you know what you're getting into before investing. The term of a bond can be from 18 months to 5.5 years and will be linked to the performance of one or more of the world's bourses such as the DAX Index in Frankfurt or the FTSE 100 in London. Again, all major banks and assurance companies market tracker bonds.

As you have to get on board by a set date with each new tracker issued, it's impossible to say what will be available by the time you're ready to invest. However, to give you an idea, here's a sample of some of the products that were on the market at the time of writing:

- AIB Secure Tracker Bond. Capital is fully secure and you invest a lump sum equivalent to $2,260 or more for a fixed period of 5.5 years. Your money is directly linked to the performance of the Euro Stoxx 50 Index. (This Index monitors the performance of the shares in 50 large companies in the Eurozone. It includes companies such as Unilever, Bayer, Siemens, Philips and Nokia.) At the end of the investment period, you will receive back the full amount of the money you invested, plus a return equal to 100 percent of the rise in the index over the period, subject to a maximum return of 50 percent.
- AIB Index Bond. Possible returns with this bond are up to 18 percent over 18 months, up to 24 percent return over two years, or up to 36 percent return over three years. Linked to major company shares in the Eurozone, at the end of the 18-month option, you will receive the full amount invested plus a return equal to the full rise of the index, up to a maximum of 18 percent. If the index falls by up to 18 percent over the period, you get the full amount invested at the outset, but no profits. However, if the index falls by more than 18 percent, the sum invested is subject to a deduction by which the fall in the index exceeds 18 percent. (For example, a 20 percent fall would result in a deduction of 2 percent.)
- TSB Bank World Tracker Series. Another capital-guaranteed tracker bond with a minimum investment equivalent to $5,700. The indices specific to this investment are the Eurostoxx 50, S&P 500 and the Nikkei 225. There are a number of options. Option One is for a three-year term. At the end of this investment period you will receive back your capital together with a return equal to 55 percent gross of the growth in the specified indices. Option Two is a five-year term. At the end of this investment period you will receive your capital together with a return equal to 75 percent gross of the growth in the specified indices.
- Bank of Ireland Combination Equity Bond. With a term of 5.75 years,

this is a tracker bond linked to a one-year deposit account. Investors get 65 percent of the composite index gain and capital is guaranteed. A deposit element pays a rate of 5.5 percent if investors keep funds on deposit for one year.

- Standard Life U.K. Property Fund. This allows Irish investors to put money into commercial property in the U.K. (since 1971, the average return has been 12.4 percent per year). The minimum investment is equivalent to almost $8,500.

Gilts and Bonds

Government gilts and bonds are other kinds of investment products that can be bought by individuals. A bond is a fixed interest investment. Basically it's a certificate of debt issued by the government or a company guaranteeing repayment of the original investment plus interest by a specified future date.

Gilts are issued by the government and offer a fixed-interest payment twice yearly, with your money back at the end of the investment term. They are traded in a similar fashion to shares and the price can fluctuate daily, thus affecting the effective return. Contact a broker for more information on these.

PART VI
Appendix

20. USEFUL RESOURCES

Useful Resources

Ever wonder what the Irish name Áine means? Or how many millimeters there are in an inch? And where you can find a tour operator offering trips to Ireland? Like an attic, an appendix is useful for storing all those bits and bobs that you can't find room for elsewhere.

Emergency Numbers

For ambulance, police, fire service or coastal, mountain and cave rescue, dial either 999 or 112 and ask the operator for the emergency service you want. Calls are free.

For non-emergency medical concerns, contact the appropriate regional health board for information on local doctors or dentists. You'll find numbers in the Golden Pages of the telephone directory under "Health Boards." If you're not sure which authority covers your area, call this freephone number from anywhere within the Republic: 1800 520520.

Other Useful Phone Numbers and Addresses

- **Embassy of the United States in Ireland:** 42 Elgin Road, Dublin 4; tel +353 (0)1 668 8777.
- **Embassy of Ireland:** 2234 Massachusetts Ave. NW, Washington, DC 20008; tel (202) 462-3939. Diplomatic representation at consulate offices is available in: Boston, tel (617) 267-9330 New York, tel (212) 319-2555 Chicago, tel (312) 337-1868 San Francisco, tel (415) 392-4214
- **Irish Business Organization of New York:** FDR Station, P.O. Box 6425, New York, NY 10150-1901; tel (212) 750-8118. Another resource for networking within the Irish and American-Irish business communities.
- **Revenue Commissioners** (Indirect Taxes), Stamping Building, Dublin Castle, Dublin 2; tel +353 (0)1 878 0000.
- **Tourist Information:** Bord Fáilte, 345 Park Ave., New York, NY 10154; tel (212) 418-0800. Also at this address are the offices of **Enterprise Ireland**, the Irish Trade Board, tel (212) 371-3600, and **Ireland's Industrial Development Agency**, tel (212) 750-4300, whose mission is to attract foreign business to Ireland.

Ireland's Provinces and Counties

THE REPUBLIC OF IRELAND

Leinster Province—counties Carlow, Dublin, Kildare, Kilkenny, Laois, Longford, Louth, Meath, Offaly, Westmeath, Wexford, Wicklow

Munster Province—counties Clare, Cork, Kerry, Limerick, Tipperary, Waterford

Connacht Province—counties Galway, Leitrim, Mayo, Roscommon, Sligo

Ulster Province—counties Cavan, Donegal, Monaghan

NORTHERN IRELAND

Ulster Province—counties Antrim, Armagh, Derry (Londonderry), Down, Fermanagh, Tyrone

Public Holidays

January 1, New Year's Day
March 17, St. Patrick's Day
Good Friday
Easter Monday
May Holiday, first Monday in May
June Bank Holiday, first Monday in June

August Bank Holiday, first Monday in August
October Bank Holiday, last Monday in October
December 25, Christmas Day
December 26, St. Stephen's Day

Tour Operators

Although some package trips to Ireland (for example, with Trafalgar Tours) are bookable only through travel agents, you can also check out the brochures from these operators:

Crystal Travel & Tours, 8 Chestnut Hill, Brighton, MA 02135; tel 617-254-4900

Round Tower Travel, 18 Central St., Norwood, MA 02062; tel toll-free 888-762-9090

Ireland Vacations, 5644 Westheimer #280, Houston, TX 77056; tel toll-free 866-433-6007

IL Discovery Tours, Agora South, 1050 SE 5th Ave., Suite 100, Delray Beach, FL 33483; tel 561-243-6276

Brian Moore International Tours, 150 Wood Road, Suite 100, Braintree, MA 02184; tel toll-free 800-982-2299

Irish Festival Tours, P.O. Box 169, Warminster, PA 18974; tel 215-675-3117

Celtica Tours, 430 Franklin Village Drive, Franklin, MA 02038; tel toll-free 800-299-CELT

TWA Getaway Vacations, 1415 Olive St., St Louis, MO 63103; tel 800-892-4141

Metric Conversion

WEIGHT
1 ounce (oz) = 28.3 grams (g)
1 pound (lb) = 454 grams
2.2 pounds = 1 kilogram (kg)
1 stone (14 pounds) = 6.36 kilograms

LENGTH
1 inch (in) = 25.4 millimeters (mm)
1 foot (ft) = 30.5 centimeters (cm)
1 yard (yd) = 0.914 meters (m)
1 mile (1,760 yards) = 1.61 kilometers (km)
0.39 inches = 1 centimeter
3.28 feet = 1 meter
0.62 miles = 1 kilometer

VOLUME
1 pint (pt) = 568 milliliters (ml)
1 gallon (gal) = 4.55 liters (l)
1.76 pints = 1 liter
(An Imperial gallon is larger than the U.S. gallon of 3.79 liters)

AREA
1 square foot(sq. ft.) = 929 square centimeters (cm^2)
1 square yard (sq. yd.) = 0.836 square meters (m^2)
1 acre = 0.405 hectares (ha)
1 square mile = 259 hectares
10.8 square feet = 1.0 square meter
2.47 acres = 1 hectare
247 acres = 1 square kilometer (km^2)

SPEED
1 mile per hour (mph) = 1.61 kilometers per hour (km/h)
0.621 mile per hour = 1.00 kilometer per hour

TEMPERATURE
Centigrade to Fahrenheit: multiply by 1.8 then add 32.
Fahrenheit to Centigrade: subtract 32 then multiply by 5/9.

Time Difference

Ireland sets its clocks by Greenwich Mean Time. Without taking into account daylight saving, when it's 7 A.M. in New York, it's 12 noon in Ireland. In mid-March the clocks go forward by one hour and are put back an hour at the end of October (spring forward, fall back). During midsummer evenings, the light doesn't fade until around 11 P.M. in the west of Ireland.

Recommended Reading

Angela's Ashes by Frank McCourt. Published by Scribner, 1996.

Celtic Sacred Landscapes by Nigel Campbell Pennick. Published by Thames & Hudson, 1996.

Fairy & Folk Tales of Ireland edited by W. B. Yeats. Republished by Simon & Schuster, 1998.

The Great Hunger: Ireland 1845-1849 by C. B. F. Woodham Smith. Published by Penguin USA, 1995.

Mythic Ireland by Michael Dames. Published by Thames & Hudson, 1996.

Oxford Illustrated History of Ireland edited by R. F. Foster. Published by Oxford University Press, 1991.

The Peoples of Ireland: From Prehistory to Modern Times by Liam de Paor. Published by University of Notre Dame Press, 1990.

The Tain, translated from the Irish Epic Tain Bo Cuailnge by Thomas Kinsella. Published by Oxford University Press, 1983.

To School Through the Fields: An Irish Country Childhood by Alice Taylor. Published by St. Martin's Press, 1994.

Tracing Your Irish Ancestors by John Grenham. Published by Genealogical Pub. Company, 1993.

Writer's Ireland: Landscape in Literature by William Trevor. Published by Thames & Hudson, 1986.

If you're online you can order these books through www.amazon.com. Otherwise one of the best places to source Irish-related books is Irish Books and Media, Franklin Business Center, 1433 E. Franklin Ave., Minneapolis, MN 55404; tel (612) 871-3505 or (800) 229-3505.

Clothing and Shoe Sizes

Clothing and shoe sizes may initially seem a bit confusing. My advice is try before you buy. U.S. women's wear sizes are smaller than Irish/U.K. sizes, so don't buy straight from the rack. You may find the kids can use your new dress as a tent on outdoor camping expeditions! Shoes are often imported from Germany and Italy, and these are usually always sized in European numbers.

WOMEN'S CLOTHING

American	8	10	12	14	16	18	20
Irish/U.K.	10	12	14	16	18	20	22
European	36	38	40	42	44	46	48

MEN'S SUITS AND JACKETS

American	34	36	38	40	42	44	46
Irish/U.K.	34	36	38	40	42	44	46
European	44	46	48	50	52	54	56

SHIRT COLLAR SIZES

American	14	14.5	15	15.5	16	16.5	17
Irish/U.K.	14	14.5	15	15.5	16	16.6	17
European	36	37	38	39	40	41	42

WOMEN'S SHOES

American	6	6.5	7	7.5	8	8.5	9
Irish/U.K.	4.5	5	5.5	6	6.5	7	7.5
European	36	37	38	38	38	39	40

MEN'S SHOES

American	6.5	7.5	8.5	9.5	10.5	11.5	12.5
Irish/U.K.	6	7	8	9	10	11	12
European	40	41	42	43	44	45	46

Some Irish Names and Their Meanings

GIRLS

Áine (Anne)—radiance or splendor
Aisling (Ashling)—dreamer
Aoife (Eva)—beautiful, pleasant
Bríd (Bridget)—High One
Deírdru (Deirdre)—sorrowful
Étaín (Edwina)—jealousy
Gráinne (Grace)—she who strikes fear
Medb (Maeve)—she who intoxicates
Niamh (Neeve)—brightness
Sorcha (Sara)—radiance

BOYS

Aodhán (Aidan)—fire
Aonghas (Angus)—young god
Cathal (Charles)—strong in battle
Coilín (Colin)—whelp, young pup
Eoghan (Owen)—yew-born
Fionnbhar (Finbar)—fair-haired
Lughaidh (Louis)—Lugh the god
Muiris (Maurice)—sea-strength
Ruairí (Rory)—red king
Tadgh (Todd)—poet

Index

About the Author

Steenie Harvey lives in county Roscommon in the west of Ireland. Born in the United Kingdom of Latvian and English parents, she moved to Ireland in 1988 with her Scottish husband Michael and their daughter Magdalen. After renting a house for a year, Steenie and her family decided to buy their own Irish property—a hilltop cottage overlooking the magical waters of Lough Key.

A freelance writer, Steenie writes about travel, folklore, and real estate for publications both at home and abroad. Her U.S. magazine credits include *The World of Hibernia*, *The World & I*, and *International Living*; she was IL's "Travel Writer of the Year" in 1997. *Adapter Kit: Ireland* is Steenie's second book. She is also the author of *Live Well in Ireland*. Recent travels have taken her to the Greek islands, the jungles of Malaysian Borneo, and eastern Germany.

Along with delving into Ireland's Celtic heritage, Steenie also enjoys opera, organic gardening, and countryside hikes.

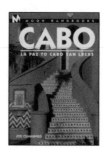

MOON HANDBOOKS
provide comprehensive coverage of a region's arts, history, land, people, and social issues in addition to detailed practical listings for accommodations, food, outdoor recreation, and entertainment. Moon Handbooks allow complete immersion in a region's culture—ideal for travelers who want to combine sightseeing with insight for an extraordinary travel experience in destinations throughout North America, Hawaii, Latin America, the Caribbean, Asia, and the Pacific.

WWW.MOON.COM

Rick Steves shows you where to travel and how to travel—all while getting the most value for your dollar. His Back Door travel philosophy is about making friends, having fun, and avoiding tourist rip-offs.

Rick has been traveling to Europe for more than 25 years and is the author of 22 guidebooks, which have sold more than a million copies. He also hosts the award-winning public television series *Rick Steves' Europe.*

WWW.RICKSTEVES.COM

ROAD TRIP USA

Getting there is half the fun, and Road Trip USA guides are your ticket to driving adventure. Taking you off the interstates and onto less-traveled, two-lane highways, each guide is filled with fascinating trivia, historical information, photographs, facts about regional writers, and details on where to sleep and eat—all contributing to your exploration of the American road.

"[Books] so full of the pleasures of the American road, you can smell the upholstery."
>BBC radio

WWW.ROADTRIPUSA.COM

FOGHORN OUTDOORS guides are for campers, hikers, boaters, anglers, bikers, and golfers of all levels of daring and skill. Each guide focuses on a specific U.S. region and contains site descriptions and ratings, driving directions, facilities and fees information,and easy-to-read maps that leave only the task of deciding where to go.

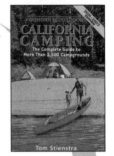

"Foghorn Outdoors has established an ecological conservation standard unmatched by any other publisher."
~Sierra Club

WWW.FOGHORN.COM

TRAVEL SMART guidebooks are accessible, route-based driving guides focusing on regions throughout the United States and Canada. Special interest tours provide the most practical routes for family fun, outdoor activities, or regional history for a trip of anywhere from two to 22 days. Travel Smarts take the guesswork out of planning a trip by recommending only the most interesting places to eat, stay, and visit.

"One of the few travel series that rates sightseeing attractions. That's a handy feature. It helps to have some guidance so that every minute counts."
~San Diego Union-Tribune

CITY·SMART™ guides are written by local authors with hometown perspectives who have personally selected the best places to eat, shop, sightsee, and simply hang out. The honest, lively, and opinionated advice is perfect for business travelers looking to relax with the locals or for longtime residents looking for something new to do Saturday night.

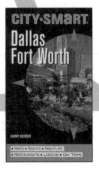